A Cultural Economic Analysis of Craft

Anna Mignosa · Priyatej Kotipalli
Editors

A Cultural Economic Analysis of Craft

palgrave
macmillan

Editors
Anna Mignosa
University of Catania
Catania, Italy

Erasmus University Rotterdam
Rotterdam, The Netherlands

Priyatej Kotipalli
Erasmus University Rotterdam
Rotterdam, The Netherlands

ISBN 978-3-030-02163-4 ISBN 978-3-030-02164-1 (eBook)
https://doi.org/10.1007/978-3-030-02164-1

Library of Congress Control Number: 2018968338

Cover illustration: Cultura Creative (RF)/Alamy Stock Photo

This Palgrave Macmillan imprint is published by the registered company Springer Nature Switzerland AG
The registered company address is: Gewerbestrasse 11, 6330 Cham, Switzerland

Preface

The crafts are back. At least, they are the world around the subject of a re-appraisal. Declared obsolete in the wake of industrialized and automated production processes they were considered a dying sector maintained only as keepsake. Now politicians are discovering the crafts as an invigorating factor in their economic policy and educators and professionals are re-evaluating the importance of developing and applying manual skills. Artists, designers, and surgeons are realizing that they are craftspeople after all. "Craftsmanship" is gaining so much clout that even policemen and judges want to be considered "craftsmen". In this groundswell of attention, scholars cannot stay behind. This book is a scholarly attempt to catch up with worldly events and to make sense of the significance of crafts in contemporary societies across the world.

Actually, most authors have been researching or even working in the world of crafts for many years. The achievement here is to rein in all their experiences and insights gained over those years and present them in a condensed way for other scholars, policymakers and other stakeholders in the world of crafts.

All authors share a keen interest in the crafts. Yet, as behooves scholars, we stress the problematics of the current state of the art. When we compare situations in a great variety of countries, we cannot help but being struck by the differences in defining and, consequently, measuring the crafts. Quite a few contributions address the definitional confusion. We are to be forgiven for that as we find a systematic and thorough analysis of a subject problematic when the boundaries of that subject are unclear. When the Germans mainly intend to discuss skilled handwork when they speak of crafts, and the Japanese have artistic craftsmanship in mind, we scholars will insist upon delineating the common subject.

A broad perspective on the crafts is called for, so we argue. This is not only to include utilitarian handwork as well as artistic craftsmanship but also to extend the discussion beyond traditional crafts and acknowledge new crafts, the use of new techniques and designs: i.e. craftsmanship on the cutting edge. For the crafts make such a fascinating subject not only because of the awe for skills honed through the ages but also because of the spectacle of people working on new techniques, new materials, and new designs. The world of the crafts is on the move and we scholars want to capture that dynamic and make sense of it, and at the same time appreciating the precious intangible heritage that the crafts represent.

The re-appraisal of the crafts may signal, or be an expression of, a paradigmatic change in contemporary economies. After an instrumentalist period with the emphasis on increasing quantities of all kinds—such as the quantities of income, production, GDP, profit, jobs—interest turns to qualities of all kinds—such as the quality of work, of goods, of communities, of family life. The crafts are about qualities above all. The work of craftspeople is about doing a job well, to excel in applying manual skills with the best materials to make the most beautiful, effective goods. Craftsmanship is about crafting goods. Craftspeople draw satisfaction from doing a good job. The crafts cultures in countries like Japan, Italy, and Germany are about qualities of things like food, cloth, ceramics, roof work and carpentry. Such cultures also stand out with their appreciation of manual skills, expressed in well-developed and sustained master-apprentice programs. They could be exemplars for other countries to follow.

The exemplars of strong craft cultures show that a craft culture does not come about just by changing a few policies here and there, to direct more resources to the crafts, or to start a craft school. A change in values is needed, like a re-evaluation of manual skills, and a willingness to pay for quality.

Additional scholarly effort like this book will not suffice either. But we have to start somehow. If the contributions in this book are a foreboding what attention for the crafts will bring about in disciplines such as economics, we would expect far-reaching changes in the way scholars make sense of the economy. They will figure out in particular how to do justice to the qualities of work, of goods, and to societies at large. And how to acknowledge the relevance of culture in economies.

Rotterdam, The Netherlands Arjo Klamer

Contents

Notes on Contributors

John Ballyn worked for 10 years in UK manufacturing and consultancies after studying Industrial Design at the Central School of Art and Design in London, UK. From 1973 to 1979 he trained designers at the Pakistan Design Institute. He joined Oxfam Trading, UK, working with producers in South and SE Asia, Far East and Africa, designing products upgrading business management skills. From 1988, he trained designers for 2 years at National Design Centre for crafts in Sri Lanka. Since 1990, he has been a consultant to international development agencies, collaborating with artisans worldwide, upgrading product development, production, marketing processes and contributing to training manuals for cultural sector enterprises. In 1995, the Society of Designer Craftsmen in UK awarded John the William Morris Centennial Medal for his services to crafts.

Julia Bennett is the Crafts Council's Head of Research and Policy. She develops policy and advocacy strategy, writes about craft and manages research, strengthening evidence to improve the conditions for craft. Research commissions include Studying Craft 16, an analysis of craft education and training, Innovation through Crafts: opportunities for growth and Measuring the Craft Economy, which resulted in DCMS including craft data for the first time in its economic estimates. Julia has worked independently with small arts organizations, as well as for the Local Government Association, the Learning and Skills Improvement Service and the Minority Rights Group.

Ronda L. Brulotte is Associate Professor of Geography and Environmental Studies and Associate Director for Academic Programs at the Latin American and Iberian Institute at the University of New Mexico. Her areas of expertise include food systems, craft economies, tourism geography, critical heritage studies, and commodities and materialism. She is the author of *Between Art and Artifact: Archaeological Replicas and Cultural Production in Oaxaca, Mexico* (University of Texas Press, 2012) and co-editor of *Edible Identities: Food as Cultural Heritage* (Routledge, 2014). She is currently working on a book manuscript addressing the transformation of the Oaxacan mezcal industry within the context of emergent global markets.

Ashoke Chatterjee received his education at Woodstock School (Mussoorie), St. Stephen's College and Miami University (Ohio). He has a background in the engineering industry, international civil service, India Tourism Development Corporation, and 25 years in the service of the National Institute of Design (Ahmedabad) where he was Executive Director, Senior Faculty, Distinguished Fellow and Professor of communication and management. He has served a range of development institutions in India and overseas, particularly in the sectors of drinking water, sanitation, disability, livelihoods, and education as well as working with artisans in many parts of the country. He was Hon President of the Crafts Council of India for over twenty years and continues to serve CCI. An author and writer, his books include *Dances of the Golden Hall* on the art of Shanta Rao and *Rising* on empowerment efforts among deprived communities in rural Gujarat. Professor Chatterjee continues to assist design education in India and Pakistan.

Francesca Cominelli is Associate Professor at the University of Paris 1 Panthéon-Sorbonne and Director of IREST. She holds a Ph.D. in Economics and her research interests include economics of culture, cultural commons, public policies, and cultural tourism. More specifically she is interested in cultural diversity, intangible cultural heritage, creativity, innovation, and traditional craftsmanship. Previously, she worked as project specialist for INMA and the French Ministry of Culture and Communication (2008–2010), and as researcher for the European Investment Bank Institute (2013–2014) and for the University of Lille 3 (2015). She is member of ICOMOS and Vice-President for Europe of ICOMOS International Committee on Intangible Cultural Heritage.

Simon Ellis has interests in craft that stem from work as a leading Roman archaeologist from 1976–2010 as well as a senior member of UNESCO Institute for Statistics from 2001–2012. He has a D.Phil. from Lincoln College, University of Oxford. Since leaving UNESCO in 2012 his work has concentrated in Georgia, the Philippines, and Thailand, where he has been particularly concerned to provide statistical evidence to demonstrate why governments should support traditional craft production, and to identify increasing demand for craft products in OECD countries. As a consultant he has worked on several recent projects on cultural statistics for both UNESCO and the EU. He has some 85 personal publications, including books and articles in scientific journals.

Thora Fjeldsted is a Ph.D. candidate in Cultural Economics at the Erasmus University of Rotterdam, where she investigates the place of skills, practice, and artisanal making in the history of economic thought. Her research builds on the interplay of economics, crafts, and sports, to address questions such as the origin of economic value, the negative utility of work and the discounting of human making and production. Her other scholarly interests include the study of material logics, the overlaps between religious practices and traditional knowledge in Central and South Italy, and the German system of Crafts and Trades, all topics on which she has co-authored peer-reviewed publications. Thora holds a B.A. in History from the University of Iceland and an M.A. in Museum Studies from New York University, and has script-written and directed several documentary films.

Judy Frater is Founder Director of Somaiya Kala Vidya, an institute of education for artisans. She has lived in Kutch, working with artisans, for 28 years. During this time she Co-founded and operated Kala Raksha Trust, and established the Kala Raksha Textile Museum. In 2003, for her concept of design education for artisans, Ms. Frater was awarded an Ashoka Fellowship for social entrepreneurship. She founded Kala Raksha Vidhyalaya, the first design school for traditional artisans, and under her eight-year tenure as director, the program received international recognition for its unique and successful approach. Frater received the Sir Misha Black Medal for Distinguished Services to Design Education in 2009, the Crafts Council of India Kamla award in 2010, and the George B. Walter'36 Service to Society Award from Lawrence University in 2014. In 2014 she joined Somaiya group, to take design for artisans from a program to an institute and reach its full potential. Ms. Frater is author of *Threads of Identity: Embroidery and Adornment of the Nomadic Rabaris*, recipient of the Costume Society of America's Milla Davenport award. Before residing in India, she was Associate Curator of Eastern Hemisphere Collections at the Textile Museum, in Washington, DC.

Lucia Giuliano studied at the Faculty of Architecture of Palermo, where she graduated, and at the Universitat Politecnica de Catalunya in Barcelona (ETSAB). From 2000 to 2011 she worked as an architect at Arata Isozaki & Associates office in Barcelona, working to several projects developed between Barcelona and Tokyo. During her time at AIA, she has expanded her interests toward the intersections between architecture, education, territory, and society. Since 2010 she works full time as director of Abadir, a private academy based in Catania, recognized by the Italian Ministry of Education and focused on design training.

Kazuko Goto holds a Ph.D. in Economics from Kyoto University. She was Associate Professor at Saitama University, 1998–2004, and Professor at Saitama University, 2004–2014. She was Visiting Professor at Erasmus University Rotterdam, 2004–2005. Since 2014, she is Professor and Chair of the Department of Economics at Setsunan University in Osaka. She was executive board member of the Association for Cultural Economics International, 2006–2012. Professor Goto was also Editor-in-Chief of Bunka Keizaigaku (Japan Journal of Cultural Economics), and President of the Japanese Association for Cultural Economics, 2010–2012. She has been an executive board member of the Japan Institute of Public Finance since 2016.

Marleen Hofland-Mol is a goldsmith, teacher Entrepreneurship at the Albeda College and master student in Cultural Economics and Entrepreneurship at the Erasmus University, both situated in Rotterdam. It's her ambition to help enhance the position of crafts in The Netherlands. Using the rare combination of her experiences she connects craftsmanship and theory in a creative and practical way during classes and seminars. This way she helps building bridges between the wide variety of organizations the crafts field consists of.

Lili Jiang holds a Ph.D. from Erasmus University Rotterdam with a thesis on "Valuing Craftsmanship: In Particular the Crafting of Chinese Porcelain and Dutch Delft Blue". During her Ph.D. time, she tried to use the cultural economic perspective to provide suggestions for the refocusing of craftsmanship and the strengthening of the crafts culture. She did research in China and The Netherlands, and participated in multicultural projects, to explore how values of arts and crafts work in cultural, social, and political contexts and, more importantly, how different values are interconnected and realized in our daily lives.

Arjo Klamer (Prof.-Ph.D.) holds the chair of Cultural Economics at the Erasmus University, Rotterdam. His current research focuses on the cultural dimension of economic life, the values of art and culture, and the assessment of qualitative impact of artistic and social activities. His most recent book is *Doing the Right Thing: A Value Based Economy* (Ubiquity Press, 2017). He is member of the board of various cultural organizations. He is Past-President of the Association for Cultural Economics International (ACEI). He also served as a (part-time) local governor. He is currently chairman of the Dutch Craft Council.

Priyatej Kotipalli holds a Ph.D. from Erasmus University, Rotterdam, The Netherlands. His primary research interest is in the economics of intangible cultural heritage with a special focus on traditional knowledge and skills. He serves on the board of various cultural organizations in The Netherlands and India. He is also member of the National Scientific Committee of Intangible Cultural Heritage, ICOMOS India, and of the Crafts Council of Telangana, India.

Maikel H. G. Kuijpers is Assistant Professor of European Prehistory at Leiden University and research coordinator of the joint Leiden-Delft-Erasmus Centre for Global Heritage and Development. He earned his Ph.D. in archaeology from Cambridge University in 2015. He is the author of *An Archaeology of Skill* (2017) and *Bronze Age Metalworking in the Netherlands* (2008). His main interests are craftsmanship and skill, both in the past and the present. His current research explores the relationships between material culture, skill, cognition, and innovation.

Joseph Lo holds a Ph.D. and his thesis was nominated for the 2015 annual award for outstanding research. His academic contribution has been to determine self-identified markers of authenticity in the work of artisans. In the last two decades, Dr. Lo has worked for numerous UN agencies in Bangladesh, Bhutan, China, Indonesia, Laos, Mongolia, Myanmar, Pakistan, Thailand, China-Tibet and Vietnam. Currently, Dr. Lo is a curator with Centre for Folklife and Cultural Heritage, Smithsonian Institution, Washington, DC. He also sits on the Boards of Advisors for British Council's Crafting Futures programmes in Southeast Asia and World Crafts Council Asia-Pacific Region.

Anna Mignosa is Assistant Professor at the University of Catania, Italy, and Lecturer at the Erasmus University, Rotterdam, The Netherlands. Her field of research is cultural economics, specifically cultural heritage and cultural policies. Mignosa is particularly interested in the potential effect of research on society. She had been member of the Board of the Association of Cultural Economics and is one of the founders of Officine Culturali and of CREARE.

M. J. R. Montoya, Ph.D. is a Professor of global structures and international management at the University of New Mexico Anderson School of Management. Generally, he researches global political economy and is concerned with how we make the planet a meaningful part of our social and economic realities and has published work on issues ranging from international trade to creative economy. As a professor of Creative Enterprise he also focuses on how the global creative economy is evolving.

Marion Poortvliet is founder and managing director of Crafts Council Nederland (2012), the platform for contemporary craft where heritage and innovation unite and where craftsmanship is nurtured and passed on in an innovative way to new generations. She collaborates with a large network of makers, designers, museums, educational institutes, and (business) organizations. She also works as a lecturer and educational developer at the Utrecht University of the Arts. She is trained as a designer at the fashion department of ArtEZ University of the Arts, and educated as a social entrepreneur at the University of Amsterdam.

Ritu Sethi is Director, Craft Revival Trust and the editor of the largest online encyclopedia on the traditional art, craft and textile heritage of South Asia (www.asiainch.org) She speaks and writes regularly on the subject and has been the editor of several publications including "Embroidering Futures – Repurposing the Kantha"; "Designers Meet Artisans – A practical guide." Her book "Painters, Poets, Performers – the Patuas of Bengal" is currently in print. Additionally she is a member of policy groups and serves as an advisor both national and international on culture, crafts and intangible heritage.

Indrasen Vencatachellum is Former Director of UNESCO's Division for the Diversity of Cultural Expressions and Creative Industries. Since 2008, Independent Consultant in Culture and Development projects for EU, UNDP, and UNESCO. Currently based in Paris, he is the Coordinator of the "International Network for Craft Development – RIDA" (www.ridanet.org) and Secretary General of the NGO "Culture of Origins" (www.culture-origins.org). He is the Editor of UNESCO's Practical Guides – "Data Collection on Crafts", "Participation in International Craft Trade Fairs" and "Designers Meet Artisans".

List of Figures

An Economic Assessment of Asian Crafts

List of Tables

Introduction

Anna Mignosa and Priyatej Kotipalli

Winter of 2010, The Netherlands, right in the middle of the economic down turn post and the starting of the euro crises was the environment within which this book originated. This was a period where a few fundamental questions were being discussed as the world was reeling under a loss in faith in capitalism. Some of the questions that we pondered were why do we work? Why ideas of doing good work are important? How does economics shape this conversation? We tried to reflect on these topics by examining craft and craftsmanship in the contemporary world.

We constituted a research group to study the craft economies in seven nations under the leadership of prof. Arjo Klamer at Erasmus

A. Mignosa (✉)
University of Catania, Catania, Italy
e-mail: a.mignosa@unict.it

Erasmus University Rotterdam, Rotterdam, The Netherlands

P. Kotipalli
Erasmus University Rotterdam, Rotterdam, The Netherlands
e-mail: Pkotipalli@eshcc.eur.nl

A. Mignosa and P. Kotipalli (eds.), *A Cultural Economic Analysis of Craft*,
https://doi.org/10.1007/978-3-030-02164-1_1

University. The list of countries was a mix of developed-developing economies, traditional and modern societies, and the aim was to understand the status of craft in these countries. During this research, we got alerted to the fact that craft, craftsmanship and also the economic understanding varied across countries. We also realised that cultural economists had not paid much attention to this field. What also emerged is that there was a revival in interest in craft.

In different periods, craft has attracted the attention of policy agencies, museums, designers, private institutions. This has led to its 'revival' (Luckman 2015). The first time this took place with industrialisation and William Morris' *Arts and Crafts* movement. The wave of a second revival took place in the 1960–1970s with the hippy movement. Finally, we are now testifying a third revival characterised by the spreading of the Do it yourself (DIY) movement and the turning to crafts as a source of income in time of economic crisis. This 'third' revival, which is still taking place, emphasises the economic potential of crafts, though it is translated into very different policies. From being considered a mean to generate income for young craftsmen, while revitalising cities stimulating small scale production activities in advanced economies, to being considered a resource to boost the export of local products to contribute to the strengthening of the national economy of developing countries. Interestingly enough, in this second group of countries many craftsmen are abandoning their activity as they cannot survive, whereas in advanced countries many young people turn to crafts as the unique possible source of income following the crises.

These issues have been the focus of researches in different fields. However, the bulk of works analysing the craft sector come from cultural studies where books like Sennet's *The Craftsman* (2009) or Dormer's *The Culture of Craft* (1997) provide a thorough recount of the main features of the sector and its evolution. Economists, instead, have given attention to specific aspects of the craft sector, namely job organisation and the impact of the sector on the overall economy of a country. The economic approach, however, risks focussing on measuring the sector and/or its impact, overlooking its specific features. This book intends to overcome this limitation bringing in the analysis cultural economics, i.e. the application of economics to the analysis of the cultural sector. The vantage point of this perspective is that it could imply a different approach considering those characteristics that differentiate cultural objects from industrial products.

The book builds upon the results of the above-mentioned research that compared the craft sector in seven countries (China, Germany, India, Italy, Japan, the Netherlands and UK, see Klamer et al. 2012, 2013) highlighting characteristics interesting for cultural economics (e.g. the role of institutions, education and organisations, the structure of the market, the evolution of the craft sector, etc.). Using the results of this comparative analysis as a reference, the book highlights the implications of a cultural economics approach. It considers the traditional discourse about craft and craftsmanship, the economic features, the importance of policies and of the tools used to avoid short-term effects and, instead, make the craft sector effective for sustainable development.

Despite its cultural economic focus, the book involves researchers from different disciplines (in addition to cultural economics) and professionals from the sector. They are invited to help in contributing to a substantive framing of the relevance and contribution of the craft sector to economy and society at large.

The book is presented in four parts with each segment attempting to grapple with an aspect of crafts. The first segment sets the conceptual part of the book where we explore how we understand craft. There are three chapters, the first by Brulotte and Montoya, who take a hermeneutics approach to make sense of craft. The second contribution, by Vencatachellum, explores how UNESCO has shaped the conversation around craft, and the last chapter by Kotipalli presents the various economic approaches that have influenced our understanding of the craft sector. The second segment of the book deals with policies that have shaped the craft sector in various countries. It includes a survey of policies for craft in: China (Jiang), France (Cominelli), Germany (Fjeldsted), India (Sethi), Japan (Goto), the Netherlands (Hofland-Mol and Poortvliet), U.K (Bennet), U.S.A (Montoya), and a chapter by Mignosa that outlines the rationale of the various policies and the tools that are used. Issues on the economic assessment of crafts form the third segment of the book. Ellis and Lo deal with crafts in Asia. Ballyn explores and critically analyses the role of Intellectual Property for crafts across countries. The contribution from Chatterjee is concerned with how institutions like crafts councils are engaged in advocating and aiding in the collection of reliable economic data with the example of India. Ellis presents various issues concerned with the measurement of the craft sector. The fourth, and final, segment of the book presents yet again a conceptual view of craft with the contribution by Klamer, who views craft as a shared practice and advocates for a craft culture around it. The chapter by Giuliano explores the line between craft and design, while the chapter from Kuijpers reflects on the importance of materials for craft, proposing a different approach. Finally, Frater presents a case about what ideal education for artisans looks like with examples from India.

Some of the topics are transversal to the whole book and in what follows we would like to illustrate these shared features.

Definition of Craft

The importance of identifying craft in order to proceed with its analysis is a recurrent topic in the various chapters. Craft creates a liaison between the past and the future: it derives from the industrial revolution but, at the same time, it is a critique to it, an alternative to mechanisation. Chatterjee, however, notices also how this has become a problem for crafts in India, where the sector has been defined a 'sunset industry'. Several authors (e.g. Ballyn, Kuijpers) underline the link with tradition. This connection with the past makes it difficult to clearly defining the craft sector.

Ellis talk of an elusive concept, which makes it impossible to agree on its 'key qualities'. Brulotte and Montoya suggest that crafts 'vary across time, geographic space and social configuration'. In fact, the World Crafts Council identified five regions to be capable of grasping the specific feature of crafts in each of them. Brulotte and Montoya notice the existence of differences among countries and, especially, a separation North-South that affects the way of perceiving craft products and their values. Ellis and Lo, confirm this in their illustration of the Asian crafts as they suggest that craft in this region is based on specific materials, skills and modes of production, and 'remains an activity that produces objects that have a key function/role in local economies in which local artisans use local materials and manage local ecosystems' (Ellis and Lo). This contrasts with OECD countries where crafts were long considered as souvenirs to sell to tourists, though now there is a growing appreciation for craft object connected to the request of unique products of high quality, which, as Hofland-Mol and Poortvliet notice for the Netherland, people are willing to buy. This new demand could represent the future of craft production, as Chatterjee suggests when describing those craft companies capable to present 'hand production as a contemporary lifestyle that could communicate to new generations in new markets'. Klamer pushes further the appreciation of craft of those consumers that demand it, and suggest that they coproduce the practice of craft.

The difficulty in getting to a univocal definition of craft also relates to the organisation that uses this definition. For instance, the differences in scope of UNESCO and ILO explain the discrepancy between the two as for the notion of craft they use. In fact, the importance of definitions from a policy point of view, as it is necessary to define the sector in order to intervene in its favour, is highlighted also by Goto.

Talking of the definition of craft a twofold interpretation emerges; craft as intangible cultural heritage and craft as Cultural and Creative Industries (CCI). According to Vencatachellum, 'The holistic approach of UNESCO implies a due recognition of the dual role of craft as part of the Cultural Heritage and of the creative industries side (…)'. The difficulty in defining the sector has stimulated the creation of organisations aiming to support the sector by providing data and research (American Crafts Council, World Crafts Council).

Classification of the Craft Sector

Various contributors to the book consider craft as part of the Cultural and Creative Industries (CCI). Putting craft under the CCI category, favours an approach that considers the economic impact of the CCI and, hence, of crafts. The prevailing approach, then, considers craft part of the economy, but, its ever evolving character makes it difficult to identify and then measure it. There are reports assessing the dimension of the sector both at the international (UNESCO) and national (Buthan, Thailand, Philippines) level. UNESCO states that data on crafts are fundamental for the development of the sector. Ellis agrees on the need for a systematic classification of crafts. He suggests that this would help 'standardise what is meant by crafts' and therefore allow to have a clear measure of the dimension of the sector. His thorough illustration of the categorisations actually in place, shows, however, how far we still are from getting a clear classification of the sector, and thus, of its dimension. If it is possible to get an idea of the production, it is not easy to assess the number of artisans and the demand of craft products. As a matter of fact, Ballyin confirms this opinion. He provides some data on the dimension of the sector in India and China, but then recognises that, in fact, 'nobody knows' how many craft producers are there. In fact, Chatterjee underlines the problems related to a thorough collection of data on crafts in India. When data are available, however, the existing categories still present some ambiguities.

Differences in the definition of craft, actually, can be noticed also within countries. When looking at the development of policies for crafts in various countries, it is not rare to notice shifts in the focus on the main qualities or in the objectives of the policies themselves.

Handmade

Contributors, generally, agree on the handmade feature of crafts. However, Sethi shows that in India the first policies for crafts emphasised the handmade aspect and protected this feature against the mechanisation of craft production, whereas the more recent policies turn the situation upside down. A similar pattern seems to have characterised China (Jiang), where until 1997 policies focused on the handmade quality of crafts, but afterwards opened up to the use of machines. In the Dutch definition of the crafts, Hofland-Mol and Poortvliet notice that the handmade component is one of the defining characteristics. Germany constitutes an interesting case (Fjeldsted). Here, craft, or *Handwerk*, constitutes an educational and economic force, and has a special position as it is considered 'essential to integrity in the production of the general material environment, rather than being an optional or alternative way of production'. The human maker still has a central position, which has been guaranteed by the policies put in place in the country.

Interestingly, Kuijpers, through his approach, questions the definition of craft as uniquely handmade objects opposed to mass production. Referring to ancient objects he shows how copying was normal already in the Bronze age. He also questions the definition of craft as heritage. Thus he proposes to shift attention to materials and consider craft as the 'heritage of materials': craft becomes 'a way of exploring and understanding', a heuristic.

Despite the focus on the role of craft for the economy (to fight poverty, create employment, increase export), various authors, acknowledging that profitability and economic return are not all that matter in the cultural economics approach, anticipate the main point stated in Chapter 4 where Kotipalli illustrates the potential of the cultural economic analysis of the craft sector. The difference is that cultural economics is also capable of considering the qualities of crafts, providing a fuller framework and a strong basis for the development of a craft culture.

Policies

Policies are important for crafts. Bennet emphasises this in her contribution, pointing at the uncertainty that follows Brexit. The focus on the role of craft for economic development is common in both Eastern and Western countries. The eradication of poverty is commonly stated as one of the aim of craft. However, it is also interesting to notice some nuances implying differences among countries. For instance, in Montoya's description of the development of policies in the United States, the evolution from a focus on the role of craft for the industry and, thus, for the economy to the importance for civil rights to fight the marginalisation of some citizens stands out. The World Crafts Council, recognises the importance of this latter characteristic. The contribution of craft to CH and the identity of a community represents its added value on a global market or for the national culture (Bennet). Craft can be a weapon to fight standardisation of production, mechanisation, industrialisation, globalisation. Data shows that crafts can indeed improve living conditions as artisans have an income higher than the average in their community (Ellis and Lo).

Policy Tools

Public support to the craft sector takes place under various forms. The most common support is for the transmission of skills which may translate into: the organisation of formal education (Germany, Fjeldsted, France, UK); the use of apprenticeships (Germany) and practice (The Netherlands); the introduction of measures to facilitate the transmission of skills from older to younger generations (as in Japan with the Master title—see Goto—or in France with traditional manufactures that often date back to the seventeenth century—see Cominelli). Interestingly, Ellis and Lo in their analysis found that most artisans do not have a formal education but learn from family, friend and peers, somehow confirming the importance of apprenticeship for craft. The opposite seems to hold in OECD countries where education plays a fundamental role (e.g. in Germany where it is the prerequisite to get the Master title, see Fieldsted, and Ballyn). UNESCO considers education fundamental to support craft and put it among the fundamental policy tools (Ventachachellum). As we will see below, Giuliano proposes an interesting form of education where the interaction between craft and design benefits both. Interestingly, Frater suggests that education as a way to make people know about craft techniques can also be an instrument to develop the appreciation of crafts and, hence, demand.

Support to artisans to improve their business skills is also something necessary (Ballyn), and, in fact, it takes place in various cases (e.g. USA–Montoya). The creation of organisations capable of advocating for the sector is also a tool that can facilitate the development of the sector as it is the case with the German Crafts and Trades system, the Crafts

Council in UK (Bennet) and the Dutch Hoofd Bedrijfsschap Ambacht first and then the Dutch Crafts Council (Hofland-Mol and Poortvliet).

Of course, financing is an important tool to support the sector; however, data show that most artisans do not get external funds to start their activity (Ellis and Lo). An interesting example of indirect support comes from the Netherlands where a lower (i.e. 6%) VAT rate is applied on craft products (Hofland-Mol and Poortvliet).

Among the tools to be used in favour of the craft sector, Intellectual Property Protection is not widespread yet (Mignosa). Ballyin provides an extensive overview of the various types of IPP available, the organisations already in place to help artisans adopt these tools, and the issues related to their use. He notices, once more, the differences connected to the geographical location of the artisan.

Another feature, which can be found worldwide, is the use of crafts for cultural diplomacy. It happens in the United States where craft is seen as a 'mediator of cultural exchange' (Montoya), in China (Jiang) and in India (Sethi).

The Master title is another possible tool of intervention and, in fact, it is present in various countries with differences in the way is it assigned: in Germany (Fjeldsted) it follows an education trajectory, whereas in India (Sethi) and France (Cominelli) is a title granted by the government. Jiang notices two interesting aspects related to the attribution of the master title in China. The first is the possibility to get the title by 'influencing' the authority that should grant it, even when skills are missing. The second relates to the influence that the title has on the price of the crafts produced by a Master.

In France, Cominelli underlines the liaison between the master title, introduced in 1994, and the protection of the intangible heritage aspects of craft. The title entitled the holder to get funds for the transmission of skills. It presents several similarities with the Japanese Living Heritage title (Goto), in both cases the holder gets funds to transmit skills to younger people. Interestingly, however, in France there is also the living heritage title, it is an attribute that can be assigned to companies (label EPV—Entreprise du Patrimoine Vivant) acknowledging their skills, which entitles them to some tax incentives; though for a limited amount of time (5 years).

Prizes are among the tools used to try to stimulate craft. While there are several prizes set by public organisations, Giuliano mentions a prize that a small private art academy organises in Italy. It is a small, local experience, yet this prize is interesting as it shows that if we want to talk of a craft culture, it is necessary to involve a wider set of stakeholders including the private ones, who sometimes, are better equipped to identify interesting forms of craft and valorise them.

Role of Design

Several contributions to the book refer to design and its 'complicated/ambiguous' relationship with craft. Vencatachellum and Frater both point at the risk that artisans are simply considered as factors of production with the risk of putting aside tradition. Interestingly, Giuliano proposes a different view, one where she talks of a 'shared authorship' because 'the role of the craftsmen could not simply be that of bringing the design process to completion'. As Kuijpers suggests, craft is an exploration. Based on several international experiences of collaboration between designers and artisans, Giuliano proposes a new role for designers, they can steer a process that allows the preservation of traditional craft skills, while positioning the craft objects on the market. The experiences she recounts seem to confirm Vencatachellum's mild optimism about the relationship artisans-design. This also seems a possible solution for Frater's worry of an excessive commercialisation of crafts.

Sustainable Development

The various experiences and points of view collected in the book show how important craft can be but, also, how difficult it is to set a long term strategy to support it. Frates's chapter on her experience in India, clearly demonstrates how it is impossible to design long term policies and never modify them. On the contrary, strategies and policies for crafts need to be constantly fine-tuned to guarantee the valorisation of the sector and its development.

The notion of craft is often matched with that of sustainability. For instance, crafts could be part of a viable model of economic sustainability for Asian artisans. If adequately supported, they can become a key cultural and economic asset for the region. In the case of crafts, environmental sustainability is also often addressed. The materials used (or that should be used) the techniques followed, and the lasting quality of the final product relate to a mode of production that respects the environment. Cominelli argues that supporting crafts '(…) means to support alternative economic models of development in a global economy oriented to the standardization of shapes, needs, fabrication processes, markets and to the programming of product's lifespan'.

Craft Culture

The prevailing approach, evident from the chapters of this book, is an economic one based on 'profitability and economic return' (Brulotte and Montoya). The book argues, however, that cultural economics could provide a different look capable of taking into consideration also the qualitative aspects of crafts. Kotipalli illustrates, therefore, the characteristics of cultural economics and how it helps to understand how policies for craft are designed and implemented. However, the author also acknowledges the differences within cultural economics, whereas some authors tend to be more heterodox and provide an even wider perspective. Such an approach is proposed by Klamer. He uses the value-based approach to 'make sense of the crafts', focusing on its values and qualities. Klamer claims that craft is a shared practice. As both artisans and crafts' consumers valorize what is important to them, the latter become participants in the practice of craft. This creates a craft culture. However, generally, governmental policies are not capable of understanding this culture and, therefore, fall short in their support to the sectors. The book emphasises the need for a craft culture capable to go beyond the economic discourse on crafts (Kotipalli) and favour a rounded development of the sector. Vencatachellum suggests it is necessary to consider the demand side, and the importance of a social recognition of artisans comparable to that of movie stars, to acknowledge their creative contribution to society. It becomes evident that it is necessary to have a more holistic approach to and view of the sector. That is, it is necessary to develop a craft culture to have a sustainable development of the sector as Frater, Klamer, Mignosa and Kotipalli suggest. Klamer calls then for social changes to realise a cultural change that would put the notion of craft culture to the fore. Craft culture requires attention, work, and participation to make crafts meaningful in the future.

References

Klamer, A., P. Kotipalli, L. Jiang, T. Fjeldsted, K. Goto, and A. Mignosa. 2012. *Creatief vakmanschap in internationaal perspectief.* Stiching Economie en Cultuur, Erasmus University Rotterdam.

Klamer, A., P. Kotipalli, L. Jiang, T. Fjeldsted, and A. Mignosa. 2013. *Herwaardering Ambachtscultuur Hoofdzaak.* Stiching Economie en Cultuur, Erasmus University Rotterdam.

Luckman, S. 2015. *Craft and the Creative Economy.* Palgrave Macmillan.

Part I

Definitional Issues

Defining Craft: Hermeneutics and Economy

Ronda L. Brulotte and M. J. R. Montoya

There are few words in our contemporary economic vocabulary that contain the complexity of the word "craft." A word normally associated with handmade objects, it has historically been used to celebrate the mastery of handmade goods while simultaneously used to render them quaint, often diminishing their social and economic value. It is a word that evokes continuity with the historical past while restoring human qualities to modern technologies. It is a word that situates objects and the embodied knowledge required for their creation within a self-aware framework that references pre-industrial social formations; this includes the emphasis on apprenticeship as a form of preserving community identity in relation to evolving economic realities and new social relations. Craft is a word that is both devoted to the old and invested with meaning through its tension with the new.

R. L. Brulotte (✉) · M. J. R. Montoya
University of New Mexico, Albuquerque, NM, USA
e-mail: brulotte@unm.edu

M. J. R. Montoya
e-mail: mrmonto@unm.edu

A. Mignosa and P. Kotipalli (eds.), *A Cultural Economic Analysis of Craft*,
https://doi.org/10.1007/978-3-030-02164-1_2

Therefore, as an economic concept it resists the ability to neatly categorize, which makes the craft economy difficult to enumerate and prioritize. So then, what is craft—and, by extension, who are "craftsmen"—and how is it part of the larger discussion on the global creative and cultural economy? In what follows we define and describe the craft economy as both a philosophical problem and a feature of the global political economy. To achieve this, we explore the concept of craft as a non-linear hermeneutic question and situate this in relation to institutional descriptions of craft economy.

Why Is Craft a Hermeneutic Problem?

Craft is a very complex word, grounded in modernity, but also defined in opposition to the modern. Craft has origins in the Germanic word *kraft*, which translates into "skill." Later the word would evolve into Dutch, Swedish, and Old English renderings that meant skill, strength, or both.[1] By the late seventeenth century the word's singular form represented the act of apprenticeship and the noun itself was also used to represent a vessel, likely to convey the skill and risk associated with building something used to navigate the seas.[2] As a modifier, the contemporary phrasing describes food or drink made in either a nonconventional manner, or that is reproduced by hand or non-mechanized (or minimally mechanized) means. Its conflation with the unconventional reveals the tension the word contains. As an antonym, the word craft responds to a word like "cliché," a nineteenth-century French word to describe the sound a printing press made when it processed documents.[3] Similarly, the idea of craft has been used in storytelling to reveal the authentic, human dimension of work. Much like the mythical John Henry in African-American folklore, who is described as a "crafty and steady soul," the "steel-drivin' man" became a folk-hero narrative about

---

[1]"Craft" Oxford English Dictionary, 2017 Online Ed.

[2]Ibid.

[3]"Cliché" Oxford English Dictionary, 2017 Online Ed.

the value of labor as it competed with mechanical tools. This description implies the exploitation of human labor, including the legacy of slavery (Nelson 2006). Craft expresses the battle between human and machine, not merely as a description of what is produced, but also the environment that shaped its production (Benjamin 1968). It is a word that emanated from the same time and place as the Western concept of the nation-state and it corresponds with the era of transcontinental commerce, debates about a secularized society, and the expansion of European and later US imperialism.

This brief genealogy speaks to the paradox represented by the contemporary notion of craft: the category itself is a historic product of capitalist modernity, one that critiqued and aspired to provide an alternative to the industrial manufacture that was the hallmark of modernity itself. For many Western societies, craft represented an antidote to what sociologist Max Weber (1976) described as the progressive "disenchantment of the world"—the replacement of a pre-modern social order, with its mythical orientation to the world, by a bureaucratized, secular modernity.[4] Nevertheless, while craft may be premised on ideas about pre- or non-industrial modes of production, the forms it takes vary across time, geographic space, and social configurations. This is why we pose craft as a hermeneutic problem.

A hermeneutic approach to craft—and its attendant terms such as authenticity, heritage, and tradition—takes as its starting point that the concept of craft itself has no fixed referent. Such an analysis entails moving beyond craft as a specific category of object or practice in order to understand it as a concept emerging out of specific socioeconomic relationships. Critical to defining craft is identifying how ideas about past modes of production are mobilized in the present moment to specific economic or political ends. A hermeneutics of craft therefore allows us to examine how the term is being operationalized in today's global economy. As contributions to this volume demonstrate, both public

[4]Although Weber's concept of disenchantment is framed as a sociological condition (i.e., the retreat of magic and myth from social life through processes of secularization and rationalization), the term originates with Friedrich Schiller's philosophical treatise on modern fragmentation and the role of aesthetics (Angus 1983).

institutions and private enterprises are investing in localized cultural products. How is craft imbued with meaning and value in this post-nationalist age, characterized by digital technologies, emerging legal frameworks for intellectual and cultural property, and a consumer market simultaneously driven by novelty and nostalgia?

In this vein, we would stress that craft does not look the same from all vantage points. It may seem obvious that the conditions that defined craft in nineteenth-century Germany are different from those that presently circumscribe craft production in Mexico; however, the distinctions are not simply a function of historical period and national territory. Within these time-spaces, we must also consider who has the power to define, or, better yet, claim craft: the maker, the consumer, or some other intermediary, such as the World Crafts Council discussed below. Furthermore, the power dimension must not be overlooked. Craft exists in a world that continues to operate along the resilient axes of class, racial/ethnic, and gender formations. A craft cheese maker in France, for instance, arguably has a different relationship to global markets and consumers than an indigenous women's textile cooperative in Guatemala. To point: we rarely question the economic or symbolic value of goods like an exquisite Abbaye du Mont des Cats cheese, handcrafted by monks in a French monastery. Meanwhile, a Mayan weaver may struggle to convince her audience that the cloth painstakingly woven on a backstrap loom warrants a price that translates to a livable wage. The Global North-South divide has real material consequences for producers, whose products are not subject to the same standards of value-creation (Appadurai 1990).

Craft is ultimately a philosophical problem—a question of interpretation—embedded in economic realities. Returning to Weber's notion of disenchantment and the "iron cage"[5] of modernity, craft is invoked as part of the structural asymmetry of modern progress. Does the current vocabulary of craft as a driver of the creative and cultural economy move beyond this structural asymmetry and modern/traditional

---

[5]Weber conceptualized bureaucratized, rationalized modern society as an "iron cage" that limited the human capacity to live freely.

dichotomy or does it merely serve to reinforce them in new ways? Does craft in the creative economy hold the potential for the re-enchantment of the world, or does it replace one "iron cage" with another?

Craft and the Creative Economy

Craft has been measured as a significant part of the cultural and creative economy (Henry 2007). UNESCO's most recent report on the creative economy highlights the craft sector as over half of all cultural and creative productivity (2013). This takes the form of handcrafted goods that make use of media such as glass, textiles, woods, metal, clay, paper, or ceramics. In terms of global economic output, it is estimated that the cultural and creative economy constitutes over 5% of global GDP (Buitrago Restrepo and Duque Márquez 2013). Now popularly referred to as the "Orange Economy," the creative economy has incorporated trends and growth in the global economy, particularly in places where systemic poverty rendered these economies invisible. Moreover, the scale of growth at "the base of global income" is now looked upon as the future of the global economy, and once-dominant economies now share the conversation on future economic growth, productivity, and sustainability (Prahalad and Hart 2002). Educational services, including apprenticeships (in which craft plays a large role) for which other types of knowledge transfer activities are unaccounted, may have a significant effect on our understanding of the overall economic impact of creative industries (Henry 2007). Each of these indicators expresses important features of the cultural and creative economy and the agenda it will shape over the next century. As other types of design and technology are identified and supported, and as new materials are used in forms of production, the evolution of craft will become more difficult to measure.

To understand this problem further, one can see how defining craft has evolved among various institutions that support the craft economy. Artisan and craft guilds, for example, focus on specific forms of craft production. Non-profits such as the American Crafts Council and Aid to Artisans often introduce information about craft societies to larger national and international fora. Other organizations, such as the New England Foundation for the Arts (NEFA), produce regionally specific research and data. However, NEFA's definition of creative economy has become a standard used by other organizations throughout the United States, particularly because of the demonstrated impact of the creative sector on their own regional economy (NEFA 2007). Together, the discussion of craft supported by sector-specific artisan guilds and the information produced by research institutions (including universities and think-tanks) and the non-profit sector have established an ecosystem to organize people around the various craft industries of the world. As institutions internationalized post-World War II, so too did the complexity of these networks. The need for a wider umbrella prompted organizations like the American Crafts Council to form the World Crafts Council (WCC) in 1964. The inaugural assembly of the WCC took place in New York City, where representatives from 46 nations gathered to determine how to support the craft economy. Almost immediately, the problems in defining craft became apparent.

The World Crafts Council: The Problem of Defining Craft

During that inaugural assembly, craft was defined as emphasizing "sophisticated technique," while the arts were distinguished as emphasizing "intuitive sense" and science as emphasizing "the transfer of knowledge." It became increasingly clear that this definition, while useful in identifying the mastery of production in craft labor, was largely inadequate and would be more problematic as new technology and work patterns evolved (WCC 1964). Because techniques were not segregated from elements of arts and sciences, the WCC determined that these categories were culturally specific and would require constant re-visitation. Consequently, the WCC was separated into five distinct regions: Africa, Asia Pacific, Europe, Latin America, and North America so that smaller discussions could be organized regionally to deliver to assemblies as needed. During the 6th General Assembly, craft was reiterated as any "form of production that requires skill or skilled work," a consistent phrasing used until today (WCC 1974). The forum has since wrestled with the question of craft as a tool to critique and revise history. For example, during the 17th Assembly, discussions about how craft is a form of cultural preservation prompted discussions about social innovation and how craftspeople are cultural entrepreneurs who "support vulnerable economies" and "empower those who have suffered or who are excluded" from society (WCC 2012a, b). In total, the various assemblies' attempts to define craft can be summarized as follows. Craft:

- is a by-product of "skilled technique."
- is connected to materials. Regardless of the form of materials, the skill in manipulating or transforming those materials is part of what constitutes the skill of craft production.
- is a human process. The act of creating "by hand" is what defines human consumption and production and is the index of our relationship to the world.
- requires the teaching of such technique and the development of mastery specific to that technique.
- has a strong relationship to the past and is a visible marker of ancestral knowledge.
- is a vehicle for social mobility among vulnerable populations and a source of empowerment.

These definitions, again, rely on an evolving, hermeneutic discussion of craft. While this complicates the desire to measure the impact of the craft economy, it also reveals the resilience of its value to the global economy. Craft economy is not a set of immutable objects but it is also a problem that navigates the role of the human in relation to the passing of time and the changing of place.

So what then is the future of the craft economy? There is no doubt that the word craft cannot be separated from the problem of "being modern." The concept of skill can be seen as a by-product of the industrial revolution, where the separation of labor and leisure fractured creative work into class distinctions. It is also a by-product of mass production which has turned craft into a word that represents the battle between the handmade and its mechanized counterparts. It challenges the theory of absolute advantage that came from nineteenth-century imperial power, and it makes words like "supply chain transparency" (telling the story of your stuff) and "value-chain equity" (being included in the valuation of a product) terms that craft workers strategically employ. At each point, craft's use as a term plays an important role in the overall discussion of cultural economy. While human productivity is limitless, its manifestation in relation to place and time is not necessarily so, especially in a complex, globalized world. By maintaining a critical, non-linear definition of craft, we challenge ourselves to ask: how is craft being used today, who gets to participate in craft economy and who is being excluded (or worse yet) exploited? In the twenty-first century, there will be a convergence of ideas made possible by globalization but without a universally tested vocabulary. Craft will play a role in testing these ideas, revealing how cultural economics and cultural economy are not exclusively defined by profitability and economic return. As public and private spaces are reconfigured, so too will ideas of resourcefulness, ownership, scarcity, and abundance, and by extension ideas about what it means, as John Henry once demonstrated (Nelson 2006), to be "crafty and steady souls."

References

Angus, Ian H. 1983. Disenchantment and Modernity: The Mirror of Technique. *Human Studies* 6: 141–166.

Appadurai, A. 1990. Difference and Disjuncture in the Global Cultural Economy. *Public Culture* 2 (2): 1–24.

Benjamin, W. 1968. The Work of Art in the Age of Mechanical Reproduction. In *Illuminations*, ed. H. Arendt, 214–218. London: Fontana.

Buitrago Restrepo, F., and I. Duque Márquez. 2013. *The Orange Economy: An Infinite Opportunity*. Washington, DC: Inter-American Development Bank.

Henry, C. 2007. *Entrepreneurship in the Creative Industries: An International Perspective*. London: Edward Elgar Press.

Nelson, S.R. 2006. *Steel Drivin' Man: John Henry, the Untold Story of an American Legend*. Oxford: Oxford University Press.

New England Foundation for the Arts (NEFA). 2007. The Creative Economy: A New Definition. https://www.nefa.org/sites/default/files/ResearchCreativeEconReport2007.pdf.

Prahalad, C.K., and S. Hart. 2002. The Fortune at the Bottom of the Pyramid. *Strategy + Business* 26 (1): 35–42.

UNESCO. 2013. *Creative Economy Report: Widening Local Development Pathways*. New York: UNESCO.

Weber, M. 1976. *The Protestant Ethic and the Spirit of Capitalism*, 2nd ed. London: George Allen & Unwin.

World Crafts Council. 1964. Proceedings of the 1st General Assembly of the World Crafts Council. New York, NY.

World Crafts Council. 1974. Proceedings of the 6th General Assembly of the World Crafts Council. Toronto, Canada.

World Crafts Council. 2012a. Proceedings of the 17th General Assembly of the World Crafts Council. New York, NY.

World Crafts Council. 2012b. World Crafts Council: Finding Aid. https://craftcouncil.org/sites/default/files/2017-04/WCC_FindingAid_0.pdf.

UNESCO Approach to Crafts

Indrasen Vencatachellum

Background and Framework

Contemporary, utilitarian or artistic crafts inspired by tradition, represent a highly valuable form of cultural expression, a capital of self-confidence which is especially significant in the developing countries. Re-emphasizing the value of hand work is also important for many developed countries where the quality of life is often threatened by excessive industrial standardization.

Among the UN specialized agencies, UNESCO is the only one which has devoted a specific programme to crafts. With a global vision of the socio-cultural and economic role played by crafts in the society, UNESCO has, for many years now, endeavoured to develop well-balanced, coherent and concerted action by combining training, production and promotional activities and stimulating the necessary cooperation between the concerned national institutions, regional, international, governmental and non-governmental organizations.

I. Vencatachellum (✉)
International Network for Craft Development—RIDA, Paris, France

A. Mignosa and P. Kotipalli (eds.), *A Cultural Economic Analysis of Craft*,
https://doi.org/10.1007/978-3-030-02164-1_3

Without going into the intricate discussion on the meaning of the word 'crafts', it is useful to specify, on the one hand, that in this chapter UNESCO's intervention is **limited to utilitarian and artistic crafts**, excluding service or production crafts (bakers, tailors, electricians, and so on) which are covered by other Organizations, namely the International Labour Organization (ILO). On the other hand, although there is no universally acceptable understanding of the term "artisanal products" because of a set of variables, we will refer to the most commonly quoted following definition, adopted by the UNESCO/ITC International Symposium on "Crafts and the International Market: Trade and Customs Codification" (Manila, October 1997) and applicable to a wide range of the world's crafts:

> Artisanal products are those produced by artisans, either completely by hand, or with the help of hand tools or even mechanical means, as long as the direct manual contribution of the artisan remains the most substantial component of the finished product. These are produced without restriction in terms of quantity and using raw materials from sustainable resources. The special nature of artisanal products derives from their distinctive features, which can be utilitarian, aesthetic, artistic, creative, culturally attached, decorative, functional, traditional, religiously and socially symbolic and significant.

Such a diversity of the characteristics of artisanal products is the result of a consensus, taking into account the specific concerns of all the geographical regions represented at this Symposium: for example, the religious significance for the Arab region and the culturally attached symbol for the indigenous artisans of Latina America.

It is at the World Conference on Cultural Policies (Mexico City, 26 July–6 August 1982) that the International Community gave, for the first time, due recognition to the potential role, both economic and cultural, of crafts in national development. The Conference adopted a specific Recommendation (No. 6) calling on UNESCO "*to identify sources of basic data on the current situation of crafts throughout the world, on a national, regional or global basis*" and "*to draw to the attention of the United Nations System as a whole the importance of crafts in the development process*".

As a follow-up to this Recommendation, UNESCO convened the 1st International Consultation of Experts on the Preservation and Development of Crafts in the Contemporary World (Rio de Janeiro, Brazil, 27–31 August 1984). Among the recommendations adopted at this Conference, mention should be made of: data banks on crafts, the introduction of arts and crafts education in primary and secondary schools and the organization of pilot workshops for skills upgrading of craftspeople.

These recommendations were duly taken into account by the UNESCO Meeting of Experts for the Preparation of the "Ten-Year Plan of Action for Craft Development in the World 1990–1998" held in Hammamet, Tunisia, in 1989. It is significant that the two priorities in this Plan were given to Data collection and to the Training of craftspeople. An evaluation of the achievements of the Plan of Action carried out in 2000 by a team of external specialists from the 5 regions revealed that the objectives chosen by UNESCO were the correct ones and should continue to be promoted. It was also recommended that UNESCO's future Crafts Programme should be related to the general concern for the eradication of poverty, the protection of the environment and the indispensable linkages between culture and sustainable development.

UNESCO's Craft Policy and Programme is also to be situated in the light of the following **reference documents**:

- The *Universal Declaration on Cultural Diversity* adopted by the UNESCO General Conference in 2001 testifies to the determination of the Member States to define, within the context of globalization, an instrument to devise national cultural policies and ensure respect for all cultural identities. Artists and artisans of all cultures are the privileged actors of cultural diversity and craftworks represent the most visible manifestation of this diversity which needs to be promoted. In this connection, Article 9 of the Declaration ("Cultural policies as catalysts of creativity") stipulates: "*while ensuring the free circulation of ideas and works, cultural policies must create conditions conducive to the production and dissemination of diversified cultural goods and services through cultural industries that have the means to assert themselves at the local and global levels*".

- The 2003 *UNESCO Convention for the Safeguarding of the Intangible Heritage* is another important recognition of the need to preserve and promote crafts as a distinctive embodiment of traditional knowledge and skills. Article 22 of the Convention specifies that the "*intangible cultural heritage is manifested inter alia in traditional craftsmanship*". These traditional skills are in danger of disappearing due to the declining number of practitioners, lack of funds and the negative effects of globalization. One of the effective ways to achieve their safeguard is to guarantee that the bearers of the intangible cultural heritage continue to further develop their knowledge and skills and transmit them to younger generations. That is why UNESCO encourages the establishment by Member States of national systems of "Living Human Treasures" and the registration of unique craft traditions and techniques in the 'Representative List of the Intangible Cultural Heritage of Humanity'[1]
- Finally, the Craft Development Policy and Programme falls within UNESCO's strategy for implementing the "United Nations Decade for Poverty Eradication" (1996–2005). Indeed, crafts contribute to a fundamental step in the fight against poverty through the empowerment of people, especially youth and women, the imparting of knowledge and skills for income generation. That is why UNESCO launched an inter-sectoral programme in the poorest countries entitled "Crafts as a window for employment and income generation".

The holistic approach of UNESCO implies a due recognition of the dual role of crafts as part of the Cultural Heritage and of the creative industries side by side with the establishment of linkages between designers and artisans.

[1]Such as 'Craftmanship of Nanjing Yunjun brocade' (China), 'Woodcrafting knowledge of the Zafimaniry community' (Madagascar) and 'Indonesian Batik'. Cumulative List available on www.unesco.org/culture/ich/en/lists.

The Cultural Heritage Framework

Everywhere in the world, traditional crafts represent the living manifestation of the ways of life, customs and rituals of communities and groups. As previously mentioned, the importance of crafts in the cultural heritage has been formally recognized by the international community in the UNESCO '*Convention for the Safeguarding of the Intangible Cultural Heritage*' (2003). Article 1 of the Convention defines the 'intangible cultural heritage' as being the "practices, representations, expressions, knowledge, skills – as well as the instruments, **artefacts** and cultural spaces associated therewith- that communities, groups and, in some cases, individuals recognize as part of their cultural heritage(….)."

The UNESCO Convention further defines intangible cultural heritage as: being **transmitted** from generation to generation; **constantly recreated** by communities and groups, in response to their environment, their interaction with nature and their history; providing communities and groups with a sense of **identity and continuity**.

The following implications of this definition need to be highlighted:

- Craft items are tangible but the **knowledge and skills** to create them are intangible. It is therefore important to research and document traditional craft techniques, especially those in danger of disappearing.
- Artisans should be motivated to **constantly recreate** and adapt their products to the needs of the local and external markets. They need technical and financial assistance to move from a supply to a demand strategy;
- The reference to the identity and heritage of a community and group constitutes the **added-value** of a craft item in the global market. This represents the concrete contribution of crafts to cultural diversity.
- Children and the youth in schools should be introduced to crafts as a significant element of the national Cultural Heritage and as a source of employment. Hence the pilot, interregional Project "Education and Craft Professions" which I jointly organized with the Education Sector (Associated Schools Section) in the 5 continents.

The Creative Industries Framework

The term "creative industries" is nowadays more and more used instead of that of "cultural industries" as it includes a wider range of sub-sectors than the latter, namely crafts and design. Moreover, the concept of creative industries has the advantage of giving as much importance to the "creative" elements of the sector as to the "industrial", to the development of content as well as to production and distribution.

The most commonly quoted definition is the one used by the United Nations Conference on Trade and Commerce (UNCTAD):

> Creative industries can be defined as the **cycle of creation, production and commercialization** of products and services that uses **knowledge and intellectual capital as primary inputs**. They deal with the **interplay of various sub-sectors** ranging from **traditional crafts**, books, visual and performing arts to more technology-intensive and services-oriented fields such as the music and film industries, television and radio broadcasting, new media and design.[2]

This definition has important **implications for the Crafts sector**:

- Creative industries have their origin in **individual creativity, skill and talent**. Now, creativity is the only resource which is equally distributed around the world, whether in developing/developed countries, among rich/poor or by men/women. However, the inequality lies in the existence or not of a favourable environment to stimulate, develop and promote the creativity of craftspeople. This implies in turn a concerted effort by all the concerned partners: government institutions, private sector, NGOS and crafts associations;
- Innovative craft development projects can be developed in **synergy with other sectors of creative industries**, such as films, television and music, for example, in the creation of costumes and musical instruments.

[2]Background paper by UNCTAD Secretariat for the meeting of the High-level panel on the creative economy and industries for development, Accra, Ghana, 20–25 April 2008.

- Creative enterprises are those which have a **potential for wealth and job creation through the generation of intellectual property**. Indeed, one of the key characteristics of the Crafts sector is its capacity to provide employment and income generation with comparatively less investments than in other sectors, such as Agriculture or Tourism. For example, Tunisia's 300,000 craft workers produce 3.8% of the country's annual GDP or an annual income per family of US$ 2400. In Morocco, crafts production represents 19% of its GDP, including exports estimated at US$ 63 million.[3] In Jordan, the revenues of Ghor El Safi Women Association tripled from 4300 Jordanian dinars in 2014 to 14,000 JD in 2015! Hence the increasing interest of some international cooperation agencies to *support* crafts as a creative industry, namely the European Union, UNDP (under the Millenium Development Goals) and the World Bank (through its artisan-centric projects in South Asia, Africa and Latin America).
- Craft development projects should take into account **the value-chain: creation-production-distribution-consumption**. Unfortunately, these segments of the chain are too often considered separately. Now, the future of crafts depends on the way the key problems of marketing are solved, these in turn being dependent on the production and consumption of authentic, high-quality products which depend on the level of training of the crafts people. In short, UNESCO commends a circular approach rather than a linear one.

Linkages Between Artisans and Designers

The two visions of crafts, as part of the cultural heritage and as a creative industry are, indeed, more complementary than opposite from an operational point of view. Craftspeople do not simply preserve and safeguard cultural heritage but also enrich and adapt this heritage to the contemporary needs of societies.

[3]Source: UNESCO World Report "Investing in Cultural Diversity and Intercultural Dialogue", 2009.

The issue of design intervention in crafts is a controversial and complex one and gives way to as many concerns as hopes, depending on whether one thinks the glass is half full or half empty! The benefits brought by the alliance between design and craft as well as the existing risks and problems have been fully analysed and described in the published by UNESCO *Practical Guide 'Designers Meet Artisans'* in cooperation with the NGO 'Craft Revival Trust' (India) and 'Artesanias de Colombia'.

In today's 'global' village, the artisan is, paradoxically, more and more disconnected with consumer needs and tastes. With the extension of markets and the spectacular growth of tourism, the traditional direct personal contact between makers and users is disrupted. The artisan can no longer assume, as in the past, the combined role of a designer, producer and marketer.

Hence the concerns expressed, across all geographical borders, by craft promoters and organizations for closer links between designers and artisans. In front of the communication gap between producers and consumers, the designer is seen as an indispensable intermediate, a "bridge" between the artisan's know-how and his knowledge of what to produce. Innovative approaches to crafts can no doubt be triggered off by the introduction of design in various aspects, for example, as regards the choice of alternate materials and appropriate technologies or the definition of new product lines.

However, if Design intervention in crafts is most welcomed by some as an opportunity, it is often considered by others as a threat. The reduction of the artisan's role to that of a mere producer and the lack of reference to the cultural context in products designed for an alien, volatile market are among the commonly expressed concerns. What is the nature of the loss and/or gain in the adaptation to market forces? How to adapt and/or modify existing products or create new products from local design motifs without obliterating traditions? Can there be a well-balanced and mutually beneficial interaction between designers and artisans?

Without being over-optimistic, I submit that we respond positively to these questions. As artisans are caught in the ambiguous position of being pressured to adjust to market demands while also encouraged to remain true to their ancient traditions, designers can become partners for the preservation, development and marketing of crafts, provided that there is a shared vision and a spirit of mutual respect.

In this connection, let us not forget that the design profession itself is reviewing the sense (or non-sense) of its mission in the globalized world where frontiers are fastly disappearing not only between countries but also between creative disciplines. **Today, art uses fashion, fashion uses crafts, design becomes closer to art**. The product is no longer an end itself but a means at the service of Happiness. Innovative concepts have gained grounds, such as Bio-Design, Ethno-Design, Social Design. We observe a new trend bridging crafts and design, local and foreign cultures, traditional and contemporary forms. The "Artsy Craftsy" movement, for example, reflects a new aesthetics which offers, from design to ethnic art, a series of unique items promoting traditional know-how, small production and craft enterprises. The relationships between artisans and designers are becoming more evident in the Fashion world where accessories are now the 'stars' and in the art of recycling materials as a "second life".

There is definitely no reason why crafts should be separated from the more lively design field. Instead of looking at one another with suspicion, artisans need to work closely with designers for several practical reasons:

- To adapt to the change from the local market to the 'global' village (Fig. 1)
- To facilitate access, adaptation and use of traditional motifs and designs: artisans have their data banks in their minds and at their fingertips while it is indispensable to *ensure the transmission of knowledge and know-how*
- To respond to changes in consumer needs, fashion trends and usage preferences: artisans have the skills but need more awareness of products they can make, modify or easily develop to meet new needs
- To reactivate local organic markets and develop urban and export market niches: to be sustainable, crafts cannot depend only on competitive and fleeting outside markets.

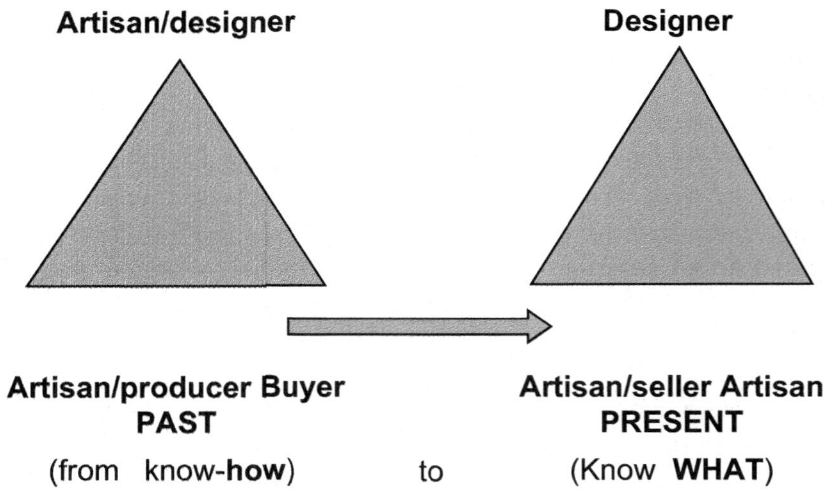

Fig. 1 Adapting and changing from the local market to the 'global' village (*Source* Authors own elaboration)

The survival of crafts as a living tradition depends on the existence of a market environment that **stimulates, supports, and promotes the artisan's creativity** and not only his or her product. Since my first contact with craftspeople some thirty-five years ago in Africa, I have been struck by the huge gap between their talent and their recognition in society. They are creators of beauty—and of revenue—yet they do not enjoy the social status and protection they deserve; they are at best regarded as persons, very rarely as personalities, in their communities, regions, and countries. By contrast, it is striking that in a world of global mass culture, the "stars" of the day, whether film celebrities, musicians, or sports champions, are idolized disproportionately to their creative role in society.

The aim of the **UNESCO Crafts Prize** is precisely to represent the recognition by the international community of the ability of crafts persons, either individually or collectively, to create, innovate and reconcile tradition and modernity. Since 1990, this Prize has been awarded on the occasion of Regional Crafts Trade Shows/Exhibitions in Africa, Asia, the Arab States and Latin America.

Policy Framework

Of course, a trade fair or an award once a year cannot pretend to ensure the sustainable promotion and development of crafts. This objective requires a comprehensive policy based on three pillars that are indispensable for the future: coordination, complementarity, and cooperation.

Coordination is necessary as the human, material, and financial means available in developing countries are insufficient to address the common problems facing craft persons: training and skills development, regular provision of imported raw materials, and the need for product development and proper marketing at national, regional, and international levels.

The cultural and socio-economic role of the Crafts Sector favours the interventions of diverse Regional and International Organizations. It also implies at the national level a coordinated approach for the sake of efficiency. There are, indeed, too many craft programmes launched separately by numerous ministries/departments (up to 13 according to a UNESCO survey!). Besides, there is generally a lack of accompanying measures in terms of legislation and regulation, institutional support, access to credit and funding, etc.

The need to create a coordination mechanism to avoid the dispersion of human and financial means and to ensure the complementarity of external interventions must be emphasized over and over again. This could be envisaged, for example, by a Public institution outside of a specific Ministry, supported by the Government but with its own Administrative Board and free to apply for funds from Regional or International Organizations. In this connection, the Public Authority for Craft Industries-PACI in the Sultanate of Oman, the 'Institut National des Métiers d'Art-INMA' in France and 'Artesanias de Colombia' or "FONART" in Mexico are interesting case studies.

The fact that crafts, and the market for it, is a multi-faceted arena where cultural, social and economic concerns all meet calls for **complementarity**. As I mentioned at the beginning of this presentation, the crafts sector cannot develop fully without connections to other key sectors, such as education (for the transmission of traditional knowledge), environment (for renewable raw materials), tourism (namely cultural and eco-tourism) and trade (for exports of representative products).

International organizations such as the European Union, the World Bank, and the United Nations Development Programme (UNDP) are sensitive and open to initiatives that demonstrate the cultural, social, and economic impact of crafts on national development plans.

The *'Creative Economy Report 2013' by UNESCO and UNDP* argues, with facts and figures, that creativity and culture have monetary and non-monetary benefits that can contribute to human development. It is, therefore, essential to insert consideration of crafts into these broad frameworks and to relate it to issues such as youth employment, gender equality, and poverty eradication.

Finally, the fierce competition in the global marketplace demands strategic **cooperation**. This means networking among artisans, entrepreneurs, private and public sectors, NGOs. Craft networks can be of three types: Local (Associations, Guilds, Cooperatives); Regional (such as the Central Asian Craft Support Association-CACSA) and International (World Crafts Council-WCC; IRCICA). The common objective of all the concerned partners should be to highlight the role of crafts as the expression of a rich cultural heritage and as a cultural industry ensuring a means of earning a living for craft persons and their families.

Conclusion

UNESCO's policy and programme is based on the two pillars—Tradition and Modernity—and on a global approach to the impact of the Craft Sector in national development. It is, indeed, vital to recognize, protect and promote the dual role of crafts: in its blending of past traditional know-how and modern creativity, in its economic and socio-cultural impact. Let us not forget that tradition today is good innovation of yesterday.

For crafts to achieve its full potential, a concerted, coherent and complementary approach is indispensable. While the various public and private institutions, organizations and agencies involved can and should play individual roles in the development process, it is important to link their activities in a comprehensive programme attuned to the changing needs of the sector. The challenge facing all those agencies which view craft as a sustainable development activity is how to adapt and/or modify existing products or create new products without obliterating tradition.

At the beginning of the twenty-first century, there are many signs that in the coming years we will witness an increased awareness of the possibilities offered by crafts for sustainable development which focuses on cultural heritage, readily available materials and the hand skills of individuals. The very qualities we take for granted in crafts will be in increased demand on the global market—qualities of timelessness and permanence, the adaptability of craftspeople and their materials to changing needs and, above all, the human, spiritual dimension of crafts.

References

UNESCO. 1982. *World Conference on Cultural Policies—Final Report*. Paris: UNESCO Publishing.

UNESCO. 2001. Universal Declaration on Cultural Diversity. Available at http://Unescodoc.unesco.org/images/0012/001271/127160m.pdf.

UNESCO. 2003. *Convention for the Safeguarding of the Intangible Heritage*. Paris: UNESCO Publishing.

UNESCO. 2009. *World Culture Report on Investing in Cultural Diversity and Intercultural Dialogue*. Paris: UNESCO Publishing.

UNESCO/Craft Revival Trust/Artesanias De Colombia. 2005. *Designers Meet Artisans: A Practical Guide*. New Delhi, India: Published by Craft Revival Trust. Available at http://www.unesco.org/new/en/unesco/resources/online-materials/publications/unesdoc-database/pdf.

UNESCO/Internationa Trade Centre. 1997. International Symposium on Crafts and the International Market: Trade and Customs Codification. Unpublshed Final Report.

UNESCO/UNDP. 2013. Creative Economy Report: Special Edition 'Widening Local Development Pathways'. Joint United Nations/UNDP/UNESCO Publication. Available at http://www.unesco.org/culture/pdf/creative-economy-report-2013.pdf.

United Nations Conference on Trade and Commerce-UNCTAD. 2008. Background Paper on the Creative Economy and Creative Industries Prepared by UNCTAD Secretariat for the Meeting of the High-Level Panel, Apr 20–25, Accra, Ghana.

Making Sense of Craft Using Cultural Economics

Priyatej Kotipalli

Introduction

Craft has been the focus of researches and books in different fields. However, economics as a discipline has paid limited attention to the sector. The focus has been towards specific aspects, namely job organisation and the impact of the sector on the overall economy of a country. This approach, then, risks focusing only on measuring the sector and/or its impact, overlooking the specific features which makes crafts and other forms of cultural creative goods unique.

The production and consumption of these kinds of goods is linked to culture, an approach that can bring out these nuances is necessary. In this context Cultural economics can offer a different approach to make sense of the cultural sector that might result helpful to support it. The cultural economics lenses could imply/realise a different approach to economics, which is capable of including those characteristics that

P. Kotipalli (✉)
Erasmus University Rotterdam, Rotterdam, The Netherlands
e-mail: Pkotipalli@eshcc.eur.nl

A. Mignosa and P. Kotipalli (eds.), *A Cultural Economic Analysis of Craft*,
https://doi.org/10.1007/978-3-030-02164-1_4

differentiate cultural objects from industrial products. It could also bring together the separate approaches that have so far characterised the sector. This branch of economics could try to solve some of the problems of the sector, and eventually guarantee its own survival.

There is a common misunderstanding about cultural economics: it is thought to focus only on profitability and economic return. However, the chapter will show the capacity of cultural economics of considering the specific features of craft and move beyond production, consumption, price. The chapter will, thus, briefly introduce cultural economics, providing an overview of its development and its focus. The chapter will refer to the different definitions of crafts to highlight how the way of conceiving the sector has consequences for the cultural economics approach.[1] It will also introduce the differences existing within cultural economics showing how the more heterodox approach could be ideal to identify and analyse the same issues highlighted in other disciplines and among practitioners, and to support the development of a crafts culture to valorize crafts beyond price.

Cultural Economics a Brief Overview

Cultural economics has been developing and is constantly evolving. In its relatively young life,[2] it has investigated various cultural sectors: from orchestras to museums, from heritage to the cultural and creative industries, from opera to festivals, etc. Cultural economics developed within neoclassical economics and, thus, studies the cultural sector from the perspective of a market approach/theory[3] towards culture. The focus on supply and demand and price formation; efficiency, productivity and issues relating to the size of the sector are the norm. In such an analysis the cultural sector is valorized in terms of the price paid for the cultural

[1]This is something that becomes evident in the policies for crafts (cf. This chapter).

[2]Baumol and Bowen's book *Performing Arts: The Economic Dilemma* (1966) is considered as the founding text of cultural economics. The two authors provided a thorough research about orchestras, opera and ballet, introducing the 'cost disease' in the arts, which was used to justify public support to performing arts and the cultural sector in general (see Towse 2010).

[3]See Towse (2010, 2011).

object. Sill, cultural economics introduced in the analysis some specific concepts to take into consideration the specificities of the cultural sector, for instance, taste formation, gatekeeping, conspicuous consumption. Public intervention and, thus, the rationale behind it and the tools for its implementation; the art market and its characteristics compared to other markets; the peculiarities of artists' career; the economics of cultural heritage and museums and performing arts have taken most of the attention of cultural economists who underlined the role of gatekeepers in the cultural sector and used the term supply induced-demand to take into account the specificities of the cultural sector.

Cultural economics focused for some time on the 'most traditional sectors' (performing arts, cultural heritage, visual arts, the art market, broadcasting) somehow oblivious of the changes that were taking place in the cultural sector (Blaug 2001). However, the evolution of the notion of culture, the development of the concept of cultural and creative industries; the effects of digitisation and, especially, internet; the role of information; the appearance of new intermediaries, new business models and new distribution channel; the importance of copyright and, last but not least, the financial crisis profoundly transformed the cultural sector. All these changes stimulated the development of cultural economics to tackle these new issues. Market failure and the need for public intervention, which seem to characterise most of the cultural sub-sectors, require an approach based on welfare economics and public choice. The most recent developments connected to the evolution of the cultural and creative industries have implied the appearance of industrial organisation and the theory of contracts.

The analysis has, then, been constantly evolving, in terms of approaches used (neoclassical economics, market theory, welfare economics, public choice theory, industrial organisation, etc.) as well as sectors analysed, though a persistent motive has been that of finding ways to support culture. The continuous evolution that has characterised cultural economics, since its origin, shows its capacity to follow what happens in society, and the attempt to provide insights that can improve the 'state of the arts'. The discipline has been evolving to understand and mirror the developments in the cultural sector.

It is possible to evidence the presence of more than one approach within cultural economics. Thus, while some authors are adamant about using neoclassical economics tools to make sense of the world of art (Ashenfelter and Graddy 2011; Cordes and Goldfarb 1996; Towse 1994, 2010, 2011), other economists like Arjo Klamer (1996, 2017), David Throsby (2001, 2010), Michael Hutter (Hutter and Throsby 2008), and to some degree Bruno Frey (2001) argue that it is necessary to adjust economics to apply it to the arts. They propose an analysis of the arts and of cultural heritage open to other disciplines including psychology, sociology and anthropology. Frey summarises this approach when, commenting on Throsby's 2001 book, he describes it as a '…major step forward: far from a mindless application of orthodox economics to the arts, he does full justice to the special characteristics, without giving up good economic reasoning' (Frey 2001, back cover). These cultural economists have made efforts in expanding the tools and providing new framings to interpret the cultural sector beyond the realms of the orthodox economic thinking.

In other words, within cultural economics there exists a spectrum of approaches. While on the one end the dominance of neoclassical economics (market theory, welfare economics, public choice theory, industrial organisation) is evident, on the other end lies a heterodox interpretations of economics. The latter tries to make sense of the commerce of culture with an approach where economists are concerned with valorizing the agency of the cultural sector beyond price.

It is in this context that we will try to understand the economics of craft. The expectation is that if we try to understand craft just from the perspective of neoclassical economics e would leave aside an important part. The intention is to make sense of crafts as part of the present (third wave) revival and this requires a different approach capable of using what both the ends of the spectrum offer.

Cultural Economics and Craft

Crafts is receiving a growing attention, the Do It Yourself (DIY) movement as well as the focus on craft within policies for urban (re)generation and economic development seem to show that craft is also an important sector that can stimulate cultural but also social and economic development.

The attention of UNCTAD (2008, 2010) towards the sector confirms this view. Policies for crafts in India, for instance, show the same focus. They are sounded from an economic perspective, as they allow craftsmen to earn a living. Still, these policies can raise some doubts as artisans are considered as 'factors of production' whereas their skills and talent are totally neglected (Baicu et al. 2018), in other words the non-monetary values of crafts is not fully understood or represented in economic analysis. This example, shows the limitations of the neoclassical economic approach and explains the reasons for a call for a different approach. It would be useful to look beyond the 'simple' demand-supply paradigm to consider crafts culture and, thus, suggest a different way to analyse the sector and, different measures to support it. Cultural economics could provide this new approach.

However, one stylized fact to account for is the lack of interest of cultural economists for the crafts until recently (Towse 2010: 80). There are some exceptions. Some studies consider the connection with intangible heritage (Cominelli and Greffe 2013; Goto 2013) or with the cultural industries (Goto 2013), or make international comparisons of the craft sector (Klamer et al. 2012, 2013). More recently, several conferences took place that brought scholars from a variety of disciplines, including cultural economics, to explore the crafts.[4] In both cases, crafts was generally perceived as important for society and for our understanding of it. Recent researches on the values of craft in India and China suggest various reasons explaining the (cultural economics) scholarly neglect of the crafts: difficulty to record the contribution of crafts to the

[4]An International Symposium on *Values of Craft: Craft as Intangible Heritage* took place at Erasmus University, Rotterdam, in March, 2018. International scholars, experts, and practitioners in the field met with the intention to set the ground for an extensive international research aiming at identifying the main conceptual issues related to craft as well as collecting empirical evidence from best practices and interesting case studies to demonstrate the importance that a craft culture and a craft economy can have for society at large. The *Values of Craft Expert Meeting*, hosted by Leiden University and the Center for Global Heritage and Development brought together a diverse group of scholars and artisans who concluded that the study of craft could change our perception of what knowledge is and affect our understanding of societal structure, identity, valorization, and general wellbeing.

economy; impossibility of crafts to compete with industrial products because of limited productivity gains and, as a consequence, relatively high price of crafts products; decreasing interest of youngsters to take on a craft; downplaying of the role of craftsmanship in the twentieth century; marginal role of crafts in political discussions throughout the world, with a few exceptions (e.g. Germany, Japan, and the UK).

This has meant that the advancements made in cultural economics, in general, have not been applied to the specific context of the economics of crafts. Still, cultural economics can contribute to a new way of looking at the sector, capable of appraising its variegated and multifaceted character. To make this possible, however, it is important to delve into the definition of craft as it will steer the economic approach to it.

Definitions of Crafts and Economic Approaches

Definitions of crafts share a semiotic relationship with economic approaches in understanding the economics of craft. To re-cap from the previous segments and to explain this relationship let us consider the following image. To start with our experience with craft, we take the stand that crafts is a concept that is evolving and shaping with the society and culture around it. What this means is that it is a dynamic entity and system. Crafts in its various forms existed in the pre-industrial society as a form of socially and culturally embedded from of production and consumption. The application of standard economic theory to understand the economics of crafts has been a somewhat recent phenomenon when compared to the dynamic evolution of crafts as a sector.

In an international symposium organised at Erasmus University titled Values *of Craft: Craft as Intangible Heritage* various aspects about the nature of crafts were discussed. In this context, there was an effort to makes sense of crafts in terms of its national and international definitions. What emerged is that definitions exist with the idea of exclusion of items as opposed to being inclusive. This principle allows policy planners to decide which or what crafts by virtue of its meeting the criteria of the definition is allowed to obtain certain subsidies and protection;

can be measured. As evidenced by the presentation of Francesca Cominelli the urgency of defining crafts is a governmental issue, for the purpose of getting good statistics and setting a basis for policy. This aspect emerged also from the presentation of the Japanese case from Kazuko Goto who, acknowledging that budget constraints limit the list of Living Heritage, underlined the need of definitions to be able to have access to funds.

During the symposium, it became evident that the economic approach tends to be instrumental with a tendency to understand the values of craft in a reductionist manner. The dominance of standard economics and instrumental thinking also produces plans, policies and definitions that tend to have instrumental goals. What is interesting to note (Fig. 1) is that neoclassical economics overlaps, at least partially, with cultural economics. Hence when there is an intention to make instrumental sense of the values of crafts the approach tends to move towards a standard economic approach. This way of making sense of the values of crafts is the predominant way and it is not without its limitations.

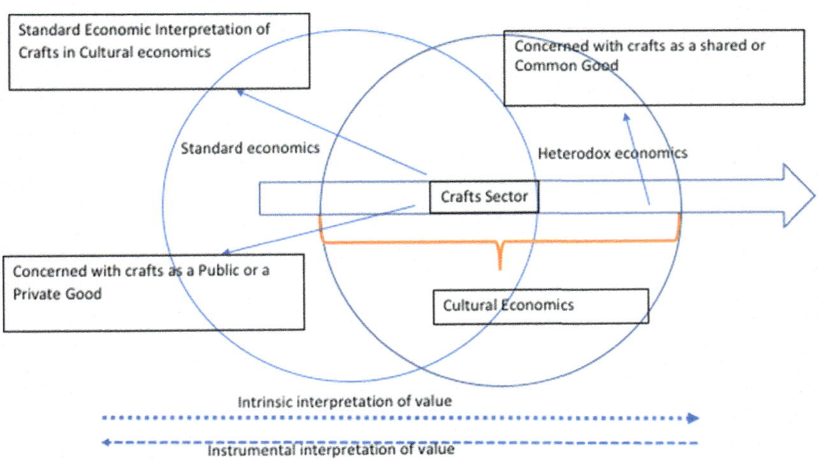

Fig. 1 The neoclassical and heterodox approach in the cultural economics analysis of craft (*Source* Authors' elaboration)

For instance, Kotipalli (2018) points out that the application of standard economics to crafts leads to paradoxes. To overcome them a different approach is required where one tries to bring to the forefront the intrinsic values of craft. The need to understand the intrinsic values of crafts is seen in the appropriation of words like crafts, craftsmen, craftsmanship, handwork by subjects and groups, which have not traditionally been considered related to crafts. Examples of this can be seen in the craft beer movements, the maker movements, and the DIY movement, each trying to invoke the intangibles aspects of crafts with notions of quality, uniqueness and so on. When one thinks about the reasons for this appropriation what emerges is that these intangible aspects reflect the wide set of values of craft beyond the economic ones. We then use the term economic value to encompass all these intangible aspects which are not explored in the neoclassical approach to crafts.

Kotipalli (2018) argues that these intangible elements make the production and consumption of crafts unique and suggests that crafts allow for the production of shared goods. In this context, the economics of crafts cannot be limited to a neoclassical interpretation that understands crafts as a public or private good. What this might also imply is that the current definitions of crafts is more concerned with understanding the output in terms of crafts objects. It fails to see it as a system where values are exchanged beyond the price paid for the craft object. In this context, it can be useful to consider an approach that develops an intrinsic understanding of the value of crafts. This leads us towards a heterodox approach to cultural economics. One of these alternative approach is the value-based approach by Arjo Klamer (2017). It is concerned with casting crafts as being a medium to produce shared goods, opening a new conversation about the economics of crafts.

Conclusion

Cultural economics with few exceptions (Cominelli and Greffe 2013; Goto 2013; Klamer 2012; Klamer et al. 2012, 2013; Jiang 2018) has not paid much attention to crafts. The economic approach to craft thus has mainly focused on the impact of the sector on export and the possibility to make artisans earn a living. Such an approach has influenced the policies which have been undertaken for crafts until now (cf. This chapter). We suggest that the cultural economic approach could help deepening the analysis of the sector and could allow taking into consideration not only the economic value of crafts but the whole set of intangible aspects of the sector. We suggest, however, that such an analysis would be possible through a heterodox approach capable of grasping the whole set of values of the sector (cf. Chapter 17).

References

Ashenfelter, O., and K. Graddy. 2011. Art Auctions. In *The Handbook of Cultural Economics*, ed. R. Towse. Cheltenham: Edward Elgar.

Baicu, R., A. Klamer, and A. Mignosa. 2018. International Symposium Values of Craft: Craft as Intangible Heritage, Rotterdam, 1–2 March 2018—Final Report.

Baumol, W., and W. Bowen. 1966. *Performing Arts: The Economic Dilemma.* Hartford, CT: Twentieth Century Fund.

Blaug, M. 2001. Where Are We Now on Cultural Economics. *Journal of Economic Surveys* 15 (2): 123–143.

Cominelli, F., and X. Greffe. 2013. Why and How Intangible Cultural Heritage Should Be Safeguarded. In *Handbook on the Economics of Cultural Heritage*, ed. I. Rizzo and A. Mignosa, 402–421. Cheltenham: Edward Elgar.

Cordes, Joseph J., and Robert S. Goldfarb. 1996. The Value of Public Art as Public Culture. In *Economics and Culture*, ed. B. Frey and D. Throsby. Cambridge, UK: Cambridge University Press.

Frey, B.S., and R. Jegen. 2001. Motivation Crowding Theory. *Journal of Economic Surveys* 15 (5): 589–611.

Goto, K. 2013. Policy for Intangible Cultural Heritage in Japan: How It Relates to Creativity. In *Handbook on the Economics of Cultural Heritage*, 1–1. Edward Elgar Publishing. (Chapters).

Hutter, M., and D. Throsby (eds.). 2008. *Beyond Price: Value in Culture, Economics, and the Arts*. Cambridge: Cambridge University Press.

Jiang, L. 2018. *Valuing Craftsmanship: In Particular the Crafting of Chinese Porcelain and Dutch Delft Blue*. Rotterdam: Erasmus University.

Klamer, A. (ed.). 1996. *The Value of Culture—On the Relationship Between Economics and the Arts*. Amsterdam: Amsterdam University Press.

Klamer, A. 2012. *Crafting Culture: The Importance of Craftsmanship for the World of the Arts and the Economy at Large*. Mimeo: Kyoto.

Klamer, A. 2017. *Doing the Right Thing: A Value Based Economy*, 266. Ubiquity Press.

Klamer, A., P. Kotipalli, L. Jiang, T. Fjeldsted, K. Goto, and A. Mignosa. 2012. *Creatief vakmanschap in internationaal perspectief*. Rotterdam: Stiching Economie en Cultuur, Erasmus University Rotterdam.

Klamer, A., P. Kotipalli, L. Jiang, T. Fjeldsted, and A. Mignosa. 2013. *Herwaardering Ambachtscultuur Hoofdzaak*. Rotterdam: Stiching Economie en Cultuur, Erasmus University Rotterdam.

Kotipalli, P. 2018. *The Values of Craft: The Indian Case*. Rotterdam: Erasmus University.

Throsby, D. 2001. *Economics and Culture*. Cambridge, UK: Cambridge University Press.

Throsby, D. 2010. *The Economics of Cultural Policy*. Cambridge: Cambridge University Press.

Towse, R. 1994. Achieving Public Policy Objectives in the Arts and Heritage. In *Cultural Economics and Cultural Policies*, ed. A. Peacock and I. Rizzo. Dordrecht: Kluwer.

Towse, R. 2010. *A Textbook of Cultural Economics*. Cambridge: Cambridge University Press.

Towse, R. 2011. *The Handbook of Cultural Economics*. Cheltenham: Edward Elgar.

UNCTAD, and UNDP. 2008. *Creative Economy Report 2008: The Challenge of Assessing the Creative Economy: Towards Informed Policy-Making* (No. UNCTAD/DITC/2008/2). Geneva: United Nations.

UNCTAD, and UNDP. 2010. *Creative Economy Report 2010: Creative Economy: A Feasible Development Option* (No. UNCTAD/DITC/TAB/2010/3). Geneva: United Nations.

Part II

Policies for Crafts

Policies for Crafts: Rationale and Tools

Anna Mignosa

Public intervention for culture is widespread and takes place with various intensities and using disparate tools among different countries. That depends on the way of conceiving the role of the State in society and the economy, as well as the institutional framework and priorities set for cultural policies (Klamer et al. 2006). In the United States, for instance, public intervention is relatively less accepted than in most continental Europe, especially for the cultural sector. Tough, even in Europe, the economic crisis has implied a general reduction of public intervention.

When it comes to crafts, policies are also common and vary from country to county or, even, within the same country. As we will see below, the main differences relate to the way of conceiving crafts (cultural heritage or cultural and creative industries—CCI) that affects the design and implementation of policies. When considering

A. Mignosa (✉)
University of Catania, Catania, Italy
e-mail: a.mignosa@unict.it

Erasmus University Rotterdam, Rotterdam, The Netherlands

A. Mignosa and P. Kotipalli (eds.), *A Cultural Economic Analysis of Craft*,
https://doi.org/10.1007/978-3-030-02164-1_5

craft as cultural heritage, policies are normally implemented by the ministry of culture and focus on the listing and transmission of skills (e.g. Japan, France).[1] In contrast, when craft is considered to be part of the creative industries, the ministries responsible for the economy or development are responsible, and the policies, which also take listing and transmission of skills into account, include tools to facilitate the production and commercialization of crafts and the creation of jobs in the sector (Japan, India).[2]

This chapter provides an illustration of the main features of policies for craft. The next section illustrates the economic rationale for public intervention for culture, in general, and the ways it can be implemented. The analysis then focuses on craft policies evidencing the tools that can be used. The last section highlights some issues with the policies presently adopted. Some final remarks conclude the chapter.

Economic Reasons for Public Intervention for Craft

The rationale for public intervention in the cultural sector has been one of the main issues considered in cultural economics since the origin of the field.[3] Economists indicate several reasons for market failure: public goods; externalities; non-use values; risk and uncertainty; and taste formation (Baumol and Bowen 1966; Frey and Pommerhene 1989; Peacock 1994, 1998; Towse 2010).[4] Thus, the government has to step in, as the private sector alone would not guarantee the provision of the socially optimal amount of cultural goods.

According to economists, a (pure) public good is non-rival and non-excludable in consumption. This implies that, unlike private good (e.g. a bottle of water), the use from one person does not prevent

[1]See supra chapter Goto, Cominelli.

[2]Cf. Chapter Ellis and Lo, and Goto.

[3]Cf. Supra Chapter 3.

[4]For a critical survey of the arguments in favor of public support see van der Ploeg (2006).

another person from using the same good (up until the point where congestion starts),[5] and nobody can be technically or economically excluded from enjoying a public good. Clearly, such goods would induce free riding behavior: people do not have an incentive to declare their real willingness to pay for culture, knowing that their consumption cannot be excluded, and they will benefit anyway, should the good be provided by somebody else.[6] The government will, therefore, have to step in to guarantee that provision of these goods is efficient, namely consistent with social welfare maximization (rather than individual maximization of just one's utility).[7] There are, however, doubts among economists as to the extent of publicness of culture. In case of exceptions to indivisibility and non-excludability, economists talk of impure public goods. In fact, this is often the case in culture, for instance, a person can be excluded from entering museums, when an entrance fee is applicable, and consumption may become rival in case of congestion. However, there are additional reasons for public intervention, as indicated next.

Externalities are the benefits or costs of an economic good that are not accounted for by the market. Externalities can be positive (e.g. benefits deriving to society from cultural consumption) or negative (e.g. threats to cultural heritage due to tourist congestion). Since externalities deriving from production and/or consumption are generally not traded in the market, there are no prices to signal the negative or positive external effects to those causing them. This implies an over- or underproduction of these goods and services. Governments, thus, intervene to account for externalities and stimulate the production of the goods that would be demanded if their actual total cost or benefit would be known.

[5]Congestion due to the increase in the number of people benefiting from the good at a time may reduce individual benefit.

[6]Typical examples of this are public defense, firework, public lights: all people benefit from them even when they do not contribute to their provision.

[7]See Stiglitz and Rosengard (2015).

Culture bears a wide set of non-use values (bequest, existence, option),[8] which cannot be expressed through price mechanisms and vary from person to person. Again, governments may want to supply these goods, or the non-profit sector may step in, as people would directly provide those cultural goods they consider important.[9]

There are also equity issues that come into play to justify public intervention. The idea is that everybody should be allowed to benefit from culture and that people working in the cultural sector should earn as much as people with the same level of education who work in other sectors. All the previous issues help to explain why in some countries entrance to public museums is free (e.g. England); VAT on cultural goods is lower; or subsidies for artists are in place.

It is true that public intervention in favor of the CCI is sometimes questioned. In fact, we talk of industries and cultural products, which are often reproducible and exchanged on the market. However, in this case, other issues might be considered. The neutrality of information and the need to avoid the risk of private control justify support to public broadcasting. Finally, the role of CCI in creating employment, contributing to the exports of a country explain why governments often intervene to support them.

Once agreed that there are reasons justifying public intervention for the cultural sector, it is necessary to understand which tools are available. Public intervention takes place through direct and indirect spending and regulation. When we talk of direct spending we, first of all, refer to the direct provision of culture from the public sector; public museums are a clear example of this form of intervention. It is the government (national, regional, local) that directly manages the museums, covering the costs related to their operations.[10] Sometimes the governance of cultural

[8]Bequest, option and existence values are the most commonly referred to next to prestige, identity, historical values. See Throsby (2010).

[9]The reduction of public funds for culture have stimulated the direct participation of people in the provision of culture.

[10]This model has practically disappeared as, nowadays, the financing of public museums and cultural organizations in general takes place through a combination of public and private funds. This mixed model has been developing with increased speed since the financial crisis.

organizations is delegated to arm's length bodies in order to reduce the risk of political influence on culture (Van der Ploeg 2006). Direct support also takes place in the form of subsidies (matching grants, vouchers) to public and private cultural organizations and individuals. Direct support can also take place in kind when the public sector instead of giving funds, provides its expertise/knowledge. Governments may otherwise decide to use incentives to bring the action of private actors in line with the desired policy. The use of tax incentives can stimulate private intervention in favor of the cultural sector getting a tax reduction in exchange. This form of support is indirect because the government gives up revenues when allowing tax rebates. Regulation is a form of non-monetary intervention from the government to limit the activities of other stakeholders (public actors, companies in the private sector, non-profit organizations) interested in culture (Rizzo 2011). Those stakeholders have to comply with the rules set by the public administration responsible for culture. Regulation is the least favored tool of public intervention for economists because of the high indirect costs it can cause. Regulation can be hard (laws, lists, etc.) when it legally bounds people and organizations to comply with it, or soft (conventions, treaties, recommendations) when no legal actions follow if the latter do not observe them (Throsby 1997).[11]

These tools translate in concrete forms of interventions in favor of the cultural sector. When we talk of direct support, we can think of the direct ownership and operation of museums, theater, opera companies, TV channels, and cultural organizations in general, to the distribution of public funds to public and private entities directly or through arm's length bodies (e.g. Arts Council England). Direct support takes place also when the institutions responsible for heritage provide their expertise to private owners of heritage for its restoration or preservation; or when local governments offer spaces to cultural organizations or cultural entrepreneurs for free or for a reduced rent. Regulation can take different forms depending on the country—e.g. listing vs. constraints for the

[11]However, Dresden in Germany and the Arabian Oryx Sanctuary in Oman were delisted from UNESCO World Heritage List (respectively in 2009 and 2007) because the rules set to be part of the WHL were not respected any more (Schoch 2014; Gaillard and Rodwell 2015; UNESCO 2018a).

preservation of cultural heritage; or the sector—the use of copyright in the CCI vs. the use of trademarks. Examples of indirect support are the possibility to get tax deduction for individuals or companies who donate funds or artworks to cultural organizations, as well as the reduction of the amount of taxes to be paid by the latter.

As we will see in the next section, public intervention takes place also for crafts and the tools used vary again in order to adapt to the specific features of this sector.

Policies for Craft

The justification for public support for craft differ depending on the definition of craft adopted. As a matter of fact, this definition shifts between two main framings: on the one side, craft is considered to be part of intangible cultural heritage, on the other side, craft is seen as part of the CCI.[12] In the first case, the rationale behind support is related to public goods, externalities, identity and historical value. Crafts are to be preserved and transmitted to future generations. Examining the policies adopted in various countries, we see how difficult it is to understand which is the best policy tool to adopt. The notion of intangible cultural heritage is well established in the Eastern part of the globe. For instance, in the case of Japan, policies for the sector have been in place for decades, focusing especially on the transmission of skills and, thus, on education or the recognition of living treasures, i.e., holders of craft skills and knowledge.[13] In Western countries, where the notion of intangible heritage has gained attention and importance following the 2003 UNESCO convention (Mignosa 2016), the introduction of policies is still on the making through a process of trial and errors where policies supporting living treasures, policies proposing the listing of crafts and policies for education prevail. The main

[12]See the chapters in the 1st part of the volume.

[13]Interestingly, in Germany education and the transmission of skills have traditionally been the focus of policies for craft (cf. Fjeldsted's chapter).

worry is that the tools chosen, often adopted following tangible heritage policies, might have a boomerang effect for the craft sector and freeze it, instead of guaranteeing its ongoing evolution. The ministry for culture is, generally, the authority responsible for the design and implementation of policies in this case.

When the notion of CCI is used to define craft, policies and the authority responsible change. The economic, social and cultural spillover effects of craft come to the fore and call for government support. In this case, subsidies or other form of support to facilitate the production, distribution and export of crafts prevail. Education for the transmission of skills and to support managerial skills is also used. The introduction of trademarks or denomination of origin is sometimes considered to protect and support craft.[14] Again, Japan is emblematic to describe this difference; when crafts are seen as part of the CCI, it is the ministry of industry or economics that is responsible for the design and implementation of policies.

The chapters in this part of the book, which illustrate policies for crafts in various countries evidence these differences. The analysis is useful as it shows the presence of frequent analogies among countries, it also highlights possible best practices that could be adopted when the aim is to boost a craft culture where the whole spectrum of values of craft is considered. In this case, while the economic value might be instrumental to guarantee the survival of the sector, a wider approach would reduce the risk of oversimplifying craft reducing artisans to simple factors of production (Baicu et al. 2018, and infra Chapter 2).

Issues in Craft Policies

The differences characterising policies for crafts demonstrate that not only the definition adopted but also the institutional arrangements in place play a role in shaping them. Thus, when the role of crafts for the

[14]See Braun and Lavanga (2007) for a thorough illustration of the possible tools that can be used to support the CCI and the responsible authorities. See also Chapter 14 infra.

economy is acknowledged and the work of artisans supported, some countries create lists or registers to protect specific craft forms, whereas others prefer to use direct and indirect support by providing spaces where artisans can work paying a cheaper rent, or by introducing special tax schemes to facilitate the creation of a craft enterprises.

The measures adopted in favor of crafts are not without problems. The highly regulated German craft system got under the radar of the EU as it led to discrimination among EU citizens. A further critique to the regulation of the sector is that it creates entry barriers that hamper competition and economic performance. A study (Gathmann and Lembcke 2017) on the effects of deregulation of the German crafts that took place in 2004 (cf. Chapter 13) however, does not show huge differences between the regulated and deregulated craft sectors in term of earning and job mobility.

Listing, such as the UNESCO List of Intangible Cultural Heritage of Humanity (UNESCO 2018b), and some national equivalents (e.g. *Registro delle Eredità Immateriali* of the Sicilian Regional Government or the *Inventaire du Patrimoine Culturel Immatériel* in France),[15] raise also doubts because of the risks of freezing a specific craft expression, stopping or hindering its evolution, whereas craft is something that evolves through time. In this case, policies would reach an objective which is the opposite of the original intention: the destruction of crafts instead of their protection.

In fact, in the case of the intangible cultural heritage of humanity UNESCO does not indicate fixed rules but, instead, holds a Register of good safeguarding practices (UNESCO 2018b) that "contains programs, projects and activities that best reflect the principles and the objectives of the Convention".

Intellectual property is another tool (regulation) that can protect and support crafts. However, there is a distinction to be made as the effects vary depending on the tool chosen. Trademarks or the brand name are form of individual protection that safeguards a single producer. The denomination of origin, instead, can be considered a form of community protection as it safeguards all the producers in a given area (Santagata 2002).

---

[15]See respectively http://www.regione.sicilia.it/bbccaa/dirbenicult/info/news/REI/index.html, and http://www.culture.gouv.fr/Thematiques/Patrimoine-culturel-immateriel/L-inventaire-national.

This latter instrument together with district trademarks could be used to protect the common crafts of a specific area stimulating cooperative behaviors while increasing the competitiveness of the group. It would also improve (and guarantee) the quality standards of craft products, possibly increasing the creativity of the district (Ibidem). This type of policy might focus mainly on the economic effects, or, when integrated in a more holistic approach that includes education, could be a basis for the development of a craft culture in a region.

Concluding Remarks

The chapter has provided an overview of the reasons for public intervention for culture and, hence, for crafts and the tools that can be used. As illustrated here and in the following chapters, the aims of the government influence the type of policies and the tools used. It is evident, however, that policies focusing on a single objective (e.g. protection or economic development) risk of falling short. In designing and implementing policies, an approach to crafts that would consider all the values involved, instead, could guarantee not only the survival of the sector but also its development and, even better, the development of a craft culture.

References

Baicu, R., A. Klamer, and A. Mignosa. 2018. International Symposium Values of Crafts: Crafts as Intangible Heritage, Rotterdam, 1–2 March 2018—Final Report.

Baumol, William J., and William G. Bowen. 1966. *Performing Arts: The Economic Dilemma*. New York: The Twentieth Century Fund.

Braun, E., and M. Lavanga. 2007. *An International Comparative Quick Scan of National Policies for Creative Industries*. Rotterdam: Euricur for the Ministry of Education, Culture and Science of the Netherlands.

Frey, B., and Pommerehne. 1989. *Muses and Markets: Explorations in the Economics of the Arts*. Oxford: Blackwell.

Gaillard, B., and D. Rodwell. 2015. A Failure of Process? Comprehending the Issues Fostering Heritage Conflict in Dresden Elbe Valley and Liverpool—Maritime Mercantile City World Heritage Sites. *The Historic Environment: Policy & Practice* 6 (1): 16–40.

Gathmann, C., and F.K. Lembcke. 2017. *From Licensing to Certification: An Analysis of Germany's Crafts and Trade Sector*. Mimeo.

Klamer, A., L. Petrova, and A. Mignosa. 2006. *Financing the Arts and Culture in the European Union*. European Parliament.

Mignosa, A. 2016. Theory and Practice of Cultural Heritage Policy. In *The Artful Economist: A New Look at Cultural Economics*, ed. I. Rizzo and R. Towse, 227–244, Cheltenham, UK/Northampton, MA: Edward Elgar.

Peacock, A. 1994. *A Future for the Past: The Political Economy of Heritage*, Paper No. 44. Edinburgh: The David Hume Institute.

Peacock, A. (ed.). 1998. *Does the Past Have a Future? The Political Economy of Heritage*. London: The Institute of Economic Affairs.

Rizzo, I. 2011. Regulation. In *A Handbook of Cultural Economics*, ed. R. Towse, 386–393. Cheltenham, UK: Edward Elgar.

Santagata, W. 2002. Cultural Districts, Property Rights and Sustainable Economic Growth. *International Journal of Urban and Regional Research* 26 (1): 9–23.

Schoch, D. 2014. Whose World Heritage? Dresden's Waldschlößchen Bridge and UNESCO's Delisting of the Dresden Elbe Valley 1. *International Journal of Cultural Property* 21 (2): 199–223.

Stiglitz, J.E., and J.K. Rosengard. 2015. *Economics of the Public Sector: Fourth International Student Edition*. New York: W. W. Norton & Company, Inc.

Throsby, D. 1997. Seven Questions in the Economics of Cultural Heritage. In *Economic Perspectives of Cultural Heritage*, ed. M. Hutter and I. Rizzo, 13–30. London: Macmillan.

Throsby, D. 2010. *The Economics of Cultural Policy*. Cambridge: Cambridge University Press.

Towse, R. 2010. *A Textbook of Cultural Economics*. Cambridge University Press.

UNESCO. 2018a. World Heritage List. Available at http://whc.unesco.org/en/list. Last Retrieved August 16, 2018.

UNESCO. 2018b. Purpose of the Lists of Intangible Cultural Heritage and of the Register of Good Safeguarding Practices. Available at https://ich.unesco.org/en/purpose-of-the-lists-00807. Last Retrieved August 16, 2018.

Van der Ploeg, F. 2006. The Making of Cultural Policy: A European Perspective. In *Handbook of the Economics of Art and Culture*, ed. V.A. Ginsburgh and D. Throsby, vol. 1, 1183–1221. Amsterdam: Elsevier.

Crafts in China

Lili Jiang

Introduction

Chinese crafts are famous worldwide, reflecting China's long history, magnificent culture, aesthetic and values. Chinese culture strongly emphasizes the tangible dimension of material life, such as silk for clothing, ceramic for drinking, and jade for decorating. In China, crafts mostly are bound up with daily life and are for people's livelihood.

From the anthropological and sociological perspectives, Chinese crafts are closely connected with nature and humans. Due to China's unique geographical location and a long history as an agricultural civilization, its crafts mirror typical Chinese emotion and experiences that are practical, simple, warm, and natural. China is a country with strong local flavors, with the majority of its people living in rural areas, and as such, they were likely to pay attention to handicrafts. For thousands of years, this kind of autarkic rural life stimulated the formation and development of the Chinese traditional crafts culture. That is, crafts in

L. Jiang (✉)
Erasmus University Rotterdam, Rotterdam, The Netherlands

A. Mignosa and P. Kotipalli (eds.), *A Cultural Economic Analysis of Craft*,
https://doi.org/10.1007/978-3-030-02164-1_6

China are the essence of Chinese traditional culture, the accumulation of the Chinese work experience, and the crystallization of the Chinese life wisdom.

In the initial historical period of the People's Republic of China (1949–1957), the Chinese government put forward the slogan, 'use crafts in exchange for industrial machines' and, with its export advantage, 'Chinese Crafts' became a driving force in developing the national economy. In the 1970s and 1980s after the Cultural Revolution,[1] the Chinese government paid strong attention to the revival of Chinese crafts. Due to the policies of Reformation and Opening in 1979, the sector was confronted with new opportunities for development as well as new challenges from modern society. The government thus published *Regulations on the Protection of Traditional Crafts and Arts* in 1997 for crafts to develop with steady steps, these regulations were very important and a turning point in the development history of Chinese crafts. In sum, crafts in China carry the crucial responsibilities of preserving cultural heritage and ensuring economic development, and make great contributions to economic, cultural, and social spheres.

Yet, what are Chinese crafts? Are they different from the other countries'? Do they have special characteristics? How are they organized and developed in China? And have they contributed to our lives? We explore these issues in the following discussions.

Definition

In ancient times, 'crafts' was a term was used to describe all handmade works in China. There were no significant differences between 'crafts' and 'arts', moreover, 'crafts' was not an opposite term for 'arts', but included all the skills and forms of the 'arts'. In other words, 'arts' is a foreign word introduced in China (Qingcheng Huang 1893). After the Sino-Japanese War, 'arts' became a familiar term among Chinese scholars.

[1]The Cultural Revolution was a socio-political movement in China from 1966 to 1976.

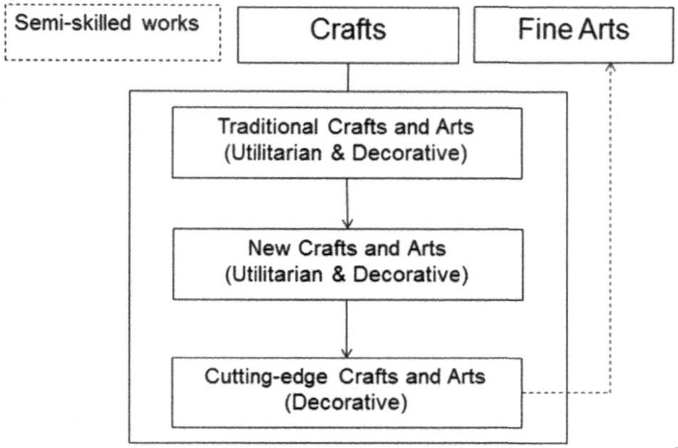

Fig. 1 The types of crafts

In 1920, 'arts and crafts' first appeared in China (Yuanpei Cai 1920), translated from the *Arts and Crafts Movement*. Cai claimed that crafts should be a combination of the function of crafts and the beauty of art. Chinese scholars subsequently wanted to emphasize crafts' utilitarian attributes and skilled technology, so they changed the term from 'arts and crafts' to 'crafts and arts', and finally 'crafts' was gradually replaced with 'crafts and arts'. In Eastern Han Dynasty (25–200), it was mentioned that every craftsman uses a certain degree of culture and skilled technology to handle different materials and languages, and create handicrafts with both tangible and intangible values (Shen Xu 100AD).

'Crafts and arts' has pragmatic and aesthetic attributes in its traditional meaning; that is, crafts must have a function that satisfies some daily needs of consumer and express different emotional values according to different conditions and environments. Therefore, 'crafts and arts' inevitably impacts on the development of cultural and economic spheres in China and records the whole of Chinese history from material to spiritual dimensions. In contrast, 'fine arts' is a vehicle for the transmission of personal experience and the aesthetic tendency of its creators.

From a taxonomical perspective based on chronology, I prefer to classify 'crafts and arts' into three types: traditional, new, and cutting-edge (Fig. 1).

Firstly, 'traditional crafts and arts' obviously has an epochal character. Compared with other kinds of crafts, hands must play an important role in the manufacturing process, not machines. According to the *Regulations on the Protection of Traditional Crafts and Arts* (1997),

> …'traditional crafts and arts' should have a long history of more than one hundred years from skill and form, and this superb craftsmanship should be handed down from generations; this type of crafts should have complete technical processes, be made with natural raw materials, reflect national styles and local characteristics, and also have high prestige in domestic and foreign domains… [Author's translation]

Hence, 'traditional crafts and arts' should have characteristics that are (i) traditional, (ii) artistic, (iii) national, (iv) natural, and (v) procedural.

Secondly, 'new crafts and arts' has no official definition in China. But after inspection and investigation in the Chinese crafts sphere, we could characterize it as having (i) new materials, (ii) new technologies, and (iii) new meanings. Even though 'new crafts and arts' must still be built on Chinese traditional culture, it also needs to satisfy new lifestyles and consumer tastes. Moreover, the characteristics of 'new crafts and arts' are driven entirely by market sales. For example, most traditional crafts workshops have already been transformed into modern craft industries by the tide of China's market economy. They keep the crucial values of traditional crafts and arts, but import advanced equipment, new management modes, and fresh creative ideas. That is, 'new crafts and arts' are a perfect union between traditional and modern, local and international, and conservative and creative.

Third, 'cutting-edge crafts and arts' are closely connected with 'fine arts' due to their similar features. In this sphere, even though creators have good knowledge of materials and sophisticated skills, and are well balanced among head, heart, and hands, they are different from other craftsmen in that they want to express personal experiences and feelings through their own work, and transform their role from craftspeople to artists. They struggle and have conflict with rules in the boundary between crafts and fine arts. Yet, if we carefully observe the market, we would find that works of cutting-edge creators still are subject to consumers' preferences, even if the creators are reluctant to admit it. Unfortunately, in China, we do not have corresponding official policies to interpret the group, and these creators are somewhere between crafts and fine arts.

What about plumbers, diggers, and roof workers? Are they craftsmen? Are their works crafts? Differently than in Germany, in China, most of them are just semi-skilled people, not artisans. In most Chinese minds, plumbers, diggers, and roof workers have less self-motive and autonomy and have the ability to handle emergencies. They need a commander to conduct them step by step, even though their works have obvious utilitarian or decorative attributes. Greatly skilled plumbers, diggers, and roof workers, however, might need to wear the craftsman's shoes.

Craftsmanship

Craftsmanship is regarded as an intrinsic value that goes beyond its economic valuation in China. It plays a crucial role in the life of craftspeople. In *Change of Traditional Crafts Culture*, Chunlin Qiu (2011) suggests dividing craftsmanship into two sorts:

i. *General Craftsmanship* is the collective wisdom and experience of generations. For a long time, selection, addition, reduction, and replacement continually improved and perfected craftsmanship from generation to generation. Craftsmanship, in general, is open to the public; anybody can know it, learn it, and control it.
ii. *Special Craftsmanship* is the secret and personal wisdom and experiences of groups. It means knowledge and skills of craftsman like 'special secret'. Outsiders can never master the secret skill or have the secret knowledge.

Craftsmanship increasingly, and fortunately, started to open to the public in modern Chinese society, providing an essential condition for the development and revival of Chinese crafts. Because craftsmen were looked down upon in the old society, they had no subsistence allowances; they had to keep their 'secret skill' for survival. Now that the position of craftsman has been raised, they need not worry that having knowledge and experience open to others will destroy their livelihoods. But we cannot deny that because awareness of copyright is weak in China's markets, some craftsmanship still wears the mysterious veil.

For the development of craftsmanship in modern society, many machines have replaced hands. When we face the impact of modernization, how do we recognize the 'craftsmanship' of Chinese crafts? Do we keep it or change it? Qiu (2011) puts forward the notion of 'core technology', and reminds craftspeople that they could use advanced knowledge and modern equipment in traditional crafts, but the 'core technology' must be inherited. Because there is a comparatively stable ideology behind every traditional craft, this ideology as 'core technology' would determine the values of craft. For example, the core technology of porcelain in Jingdezhen is about forming, decorating, and glazing by hands. It reflects surviving wisdom, public emotion, and balanced relationships between nature and humans, material and spirit, utility and decoration. In other words, if 'core technology' changes, the quality of Chinese crafts would be weakened and perhaps even disappear.

Organization Systems

Since 1950, the Chinese government has set organizations and associations for the development of Chinese crafts, such as the *Crafts and Arts Bureau* (established in 1957), which was in charge of the management of Chinese Craft; the *Crafts and Arts Company of Ministry of Light Industry* (1972) was mainly for coordinating the industry of Chinese crafts but at the end of the 1980s, its role was transformed from administrative to operative, weakening its management abilities. During that time, it was paralyzed by a lack of resources and enforcement capabilities.

To better conserve and develop Chinese crafts in modern society, the government has increasingly paid attention to the organization of Chinese crafts in recent years. It continually establishes different kinds

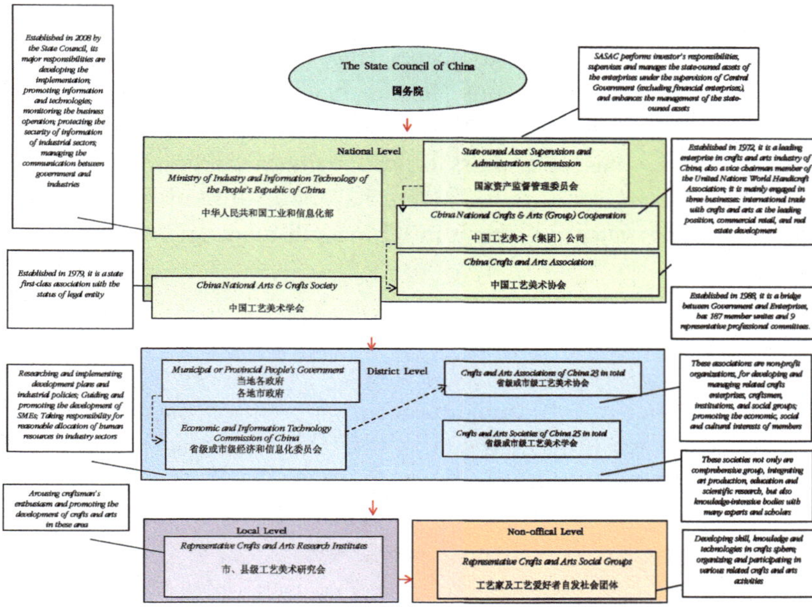

Fig. 2 Chinese 'crafts and arts' organization system

of comprehensive organizations in many provinces in China, and promulgates related policies and regulations to solve problems and stimulate the growth of Chinese crafts. As shown in Fig. 2, as a leading enterprise the *China National Crafts & Arts (Group) Cooperation* is directly managed by the State-owned Asset Supervision Administration Commission. *China Crafts & Arts Association* and *China National Arts & Crafts Society* are different organizations. The former was established in 1988 by the Ministry of Civil Affairs, it is a national non-profit organization to support the effective protection of Chinese crafts and arts, and facilitate the thriving of the crafts industry in China. The latter was ratified in 1979 by the Science and Technology Association of China, which is a non-profit social group meant to organize and educate craftspeople in China. These two organizations play very important roles to develop and revive Chinese crafts in our modern-day society.

However, because of Chinese crafts are operated by two departments of the State Council—the Ministries of Finance and Culture—serious problems are bound to arise, such as the difference of opinions on some matter, the distribution of resources, and the lack of integrated planning. Some craft organizations lack financial support and their respective craftsmen receive no benefits from them. And just a quarter of provinces of China have crafts official regulations and measurement. Even though the Chinese government has made unremitting efforts, the organization of the crafts system in China still meets many problems.

Education

Early on, 'father-to-son' and 'master-to-apprentice' succession modes were the main teaching methods in the Chinese crafts sphere. For the past 100 years or so the education of crafts has been moving toward colleges or universities. The development of crafts education has been roughly divided into three stages since 1949:

i. *1949–1980* was the primary stage of the crafts education system. The form of related crafts educational system began to take shape and gradually developed. It aimed to train and cultivate professional craftsmen with excellent talent, creativity, ability, and quality. According to the government statistics of 1983, there were at least 4500 students, 12,000 graduates, 1300 postgraduates, and 1200 teachers in the crafts education system in China.
ii. *1980–2000* was the reform and adjustment stage of the crafts education system. In the face of a rapidly developing economy, 'crafts' seemed to lag behind the requirements of modern society. The education system of crafts inevitably experienced some negative effects. Even though crafts major subjects were springing up all over China, they were inclined to design and high-technology within the industrial production milieu. Moreover, fewer and fewer people wanted to acquire the traditional skills and knowledge of crafts due to the risk of unemployment of the sector.
iii. *2000–present* has been an innovation and renovation stage for the crafts education system. Government policies and measures for education stimulated the initiative of many colleges or universities

> and the enthusiasm of students and teachers. According to the government statistics of 2007, there are at least 465 crafts colleges and universities, 310,000 students, 100,000 graduates, 46,703 teachers, 16,935 professors, and 900 comprehensive colleges and universities with arts major subjects indirectly related to crafts.

By 2006, according to *General Census Report on Chinese Crafts 2006*, in China there were 465 related crafts colleges and universities. Detailed information is listed in Table 1.

From a cultural perspective, Chinese crafts have significant artistic meanings and cultural connotations. From an economics perspective, they have enormous economic value and commercial potential. Yet, faced with the contradiction between the cultural and economic industries, arguments and disputes exist within the crafts educational system. In 1956, the 'Central Academy of Crafts and Arts' was established in Beijing but early in 1957, there was a dispute about which organization would be in charge of it. Some thought it should be the Chinese Arts and Handicrafts Administration because 'Chinese crafts' should be considered one economic industry for the development of the Chinese economy. Furthermore, the academy's education and training was to increase production and profits. Others, however, insisted that the Ministry of Culture of the People's Republic of China should be in charge because 'Chinese crafts' is one *cultural* industry for the improvement of Chinese cultural daily life. Finally, the Chinese government decided that the Ministry of Culture of the People's Republic of China should take over the Academy, but controversy on the 'ownership' of crafts education remains.

More and more related crafts colleges and universities started to rename their major subject from 'crafts and arts' to 'arts and design'. Even if some colleges and universities use their original names, the traditional skills and knowledge of crafts are beginning to dissipate. The development of the crafts educational system is suffering a bottleneck. In many Chinese minds, the social position of artists is higher than craftsman's; a student who wants to become a master would need an innate gift as well as energy and time. Most Chinese parents like to help their children select their dreams, and many children prefer industrial

Table 1 Situation of the crafts educational system in 2006

Level	Region	Public school					Private school				
		School	Teacher	Professor	Student	Graduate	School	Teacher	Professor	Student	Graduate
National		10	405	206	814	5006	–	–	–	–	–
Provincial	Beijing	2	243	113	610	2759	–	–	–	–	–
	Tianjin	7	332	14	644	2926	–	–	–	–	–
	Hebei	34	941	373	4501	20,787	1	147	42	252	1804
	Shanxi	9	374	71	1065	4920	–	–	–	–	–
	Nei Monggol	10	98	26	109	1284	–	–	–	–	–
	Liaoning	5	126	42	–	3524	1	200	2	–	500
	Jilin	11	295	79	950	4191	2	50	17	300	1500
	Heilongjiang	23	301	81	852	4415	2	116	36	23	2226
	Shanghai	73	2077	542	13,957	33,475	–	–	–	–	–
	Jiangsu	5	255	135	998	4848	–	–	–	–	–
	Zhejiang	43	25,553	10,609	4735	18,467	14	4866	1586	1165	6423
	Anhui	16	630	185	2756	12,624	–	–	–	–	–
	Fujian	14	719	62	3168	10,011	2	209	32	1239	4533
	Jiangxi	3	399	95	1285	4720	–	–	–	–	–
	Shandong	22	503	209	2400	6535	3	25	8	100	175
	Henan	16	1350	320	1537	38,770	3	125	10	330	5700
	Hubei	16	1607	448	6320	21,076	3	212	75	1970	5100
	Hunan	1	186	15	1400	4800	–	–	–	–	–
	Guangdong	26	851	200	2742	16,675	–	–	–	–	–
	Guangxi	6	152	31	1450	3865	–	–	–	–	–
	Hainan	3	81	29	–	1993	–	–	–	–	–
	Chongqing	7	227	86	657	4705	–	–	–	–	–
	Sichuan	29	1623	601	4656	35,502	1	30	4	70	300
	Guizhou	3	70	21	8800	1550	–	–	–	–	–
	Yunnan	7	264	112	1131	3505	1	7	–	54	191

(continued)

Table 1 (continued)

Level	Region	Public school					Private school				
		School	Teacher	Professor	Student	Graduate	School	Teacher	Professor	Student	Graduate
	Tibet	1	11	6	154	154	–	–	–	–	–
	Shaanxi	16	670	207	25,441	12,789	2	18	2	382	152
	Gansu	2	38	12	35	100	–	–	–	–	–
	Qinghai	2	53	16	171	598	–	–	–	–	–
	Ningxia	2	73	20	852	1501	–	–	–	–	–
	Xinjiang	6	109	21	276	482	–	–	–	–	–

design to traditional craftsmanship in accordance with their parents' advice. Such a phenomenon is bound to set up a vicious circle and raise serious problems, such as a shortage of teachers, facilities, and capital.

The Chinese Master Title

Toward the conservation and development of Chinese 'traditional crafts and arts', the government has since 1954 praised excellent craftspeople in many cities, provinces, and municipalities for strong knowledge, sophisticated skills, and outstanding craftsmanship. In 1996, 377 craftsmen were awarded the honorary title of 'Old Craftsman'. Since then the government has organized different divisions. They established the 'Chinese Crafts Master' title, which has different levels: national, provincial, municipal, and high. For a national-level title, according to *Regulations on the Protection of Traditional Crafts and Arts*, craftsman must meet certain quality characteristics and have long engaged in the crafts profession. 'Chinese Craftsman Master' national-level awards have been granted six times (1979, 1988, 1993, 1997, 2006, and 2011).

However, because most traders use the 'Chinese Crafts Master' title to set the price, the market value of a crafts item is always decided by the Master title. The 'Chinese Crafts Master' title seems to bring a considerable income for the craftsmen, many Chinese craftsmen inevitably use 'Guanxi'[2] power to get this kind of titles in the master selection process, although they are not good at transforming raw materials into valuable goods. That has once again proven that much more work is still needed if we are to revive Chinese crafts and their craftsmanship.

In China, because of economic and social rapid changes, along with the fast development of science and technology, 'crafts'[3] entered a new development stage. Even though 'Chinese crafts' had already lost its mainstream position in society, it bears the responsibility of carrying on

[2]Guanxi means that the basic dynamic in personalized networks of influence, which refers to the benefits gained from social connections and usually extends from family, friend, workmates, and members of common clubs or organization. This is an intricate and obscure network in China.

[3]<2018年中国民间手工艺品行业现状调查以及发展趋势预测报告>, 2018, China Market Report Online.

Chinese traditional connotations and ideology. Faced with economic globalization and the information age, 'crafts' should be infused with a new culture and technological system to satisfy the needs of modern people.

Thus, Chinese craftsmen increasingly try to combine 'traditional and modern', 'inheritance and creativity', 'national and international' in their crafts. Following diversified social lives and the various human needs in modern times, 'crafts' should reflect the characteristics of unique historical values and embody the tendencies of modern lifestyles. That is, in China 'crafts' should be not only the spirit of Chinese traditional culture, but also the symbol of Chinese modern civilization.

References

Cai, Yuanpei. 1920. <美术的起源> [The Origin of Arts]. *New Tide*.

Huang, Qingcheng. 黄庆澄. 1893. <东游日记> [Diary of Travel Around Japan]. China.

Qiu, C. 邱春林. 2011. <中国手工艺文化变迁> [Change of Traditional Crafts Culture]. China: Baijia Press.

The State Council, The People's Republic of China. 1997. <传统工艺美术保护条例> [Regulations on the Protection of Traditional Crafts and Arts].

Xu, Shen. 许慎. 100AD. <说文解字> [Explaining Words]. China.

Arts and Crafts Policies: Heritage *vs* Economics in France

Francesca Cominelli

In order to investigate the issue of arts and crafts policies in France, it is firstly necessary to assess what arts and crafts means and how this concept is interpreted within the French cultural, legal, and economic system. This is neither an easy nor a recent task. In 1976, Pierre Dehaye, at that time at the direction of the Coins and Medals administration, and aware of questions linking arts and industries, handed to the President of the Republic a report[1] about the difficulties crafts faced. He immediately pointed out the question of the elusive definition of crafts. There is nowhere, he wrote in his report, a satisfying definition of arts and crafts. The report was followed by the creation, the same year, of the Société d'encouragement aux métiers d'art/Society for the Encouragement of Arts and Crafts (SEMA), an association supported by the State. This organization was the evolution of the Société d'encouragement à l'art et

[1]Dehaye, P. 1976. *Les difficultés des métiers d'art*. Rapport au Président de la République, Paris: La documentation française.

F. Cominelli (✉)
IREST/EIREST, University Paris 1 Panthéon-Sorbonne, Paris, France

A. Mignosa and P. Kotipalli (eds.), *A Cultural Economic Analysis of Craft*,
https://doi.org/10.1007/978-3-030-02164-1_7

à l'industrie/Society for the Encouragement of Art and Industry (SEAI), created in 1889 by Gustave Sandoz, jeweler, and Gustave Larroumet, at that time chef of the direction of Fine Arts at the Ministry of Education. Its mission was essentially based on the organization of competitions and exhibitions of prize-winning objects, the allocation of apprenticeship grants, and the upgrading of fine arts crafts. SEMA has been transformed, 34 years later, into Institut National des Métiers d'Art/National Arts and Crafts Institute (INMA).

The question of defining the crafts remains nowadays controversial, but important steps have been accomplished: on December 12, 2003, an official list has been adopted by ministerial order[2] comprising no less than 217 craft practices including, among others, activities in the fields of architecture, clothing, jewelry, decorative arts, performing arts, musical instruments, etc. Nevertheless, this list is not exhaustive and in 2009, the report[3] dedicated to crafts of the Senator Catherine Dumas proposes to extend the field of crafts to new activities, like for example the gastronomic ones. Even if these last practices have not yet been recognized as crafts, the official list of 2003 has been updated by ministerial order on December 24, 2015.[4] The list includes nowadays 198 crafts activities and 83 specialties in 16 fields. This extension is the consequence, on the one hand, of continuous inventorying and research projects that led to a deeper knowledge of the arts and crafts sector and to a better comprehension of its diversity; on the other hand, to the demand of crafts professionals, excluded from the official list, to be recognized as practicing arts and crafts activities and to benefit of policy measures specifically designed for them. For example, some activities related to photography, like rotogravure, have been included in the 2015 list.

[2]Arrêté du 12 décembre 2003 fixant la liste des métiers de l'artisanat d'art.

[3]Dumas, C. 2009. *Les métiers d'art, d'excellence et du luxe et les savoir-faire traditionnels: l'avenir entre nos mains*. Rapport à Monsieur le Premier Ministre, Paris.

[4]Arrêté du 24 décembre 2015 fixant la liste des métiers d'art, en application de l'article 20 de la loi n° 96–603 du 5 juillet 1996 relative au développement et à la promotion du commerce et de l'artisanat.

In reason of the multiplicity of activities counted in the list of crafts, it is hard to concur on a single, clear, and shared definition of crafts and craftsmanship. In 2008, Richard Sennett in his book *The Craftsman* proposed an interesting approach to such a definition: "Craftsmanship may suggest a way of life that waned with the advent of industrial society [...]. Craftsmanship names an enduring, basic human impulse, the desire to do a job well for its own sake".[5] In France, in 2014 the law[6] concerning crafts, commerce, and very small businesses defined as craftspeople the physical persons, as well as the managers of legal persons, who exercise, as a principal or secondary job, an independent activity of production, creation, transformation, or reconstitution, repair and restoration of heritage, characterized by the mastery of skills and techniques to work the rough material and requiring an artistic effort.

These results, from a legal point of view, show the increasing political importance of a sector, still suffering from a lack of specific regulations. The existing policies in the field, that will be further presented, confirm that this political engagement is not only related to economic interests, in fact the arts and crafts activities constitute an important tangible and intangible cultural heritage (ICH), enforcing the dynamism of the French territories and their attractiveness.

Heritage *vs* Economics

Considering the complexity of this sector and the diversity of public interventions, arts and crafts policies in France might be structured into two main groups:

- Policies aiming at the economic valorization of the crafts knowledge and skills within the crafts sector, but also seeking to spread their creative potential in other sectors.

[5]Sennett, R. 2008. *The Craftsman*. New Haven and London: Yale University Press.

[6]Art. 22, Law n° 2014–626 of July 18th, 2014.

- Policies oriented toward the cultural dimension of arts and crafts, and aiming at the safeguarding of this tangible and intangible heritage.

The reasons fostering public intervention in the field of crafts from an economic perspective, are based on the idea that craftsmanship and crafts activities contribute to the development and to the dynamism of local economies. Firstly, as cultural industries, "industries that combine the creation, production and commercialization of creative content that is tangible and intangible in nature",[7] crafts are strongly concerned by the phenomenon of creativity. Arts and crafts can give new inputs to the production process of goods. Therefore, these inputs have an impact on the aesthetic and symbolic dimension of goods, on innovation, productivity and on the quality of products, as well as on demand and competitiveness. Moreover, the crafts industry is linked to job creation, exports and revenues at a local, national and international level. Despite the lack of precise data in this field, the French labor force in the arts and crafts sector is estimated involving 60,000 workers and 38,000 businesses, with an annual income of roughly 8 billion euros.[8] The incomes of crafts activities surely exceed the mentioned ones if we consider that these practices can incite the development of cultural, creative and touristic activities in the territory and ensure the restoration of cultural heritage buildings and sites. Finally, crafts products are strongly interested in exportations and therefore promote the image of a country through the circulation of its specific productions.

In this perspective, different measures seek to foster crafts economic visibility and growth. A national register[9] of crafts enterprises is kept and updated in France by INMA, in order to give visibility to craftspeople and workshops, as well as to make the public aware of their localization, and the specificity, and quality of these businesses.

---

[7]UNESCO. 2009. *Investing in Cultural Diversity and Intercultural Dialogue.* UNESCO World Report, Paris: UNESCO Publishing, p. 261.

[8]INMA. 2015. *Les métiers d'art: contexte, enjeux et acteurs.* Les cahiers de l'INMA.

[9]INMA. 2017. Annuaire officiel des métiers d'art. http://www.annuaire-metiersdart.com, 30/12/2017.

This register includes more or less 3200 professionals and it receives more than 50,000 virtual visitors per year.[10] In a similar perspective is developed the label Entreprise du Patrimoine Vivant/Living Heritage Company (EPV).[11] This is a mark recognized by the French State, meant to reward national firms for the excellence of their traditional and industrial know-how and to boost their growth. Introduced in 2005,[12] this label may be awarded to businesses that demonstrate the ownership of specific economic heritage; the possession of rare knowledge based on the mastery of traditional or technically advanced skills; and the link to a particular geographical area. The label is awarded by the Minister Delegate with responsibility for Crafts and Trade, for a duration of five years. The holders of the EPV label also benefit of two main tax incentives: the apprenticeship tax credit, up to 2200 euros per apprentice; and the creative tax credit, which concerns companies that invest in the design of new products, and can obtain a credit that corresponds to 15% of all the expenses realized in connection with the development of new products.

The two main objectives of the EPV system, valorization and innovation, are also pursued by other national measures. Concerning the visibility, we can mention the Journées Européennes des Métiers d'Art/European Arts and Crafts Days[13] (JEMA), that follow the same logic of the European Heritage Days and aim at opening and letting the public visit the greatest number of crafts workshops all over Europe. In 2017, 19 European countries took part in the event and in France 7500 workshops and 160 training centers were opened to the public, 1600 events were organized for the youngest public and 75 touristic tours were planned. While, concerning innovation, an interesting measure is the Prix pour intelligence de la main/Prize for the intelligence of the hand created in 1999 by the Fondation Bettencourt Schueller that rewards knowledge, know-how, creativity, and innovation in the crafts field.

---

[10]INMA. 2014. *Institut National des Métiers d'Art*. Presses d'Art & Caractère.

[11]Cominelli, F., and C. Virassamy. 2014. Le crédit d'impôt métiers d'art. *JurisArt*, Dalloz.

[12]Art. 23, Law on small and medium enterprises, August 2nd, 2005.

[13]Journées européennes des métiers d'art. https://www.journeesdesmetiersdart.fr, 27/12/2017.

The Prize comprises three awards: "Talents d'exception/Exceptional talents" that compensate a craftsperson for a creative work contributing to the development of his/her expertise; "Dialogue", created in 2010, that encourages the cooperation between a craftsperson and another creator to develop a new product; and finally the award "Parcours/Pathway", introduced in 2014, that recognizes the commitment of an individual (natural or legal person) for his or her contributions to the French crafts sector. Since their introduction, at the end of the 1990s, these awards have been recognized to nearly 90 people working in different arts and crafts fields.

Beyond these policies that stress the economic dimension of crafts activities, other policies valorize their cultural dimension, on the basis of the idea that arts and crafts contribute to cultural and social development as factors strengthening identity, social cohesion, and cultural capital.[14] From this perspective, craftsmanship is generally seen as the result of a long process of accumulation of ideas, knowledge, identities, and symbols in a specific territory. This cultural capital is built up and shared within a community of practitioners and transmitted from one generation to the other. It is, therefore, a strong factor for building cultural identity, allowing social cohesion, and developing creativity, besides being a component of economic growth. Arts and crafts also contribute to cultural diversity. As specified by the Convention on the protection and promotion of the diversity of cultural expressions "cultural diversity is a rich asset for individuals and societies. The protection, promotion and maintenance of cultural diversity are an essential requirement for sustainable development for the benefit of present and future generations".[15] The protection of crafts practices responds to this objective in reason of the richness and multiplicity of skills and knowledge mobilized by these activities and of the variety of products created.

---

[14]Cominelli, F. and X. Greffe. 2012. Intangible Cultural Heritage: Safeguarding for Creativity. *City, Culture and Society*, Elsevier; Matarasso, F. 2001. *Recognising Culture: Briefing Papers on Culture and Development*. Paris: UNESCO; Scott, A.J. 2000. *The Cultural Economy of Cities*. London: Sage.

[15]UNESCO. 2005. *Convention on the Protection and Promotion of the Diversity of Cultural Expressions*, 20 October, Paris, article 2, para 6.

Furthermore, those goods usually reflect the specific needs and aesthetic values of a community. Thus, the main focus of these policies is the valorization of the cultural dimension of arts and crafts, through a deep knowledge of this heritage, measures ensuring the transmission of knowledge, skills and handiworks and actions oriented to the evolution of crafts toward the centuries.

Concerning the development of researches about the crafts sector, if only a few academic works have been produced in France on this topic,[16] a number important of documents have been edited within the public framework. Firstly, by the ethnographers of the ancient Mission ethnologie/Ethnology Mission at the Ministry of culture and later by the experts and communities involved in the redaction of the inventory documents constituting the Register of ICH in France. This register directly followed the ratification of the 2003 UNESCO Convention for the Safeguarding of the ICH and was initiated in 2006. The section concerning crafts is mainly focused on specific knowledge and skills existing in France and has been realized in collaboration with the SEMA, and later with INMA. The creation of this register and the increasing importance given to ICH in France has led the local communities of practitioners, the public authorities and the State to sustain the inscription of a certain number of crafts practices on the representative list of ICH of humanity.

Since 2008, six practices have been inscribed within the domain of traditional craftsmanship: Compagnonnage, network for on-the-job transmission of knowledge and identities (2010); Craftsmanship of Alençon needle lace-making (2010); Scribing tradition in French timber framing (2009); Aubusson tapestry (2009); Art of dry stone walling, knowledge and techniques (2018); The skills related to perfume in Pays de Grasse (2018). These inscriptions on the UNESCO list are meant to show the diversity and the richness of ICH in France, and often pursue the objective of showing the excellence of French arts and crafts. This sense of unicity, excellence, rarity is, therefore, better pointed

[16]Cominelli, F. 2016. *Métiers d'art et savoir-faire*. Paris: Economica; Loup, S. 2003. *Stratégies et identités de l'artisanat d'art*. Thèse de sciences de gestion, Université de Montpellier I; Jourdain, A. 2014. *Du cœur à l'ouvrage*. Paris: éditions Belin.

out by another crafts measure, which is the one known as Maître d'art/ Master of Arts. This program exists in France since 1994 and has been inspired by the system of Living Human Treasures, approved in 1993 by the General Conference of UNESCO. The measure is based on the selection of crafts professionals that hold remarkable and rare skills and knowledge that can only be transmitted through informal training. They need to have a professional experience of at least fifteen years and to be engaged in the innovation of their practice and creations. To become Masters of Arts, practitioners also have to show the desire to transmit their skills and knowledge to an apprentice. Few masters are selected every year by a commission and named by the Minister of Culture. The title is associated with a pecuniary compensation and the engagement by the masters in the training of an apprentice. Since 1994, 124 Masters of Art have been named in France. This measure, even if highly selective, rejoins the objective of the 2003 UNESCO Convention of safeguarding ICH items through "measures aimed at ensuring the viability of the ICH, including the identification, documentation, research, preservation, protection, promotion, enhancement, transmission, particularly through formal and non-formal education, as well as the revitalization of the various aspects of such heritage".

If the title of Master of Arts is highly selective and based on the excellence of skills and knowledge, other training systems exists in France in order to transmit the intangible dimension of arts and crafts activities. In particular, more than 1000 establishments are specialized in the training of future professionals, often alternating courses in the school and apprenticeship in the company. The training programs include different levels, as for example the Certificat d'aptitude professionnelle/ Certificates of Professional Aptitude (CAP) that permits to acquire the basic gestures and skills, followed by the Brevet des métiers d'art/ Arts and Crafts Patent (BMA) and by the Diplôme des métiers d'art/ Arts and Crafts Diploma (DMA) which is a training of two years that follows the baccalaureate or the BMA. Some diplomas are delivered by the circuit of the Ecoles supérieures d'Arts Appliqués/Higher Schools of Applied Arts (ESAA) like for example the schools Boulle, specialized in jewelry and furniture, Duperré, in the fields of fashion and design, Estienne, for graphic arts. These trainings are the hearth of a policy aiming at safeguarding these practices, not only because of their economic potential but also in reason of their cultural value. Nevertheless, to complete this panorama of initiatives, it is important to mention the system of "manufactory".

The main manufactories existing today in the field of crafts were set up at the end of the Seventeenth century by Colbert. At that time, their objective was to organize the production, at the national level, of crafts and luxury goods. Some of these ancient manufactories, still survive becoming exhibition, training, research, and innovation centers. We can name as example the Cité de la céramique/City of Ceramic of Sèvres and Limoges, and the Mobilier National/National Forniture that includes the manufactories of Gobelins, Beauvais and the Savonnerie, and the National lace workshops in Puy-en-Velay and Alençon. Those highly specialized establishments depend on the French Ministry of Culture.

French Institutions for Arts and Crafts

The crafts policies here mentioned certainly mobilize a great number of institutions at the national, regional and local level. It is hard to draw a complete picture of crafts institutions in France,[17] because of their multiplicity, diversity, and differences in size and scope. For this reason, we will focus here mainly on institutions that act at the national level and that embrace the all sector of crafts, without making distinctions among activities and fields.

At the national level, the policy for crafts is mainly designed by two Ministries: the Ministry of Culture and the Ministry of Economics and Finances. Since 2010, their action is conveyed, as already mentioned, through the INMA, an association working under the supervision of the two Ministries and in the general interest of the crafts sector. INMA's role is to sustain the crafts sector, also anticipating its future

[17]For an extensive analysis of crafts institutions in France and their evolution since 1851 see: Jourdain, A. 2014. *Du cœur à l'ouvrage*. Paris: éditions Belin.

developments in order to establish the conditions permitting its long-term growth. Thanks to its positioning, INMA gathers the public and private actors of the crafts sector and develops expertise in both national and international matters, by means of different projects: a documentation center; conferences and meetings on the economics and development of crafts; projects fostering innovation in the field of crafts and design; promotion of the Slow Made movement; organization of competitions to award prizes to young creators or experts; actions meant to create a network of crafts actors and projects at the European and Mediterranean level. Created in 2010, the history of INMA is nevertheless more complex and can be linked to the first efforts of the movement created in 1864 within the Union central des beaux-arts appliqués à l'industrie/Central Union of Fine Arts Applied to Industry. This movement tried to associate beauty and utility and to initiate a reform of the education system in this sense. These first experiences led to the creation of the SEAI in 1889, that became the SEMA in 1976 and was finally transformed into the actual INMA in 2010.

Besides the INMA which embodies the will of the public authorities and promotes the role of crafts within the French economy, other crafts institutions exist. These institutions are often created by professionals that gather together in order to structure their sector and to promote their specific interests. A multitude of associations, federations, unions for different crafts activities exist in France. The most important institution in this sense is Atelier d'Art de France/Art Workshops of France (AAF), a professional union for crafts that associates more than 6000 craftsmen, artists, and manufactures throughout France. AAF aims to promote, represent, and defend the interests of the crafts sector and to contribute to the economic development of professionals in France and internationally. Created in 1995, its history began in 1868 with the Chambre syndicale de la Céramique et de la Verrerie/Trade Union Chamber of Ceramics and Glassworks and has evolved for almost 150 years becoming Chambre syndicale des Céramistes d'Art/Trade Union Chamber of Art Ceramists (1940–1965), Chambre syndicale des Céramistes et Ateliers d'Art de France/Trade Union Chamber of Ceramists and Art Workshops of France (1965–1984), Syndicat des Ateliers d'Art de France/Union of Art Workshops of France

(1984–1995), and finally AAF. A strong action of AAF is oriented to the economic development of the crafts market throughout the organization of crafts fairs like Maison & Objet (of which AAF is co-owner) and the Salon International du Patrimoine/International Cultural Heritage Fair that takes place every here at the Carrousel of the Louvre Museum. AAF also opened thematic shops and galleries in some French cities like Paris, Montpellier, and Pézenas.

If those institutions play an important role at the national level, a nebulous of other institution exist at the regional and local level that have the merit to take into account the territorial specificities of crafts. In Alsace, the traditional textile and organ productions, as well as the crafts activities of more than 900 craftspeople are sustained by the FREMAA, a federation of professionals, supported by the Regional Council that organizes in Strasbourg the Fair "Résonance", develops specific training programs for transmission and publishes documents to improve the knowledge of the crafts sector of the region. Some regions created innovative projects of valorization of traditional crafts: in Auvergne, the experimental poles of Nontron (1999); in Bretagne, the cluster Morbihan (2006), dedicated originally to the naval sector and then extended to the promotion of crafts all over the department; in the region Centre, a network of Chambres de métiers et de l'artisanat/ Chambers of Arts and Crafts develops project and research supporting crafts; in Lorraine, the Lorraine Mission is a structure for crafts integrated in the regional organization that coordinate some projects like the Centre International d'Art Verrier/International Glass Art Center[18] (CIAV). This center was founded in 1992, but its history began in 1704 with the birth of an ancient factory of glass making in Meisenthal, that became between 1867 and 1894, a laboratory of the School of Nancy. The CIAV is nowadays a public institution that aims to preserve the technical memory of its territory, to ensure its continuity and to inscribe the traditional glass production in the framework of contemporary creative industries. So, in all French regions the Chambers of Arts and Crafts, Regional Council, local unions, associations keep working in order to develop projects and policies to sustain and innovate the sector.

[18]CIAV. http://ciav-meisenthal.fr, consulté le 20/12/2017.

Future Perspectives

Visibly, the safeguard, the valorization, and the innovation of arts and crafts activities are a complex issue. Economic and cultural policies are extremely diversified, but intimately related since an economic development is not possible without the preservation of ancient knowledge and skills, and crafts objects exhibited in museums and galleries. On the other hand, these knowledge, skills, and objects cannot have a future without the permanent creation, recreation, and innovation that engage craftspeople.

That is why the future of crafts is strongly related to the capacity of professionals to continue creating objects that link beauty and utility interpreting the needs of contemporary generations, keeping alive the values of traditional crafts, their aesthetic dimension linked with the capacity of lasting throughout time. This means to support alternative economic models of development in a global economy oriented to the standardization of shapes, needs, fabrication processes, markets, and to the programming of product's lifespan.

Sustaining the crafts sector today means to inject new values and a new vision in contemporary economies. In this sense, it is crucial, first, to respect all the creators with policies improving their work conditions; second, to adapt the training systems to contemporary constraints and to raise the awareness of the importance of this heritage, educating generations that will be the bearers of these traditions in the framework of global and knowledge economies; third, to broadly protect and valorize the social and creative process and not only the craft's items and people themselves.

In a broader perspective, arts and crafts activities can contribute to what is pointed out today has a global priority: sustainable development. Craftsmanship can be considered a key component of this idea of growth since its practices contributes not only to "human capability expansion", reinforcing cultural and human capital and social cohesion, but also to environmental sustainability. Indeed, crafts activities are based on skills and knowledge rooted in the territory, that have had time to evolve throughout the centuries using local natural resources, without exploiting and threatening them, but in a long-time perspective.

References

Cominelli, F. 2016. *Métiers d'art et savoir-faire*. Paris: Economica.

Cominelli, F., and X. Greffe. 2012. Intangible Cultural Heritage: Safeguarding for Creativity. *City, Culture and Society*, Elsevier 3: 245–250.

Dehaye, P. 1976. *Les difficultés des métiers d'art*. Rapport au Président de la République, Paris: La documentation française.

Dumas, C. 2009. *Les métiers d'art, d'excellence et du luxe et les savoir-faire traditionnels: l'avenir entre nos mains*. Rapport à Monsieur le Premier Ministre, Paris.

INMA. 2014. *Institut National des Métiers d'Art*. Presses d'Art & Caractère.

INMA. 2015. *Les métiers d'art: contexte, enjeux et acteurs*. Les cahiers de l'INMA.

INMA. 2017. Annuaire officiel des métiers d'art. http://www.annuaire-metiersdart.com, 30/12/2017.

Jourdain, A. 2014. *Du cœur à l'ouvrage*. Paris: éditions Belin.

Loup, S. 2003. *Stratégies et identités de l'artisanat d'art*. Thèse de sciences de gestion, Université de Montpellier.

Matarasso, F. 2001. *Recognising Culture: Briefing Papers on Culture and Development*. Paris: UNESCO.

Scott, A.J. 2000. *The Cultural Economy of Cities*. London: Sage.

Sennett, R. 2008. *The Craftsman*. New Haven and London: Yale University Press.

UNESCO. 2005. *Convention on the Protection and Promotion of the Diversity of Cultural Expressions*, 20 October, Paris, article 2, para 6.

UNESCO. 2009. *Investing in Cultural Diversity and Intercultural Dialogue*. UNESCO World Report, Paris: UNESCO Publishing, p. 261.

Handwerk: Crafts and Trades in Germany

Thora Fjeldsted

Introduction

The crafts and trades as practised and maintained in Germany are a clearly defined and robust sector, collectively organized under the heading of *Handwerk*. They account for a substantial slice of the German economy. In 2016, the turnover of the sector was 561 billion euros before VAT (7.7% of national gross value), and around one million crafts companies were active and listed in the national crafts register (28.8% of active German enterprises). Around 5.45 million people were employed in the sector and 363 thousand apprentices enrolled in the vocational education and training (VET) system of the crafts, representing 12.5% of the workforce and 27.4% of those in higher education.[1] *Handwerk* is defined by extensive legislation by which enterprises

[1]Zentralverband des Deutschen Handwerks https://www.zdh.de/daten-fakten/kennzahlen-des-handwerks/. Accessed 29 June 2018.

T. Fjeldsted (✉)
Erasmus University, Rotterdam, The Netherlands

A. Mignosa and P. Kotipalli (eds.), *A Cultural Economic Analysis of Craft*,
https://doi.org/10.1007/978-3-030-02164-1_8

in 41 crafts-professions are regulated,[2] and companies in another 107 non-regulated crafts and trades[3] and "skilled crafts-like trades"[4] are represented. The *Handwerk*-run education system provides not only the crafts sector but German manufacture as a whole with a highly skilled labour force, and its organizations co-operate closely with the organs of both industry and the state in the ambit of education and skill certification. Perhaps not surprisingly, given this importance, the crafts also have an active part in politics[5] and the formation of policy on regional and national levels. In the arena of political representation they rally around the interests of what is known in German as the *Mittelstand*, which rather than mirroring the English concept of middle-class, refers to the interests of owner-managed companies in the SME sector supplying products and services.[6] At the same time, however, *Mittelstand* and artisans' own interests are also conceived to be interwoven with far wider interests: those of the larger society and even of the material environment. The notion of interdependency of the social, material and economic is an unusual one, and stands in sharp contrast with dominant conceptions of economic and political organization, where different spheres are rarely seen to overlap. *Handwerk* provides a highly interesting case study of how the interrelations between these factors can play out in a highly modern and structured context.

[2]The operating manager of a crafts-enterprise in these professions must possess a master-qualification or prove otherwise sufficient professional qualification.

[3]The range of crafts in Germany is wide, including among others plumbing, hat-making, baking, hairdressing, road-making and ceramics. A full list can be found here https://www.zdh.de/filead-min/user_upload/ZDH/0725-Berufe_englisch.pdf.

[4]https://www.zdh.de/en/trade-and-crafts-code/.

[5]This is facilitated by some of the main particularities of the German political system which are ordoliberalism, corporatism and an unusual devolution of power to local and regional bodies through a principle of subsidiarity.

[6]On its website, *Handwerk* sums up its political philosophy so: ZDH is committed to a social free market system and to an SME policy of competitive excellence that promotes independent small and medium-sized enterprises through suitable economic framework conditions and thus contributes to their ability to develop their potential as employers and providers of vocational education and further training. ZDH opposes excessive state control, a restriction on private property and the abuse of market power.

Conceptual and Historical Roots of *Handwerk*

But what is *Handwerk* exactly? *Handwerk* is a curious mix of centuries' worth of knowledge and skills and a well-defined modern legal framework. It represents a unique system ordered around the concepts of quality and skills. The meaning of quality and skills was highlighted in a 2010 television advertisement commissioned by *Handwerk* as part of a publicity campaign aimed at encouraging enrolment in its education system.[7] In the span of two minutes the material constitution of a fictional city disintegrated. Confusion reigned as tables broke to pieces, wallpaper peeled off and windows fell out. Clothes tore on the seams as textiles came undone and heels broke off shoes. Finally, roads cracked open and materials crumbled to an unbuilt state, leaving a naked, uncomfortable and scared population of humans standing on a heap of dust. 'What is the world without quality and skill in making?', the advertisement asks. The suggested answer is that it is subject to disintegration of things that are essential. Albeit exaggerated, this captures the essence of *Handwerk*. How things are made matters. They may not disintegrate with such ferocity in reality, yet lousy quality has repercussions. Not only does shoddy manufacture result in safety concerns, but it can also further encourage waste of material resources as things must be discarded in the event of flaws in making. It is the role and raison d'être of the crafts to ensure that things hold together. Unlike what might be seen as somewhat romantic or idealistic visions of the crafts as expressions of individuality, authenticity, or identity, *Handwerk* is therefore strongly grounded in a more general idea of functionality and skilled participation in the production and maintenance of the material world.[8] To be a craftsman is to be able to dependably carry out an activity well enough for a thing made or service rendered to work as intended. In the German language, this ability is captured in the figure of the *Meister* or master-craftsman whose skill, established through education, is certified

[7]https://www.youtube.com/watch?v=1TwIUgd7eb0.

[8]"Art-crafts" or *Kunsthandwerk* form a part of *Handwerk*, albeit a minor one. For a discussion see: Muthesius, S. 1998. Handwerk/Kunsthandwerk. *Journal of Design History* 11 (1): 85–95.

by *Handwerk*. However, being skilled is not an obvious proposition. Overlooking it, Adam Smith presumed, for example, that all knowledge could be transferred virtually for free. Economics followed suit, leaving skills and active learning non-essential to classical and neo-classical economic theory.[9] Yet, materials and mechanisms all have their different logics and exigencies. The knowledge and skill to understand and appropriately treat different materials can only be achieved through practice and repeated contact with both methods and materials. Over the centuries, apprenticeships have offered meeting points between those who know and can show and new generations to whom the knowledge can be passed. As such, they have been the most recurrent channel to facilitate the maintenance of material knowledge and skill.

Historical Background

The *Handwerk*-system is not so much born out of a theoretical or emotional affinity with the importance of quality, but rather as a product of the concrete consequences of the lack of skill. Two historical events have been particularly influential in its emergence. Firstly, the crafts turned out politically and materially important in the tumult of 19th century German history. From 1810, some states of what would become Germany, most notably Prussia, pursued liberalist politics with a concept of freedom of trade. Others, such as Hanover and Bavaria, rejected freedom of trade because they saw it as the reason for social erosion and mass impoverishment, which had been vividly demonstrated in Prussia. Indeed, it was only after the unification of Germany under Prussian aegis in 1870 that liberalist politics were enforced in the rest of the German states where, with freedom of trade imposed, the economic transformation process followed the same pattern. By that time, however, a strong political craft movement capable of lobbying for

[9]Epstein, S.R. 2008. Craft Guilds, Apprenticeship and Technological Change in Pre-industrial Europe. In *Guilds, Innovation and the European Economy 1400–1800*, ed. S.R. Epstein and M. Park, 57–58. Cambridge and New York: Cambridge University Press.

professional and educational interests of the craft trades had been established throughout the German states.[10]

As guild privileges such as monopolies were revoked, large industrial centres abruptly replaced what had been the crafts-based smaller and more regional modes of making. As the crafts came under pressure, also the recreation of skill ground to a halt, since industry relied completely on the training activity of the traditional craft sector and its reservoir of qualified labour: With the loss of more and more craft businesses, however, this source of qualified skilled workers disappeared, and without adequate replacement systems in place, industrial production itself went into crisis. As this combined with social unrest among industrial workers, the Imperial Government sought to ally itself with the craft movement, which had lobbied for craft regulation ever since 1848, and which was striving for economic policy significance. As a result it was decreed that the crafts should be sustained and protected so that they could keep up their traditional educational role.[11] The legal structure created for this purpose, approved in 1897, would later serve as the groundwork for the modern-day *Handwerk*.[12]

The second historical event that served to concretely demonstrate the importance of skills, then, was the challenge of rebuilding Germany after WWII. Amidst the ruins of the country's built environment there emerged pressing questions of how to rebuild. Big industry had been the engine of the German war effort and was therefore morally bankrupt, incapacitated and dismantled at the end of the war. Those who were able to successfully make and build things were the remaining craftspeople. And the combination of their knowledge and skill with the available resources proved remarkably successful in rebuilding the material environment. The sheer functionality of the crafts which thus

[10]John, P. 1987. *Handwerk im Spannungsfeld zwischen Zunftordnung und Gewerbefreiheit: Entwicklung und Politik der Selbstverwaltungsorganisationen des deutschen Handwerks bis 1933*, 170–275. Köln: Bund-Verlag.

[11]Ibid., 277–352.

[12]Thelen, K. 2004. *How Institutions Evolve: The Political Economy of Skills in Germany, Britain, the United States and Japan.* Cambridge, NY, etc.: Cambridge University Press. Chapter 2; Doran, A. 1984. *Craft Enterprises in Britain and Germany: A Sectoral Study*, 39–58. London: Anglo-German Foundation.

emerged contributed to the success of the organizations of *Handwerk* in persuading the powers reigning in Germany after the war to reinstate a legal system to protect the crafts. Against the odds they succeeded and in 1953 a robust legal framework for the crafts was approved and instated in Germany.[13] This framework has been the organizing principle of the crafts ever since.[14]

The Legal Framework of the German Crafts

Gesetz zur Ordnung des Handwerks, commonly known as the *Handwerksordnung* (Crafts Code), is the detailed and extensive legislation elaborated and passed in 1953, endowing the crafts with their elevated economic and political status.[15] It is built around a number of interrelated mechanisms aimed at ensuring that quality production is maintained through skill. This legislation lists about 150 crafts as part of *Handwerk* and, in the wake of an extensive reform in 2004, divides them into three different groups.[16]

Firstly, Annex A to the crafts code lists 41 regulated crafts professions. Work in these professions must be carried out under the auspices of a master of the craft or an equally qualified operating manager. The organizations of the crafts and the crafts enterprises working in any given of these 41 activities co-operate to maintain high-quality education in the field, including continuing education to facilitate timely updating of skills. Every practising enterprise, whether a solo operation or one with hundreds of employees, must be registered in the crafts-register (*Handwerksrolle*) and is represented by the organizations of the

[13]McKitrick, F.L. 1998. Government's Economic Role: German Artisanal Corporatism in the Postwar Period. *Business and Economic History* 27 (2): 469–476.

[14]Zentralverband des Deutschen Handwerks: Das Handwerk im 20. Jahrhundert. Available at https://www.zdh.de/fileadmin/user_upload/daten-fakten/geschichte/das-handwerk-20-jahrhundert.pdf; Kockel, T. 2011. Interview, Berlin, November 2011.

[15]The full legislation is available here in German https://www.zdh.de/daten-fakten/das-handwerk/die-handwerksordnung/.

[16]As the legislation is regularly updated this number can vary over time.

crafts. This unites them in regional, national and intra-professional associations which provide logistical support and political representation.

In the next category are the crafts listed in Annex B to the crafts code, which amount to 52. Originally, these were also regulated professions, but since 2004 the regulation has not been upheld and their practice opened up to providers without prior prove of qualification. Yet, the organization of these crafts abides by a similar logic to the first group: all practitioners must by law be registered in the register of non-regulated crafts (*Verzeichnis der zulassungsfreien Handwerke*) and *Handwerk* provides education, assistance and representation to practitioners.

The third group, finally, consists of a further 55 activities defined as 'craft-*similar*'. While, again, practitioners are required to register in the register of crafts-like trades (*Verzeichnis der handwerksähnlichen Gewerbe*), organized educational institutions are not necessarily maintained. Practitioners in these crafts, however, can still count on the common institutions of *Handwerk* for general representation.

A major element of the function of *Handwerk* is the pooling of resources on various levels. Crafts-people and -enterprises cluster by crafts, locality and region. Their major administrative organs are the chambers or *Handwerkskammer*. In addition to organizing the educational efforts,[17] the chambers employ specialists on the various logistical aspects of the running of a crafts-enterprise who are available for consultation to every member of the chamber. The specialist assistance provided covers a range of ambits, from legal to fiscal, and includes supporting enterprises in areas such as tailored filling of apprenticeships, external apprentice instruction, standardization, new technologies, ecological sustainability, research co-operations, trade fairs, design and digitization.[18] Acting as an umbrella and intermediating with the

---

[17]While the chambers are the operational organs for vocational education, the curricula is formulated by the regional- and state-level crafts—and trades associations (Innungen/Landes- und Bundesverbände).

[18]On possible analogies between such pooling of resources and the economic theory of the modern firm see: Pfizer, U. 2008. Craft Guilds, the Theory of the Firm, and Early-Modern Proto-Industry. In *Guilds, Innovation and the European Economy 1400–1800*, ed. S.R. Epstein and M. Park, 25–51. Cambridge and New York: Cambridge University Press.

national political system, then, is the Central Association of the Crafts, *Zentralverband des Deutschen Handwerks* (ZDH)[19] with headquarters in Berlin. Finally, dedicated research institutes and a political monitoring office in Brussels provide up-to-date research on the crafts and the changing world in which they operate, to inform policy-making.

The Dual Education System

Different apprenticeships, subdivided by profession and variating slightly in form and duration, represent well over a quarter of all higher education certificates completed every year, making *Handwerk* the single biggest provider of higher education in Germany.[20] The entire course of study consists of two tiers. The first level, which is completed in three to three-and-half years, results in a skill certification called *Gesellenprüfung*. The second level constitutes the *Meister*-studies: their successful completion confers on the craftsperson the master-craftsman certificate. In the 41 regulated crafts professions, this entails the possibility to operate an enterprise in that craft.[21] Further, master craftsmen are entitled to take on and oversee apprentices.

Known as dual-education, this system harkens back to the apprenticeships of old, with an emphasis on practice and organization which allows apprentices to gradually progress in acquiring their crafts. However, recognizing the need to engage with the rapid changes and new ways of understanding inherent in modern science and production methods, *Handwerk* apprenticeships were given a decidedly modern twist after the war.[22] The moniker 'dual-education' refers to the

---

[19]See https://www.zdh.de/organisationen-des-handwerks/aufbau-der-handwerksorganisation/ and https://www.zdh.de/fileadmin/user_upload/publikationen/jahresberichte/Orgaplan_2017.pdf. For a summary in english https://www.zdh.de/en/organisation/.

[20]For a description of the organization of the dual education in English see https://www.zdh.de/en/vocational-education-and-training/ more in depth information available in German here: See https://www.zdh.de/themen/bildung/ausbildung/.

[21]Non-qualified company owners have the possibility to employ an operating manager with the required professional qualification.

[22]Kockel, T. 2011. Interview, Berlin, November 2011.

inclusion of both practice and theory in the study course. Apprentices acquire practice by operating directly in a productive environment, but this training is complemented by theoretical education geared towards transmitting an up-to-date scientific understanding of each specific craft through book-based classes. Acknowledging the speed with which technology and production methods evolve, the system is highly oriented towards continuing education, offering craftspeople opportunities to disseminate and engage with new practices and materials. The examination and certification process is overseen by professional experts from the crafts companies (employers and employees) and the state, further underscoring the importance given to skill formation.[23] The success of this system clashes with the widely held assumption of mainstream economics that firms are inherently adverse to take on the cost of skill creation because of poaching problems.[24] In contrast, by its willingness to co-operate with industry and the state for purpose of maintaining quality and skill, *Handwerk* has contributed for decades to overcoming such problems and maintaining the German economy in what is considered by many a state of high-skill, high-wage equilibrium.[25]

Present Criticalities

While holding and maintaining a position of unusual strength and coherence compared to the rapid disintegration of crafts worldwide during the modern period, *Handwerk* has nonetheless been engaged in a defensive battle over recent decades. The reasons are numerous. In the first place, political and economic winds in Germany as elsewhere have blown in differing directions over time. While a decades-long push for liberalization and the

[23]For further discussion see Streeck, W. 2011. Skills and Politics. General and Specific. MPIfG Discussion Paper 11/1. The Max-Planck Institute for the Study of Societies, Köln.

[24]Thelen, K. 2004. *How Institutions Evolve*, 11–20.

[25]Soskice, D. 1991. The Institutional Infrastructure for International Competitiveness: A Comparative Analysis of the UK and Germany. In *The Economics of the New Europe*. London: Macmillan; Crouch, C., and W. Streeck. 1997. *The Political Economy of Modern Capitalism: The Future of Capitalist Diversity*. London: Sage; Thelen, K. 2004. *How Institutions Evolve*, 8–11.

imposition of free-market principles resulted in regulation of craft-activities being reduced from 94 to 41 in 2004, following the financial crisis in 2008 *Handwerk* has been hailed as the economy's 'golden floor', gaining considerably in status and appreciation.[26] There are enduring tensions, however, between Germany and the European Union about the legality of the remaining regulated professions, which are viewed by EU authorities as inhibitors to economic growth, as they supposedly block competition and give unfair advantages by restricting access to business activities.

Yet, possibly the most sustained challenge to the maintenance of the German crafts is posed on a more immediate level and regards dominating trends in quality certification. *Handwerk* insists on placing quality in the skills of human makers, which are passed on over generations through apprenticeships, and enshrined in the *Meister*-certification. In this view, quality is a past, present and future property in the production process, ensured by the maintenance of skill and knowledge. This system of quality does not exclusively rest on the tacit elements: clear written standards are set to define the appropriate production processes and resulting products. Historically, these standards have been established, monitored and continuously adjusted by the associations of the crafts themselves,[27] facilitating a dynamic and decentralized quality-standard system. More recently, however, standardization has instead come to be increasingly fixed, objective and abstract, driven and manipulated by agencies which are centralized and independent of the production process.[28] The resulting standards ostensibly require only that products be measurably the same. Therefore, they can tend to marginalize or exclude the human element in making. Furthermore, such centrally defined standards can determine how productive processes

[26]Kentzler, O. 2011. *Innovationsmotor Handwerk*. Berlin: Zentralverband des Deutsches Handwerks. Speech https://www.zdh.de/presse/reden/archiv-reden/innovationsmotor-handwerk/?L=0. Accessed 15 May 2017.

[27]As Glasman has pointed out the German legal system is organised around the concept of subsidiarity to an unusual degree, which can facilitate more decentralized monitoring and control of production. Glasman, M. 1996. *Unnecessary Suffering: Managing Market Utopia*. London and New York: Verso.

[28]For further information see, for example, the website of the International Organisation for Standardization, http://www.iso.org.

should be carried out for considerably long periods, thereby eliminating the ability to dynamically adapt or evolve production through first-hand experience of making. As this approach reserves little space for the human producer or the economic and political importance of human participation in productive processes, it poses a challenge to *Handwerk* by diminishing the possibility for apprenticeships and marginalizing the interests of the *Mittelstand*.

Conclusion

The conception of human skill as a fundamental source of quality sets the German crafts apart from many of their counterparts elsewhere. Indeed, such a conception subtends the view of the crafts as being essential to integrity in the production of the general material environment, rather than being an optional or alternative way of production. It also places fundamental importance on the presence of the human maker in the production process. *Handwerk* works on multiple levels to keep this human presence a positive force through a firm commitment to skill and quality. This effort runs contrary to the mechanistic understanding of economy which dominates economics and the contemporary drive towards automation. Yet, the continued importance of the crafts in the German political and economic landscape suggests that with concentrated effort, organization and methods tried and tested over centuries, the skilled human maker can remain a positive central figure in the material making of the world and the resulting economy.

References

Crouch, C., and W. Streeck. 1997. *The Political Economy of Modern Capitalism: The Future of Capitalist Diversity*. London: Sage.

Doran, A. 1984. *Craft Enterprises in Britain and Germany: A Sectoral Study*. London: Anglo-German Foundation.

Epstein, S.R. 2008. Craft Guilds, Apprenticeship and Technological Change in Pre-industrial Europe. In *Guilds, Innovation and the European Economy*

1400–1800, ed. S.R. Epstein and M. Park. Cambridge and New York: Cambridge University Press.

Glasman, M. 1996. *Unnecessary Suffering: Managing Market Utopia*. London and New York: Verso.

John, P. 1987. *Handwerk im Spannungsfeld zwischen Zunftordnung und Gewerbefreiheit: Entwicklung und Politik der Selbstverwaltungsorganisationen des deutschen Handwerks bis 1933*. Köln: Bund-Verlag.

Kentzler, O. 2011. *Innovationsmotor Handwerk*. Berlin: Zentralverband des Deutsches Handwerks. Speech https://www.zdh.de/presse/reden/archiv-reden/innovationsmotor-handwerk/?L=0.

Kockel, T. 2011. Interview, Berlin, November 2011.

McKitrick, F.L. 1998. Government's Economic Role: German Artisanal Corporatism in the Postwar Period. *Business and Economic History* 27 (2): 469–476.

Muthesius, S. 1998. Handwerk/Kunsthandwerk. *Journal of Design History* 11 (1): 85–95.

Pfizer, U. 2008. Craft Guilds, the Theory of the Firm, and Early-Modern Proto-Industry. In *Guilds, Innovation and the European Economy 1400–1800*, ed. S.R. Epstein and M. Park. Cambridge and New York: Cambridge University Press.

Soskice, D. 1991. The Institutional Infrastructure for International Competitiveness: A Comparative Analysis of the UK and Germany. In *The Economics of the New Europe*. London: Macmillan.

Streeck, W. 2011. Skills and Politics: General and Specific. MPIfG Discussion Paper 11/1. The Max-Planck Institute for the Study of Societies, Köln.

Thelen, K. 2004. *How Institutions Evolve: The Political Economy of Skills in Germany, Britain, the United States and Japan*. Cambridge, NY, etc.: Cambridge University Press.

Zentralverband des Handwerks

Anlage A und B. https://www.zdh.de/fileadmin/user_upload/ZDH/0725-Berufe_englisch.pdf. Accessed 29 June 2018.

Aufbau der Handwerksorganisation. https://www.zdh.de/organisationen-des-handwerks/aufbau-der-handwerksorganisation/. Accessed 29 June 2018.

Ausbildung. https://www.zdh.de/themen/bildung/ausbildung/. Accessed 29 June 2018.

Das Handwerk im 20. Jahrhundert. https://www.zdh.de/fileadmin/user_upload/daten-fakten/geschichte/das-handwerk-20-jahrhundert.pdf. Accessed 29 June 2018.

Die Handwerksordnung. https://www.zdh.de/datenfakten/das-handwerk/die-handwerksordnung/. Accessed 29 June 2018.

Made in Germany. Organisationsplan Handwerk 2017. https://www.zdh.de/fileadmin/user_upload/publikationen/jahresberichte/Orgaplan_2017.pdf. Accessed 29 June 2018.

The Skilled Crafts in Germany. https://www.zdh.de/en. Accessed 29 June 2018.

The Skilled Craft Organisation. https://www.zdh.de/en/organisation/. Accessed 29 June 2018.

The Trade and Crafts Code. https://www.zdh.de/en/trade-and-crafts-code/. Accessed 29 June 2018.

Wirtschaftlicher Stellenwert des Handwerks 2017. https://www.zdh.de/daten-fakten/kennzahlen-des-handwerks/. Accessed 29 June 2018.

The Building of Craft Policy in India

Ritu Sethi

Introduction

The Setting and the Shifting of Craft Policy: 1947 to the Present

Mahatma Gandhi had placed the centrality of hand-production within the very architecture of India's struggle for independence from British imperial rule. The bonfires of imported clothing, the hand-spinning of cotton yarn and the donning of handwoven clothing called "the livery of freedom" by Jawaharlal Nehru, the first Prime Minister of free India, were all potent symbols of the Mahatma's vision for a self-reliant India that was closely linked to the resurgence of its village industries.

In 1947, the newly independent Republic predicated its development strategies on the basis of five year plan periods that assessed needs, allocated resources, prioritized capital outlays and created frameworks

R. Sethi (✉)
Crafts Revival Trust, New Delhi, India
e-mail: r.sethi@craftrevival.org

A. Mignosa and P. Kotipalli (eds.), *A Cultural Economic Analysis of Craft*,
https://doi.org/10.1007/978-3-030-02164-1_9

within the changing economic and political order. The perspectives of the policy makers and planners was influenced by the nationalistic emphasis on economic self-reliance that prioritized providing employment, improving livelihoods and the pressing concerns of skilling, education, credit and industrialization to regenerate the economy.

In 1951 the 1st Five year plan document[1] described the on-the-ground situation of the craft sector as one that has been "…decaying, and the rural population which constitutes about 83% of the total suffers from chronic underemployment and low incomes… for the community as a whole, the economic development of the last few decades has brought no significant improvement in standards of living and opportunities for employment."[2] The policy direction set down left no room for ambiguity, stating "… for the revival of village industries, these crafts which have suffered much … will deserve special attention."[3] The plan focused on eight main areas for development that included the reorganization of the sector, availability of credit, access to raw materials, tools and equipment, an emphasis on research, the need for technical guidance and skill enhancement, welfare aspects, the importance of sales and marketing all set out under the umbrella of a protective fiscal and regulatory policy.

This pivot, with adjustments and modifications to fit shifting economic and political circumstance faced by the economy as a whole remained central to craft development policy and the thrust of government till the end of the 1980s.

Plan policies for the Sector were implemented in the initial years through a three-tier system of organization with the Ministry of Commerce and Industry at the Centre, State Departments of Industries and State Boards as implementers with the central task of "advise(ing) and assist(ing) in the formulation of policy and programmes of development for execution by state governments and to

[1]1951–1956.

[2]1st Five Year Plan. Chapter 1.11. The Determinants of Economic Development. http://planningcommission.gov.in/plans/planrel/fiveyr/index1.html.

[3]1st Five Year Plan. Chapter 24. http://planningcommission.gov.in/plans/planrel/fiveyr/index1.html.

make recommendations to the central government on all aspects of development"[4] through the agency of two powerful pan-India Boards that yielded control over handloom and handicraft development.[5] The choice of the two foundational figures appointed to Chair the boards[6]—Kamladevi Chattopadhyay[7] and Pupul Jayaker[8] in handicrafts and handlooms respectively, invigorated policy formulations on the ground. The task of setting up of institutions, the designing of frameworks for the sector to flourish and develop it was the vast undertaking faced.[9] Policy makers squarely recognized that the handlooms and handcrafts were not only an invaluable cultural tradition but equally an economic force impacting GDP and sustainable development.[10]

The early plan documents continued to reiterate the crucial role of the sector in overall development of the country which "… is not to be viewed as a static part of the economy, but rather as a progressive and efficient decentralized sector which is closely integrated, on the one hand, with agriculture and, on the other, with large-scale industry."[11]

This recognition was translated into on the ground results and by the 3rd plan (1961–1965) "…production of handloom cloth increased from about 742 million yards in 1950–1951 to about 1900 million yards in 1960–1961. Fuller employment was provided for nearly 3 million weavers … Employment, mostly part-time, was provided to nearly 11 lakh additional spinners, besides whole-time employment to

[4]3rd Five Year Plan. Chapter 25. Village and Small Industry 25.ii. Role of planned development. http://planningcommission.gov.in/plans/planrel/fiveyr/index1.html.

[5]3rd Five Year Plan—Chapter 25. II. Review of Progress. http://planningcommission.gov.in/plans/planrel/fiveyr/index1.html.

[6]By Prime Minister Jawaharlal Nehru.

[7]From 1952 till 1967.

[8]Appointed in the 1955 with a short break in between, her role in influencing culture and craft policy continued under the Prime Ministership of both Indira Gandhi and Rajiv Gandhi.

[9]Sethi, Ritu. 2015. Catalysing Crafts: Women Who Shaped the Way. Chapter 12. In *Interrogating Women's Leadership and Empowerment*, ed. Omita Goyal, 146–163. New Delhi: Sage.

[10]From the 1980s to date the sector has been administered under the umbrella of the Ministry of Textiles under the aegis of the Office of the Development Commissioner for Handicrafts and the Office of the Development Commissioner for Handlooms.

[11]2nd Five Year Plan. Chapter 20. Village and Small Industry. http://planningcommission.gov.in/plans/planrel/fiveyr/index1.html.

about 1.4 lakh weavers, carpenters, etc." Similar growth was reflected in the crafts.[12]

India's need for foreign exchange to finance its development strategies was reflected in the export thrust across sectors. For the handmade sector it was put into place in the 1st plan and based "on the study of the requirements of customers in foreign markets, not only of the wealthy but, the average citizen..... To be developed as fully as possible."[13] This attention on exports continued to be repeated as the need for forex remained critical for the fulfillment of the larger goals of the national economy. The 6th Plan document (1980–1985) stating "A major task facing the country is to ... promote exports ... This calls for an all-out effort..."[14] The development of an infrastructure to support this included the setting up of testing laboratories, participation and organization of trade fairs and buyer–seller meets both in India and overseas to promote, support and increase exports. The mandate for this was led by Export Promotion Council for Handicrafts (EPCH) established in 1986. To ensure a targeted and focused segmented approach councils for specific craft categories like carpets, handlooms, silk, leather, jewelry and others were also established. EPCH continues to be a successful focal point as reflected in the rising handicrafts export earning graph from US$ 35,659 million in 1998–1999 to $261,136 million in 2015–2016.[15]

In addition the policy mix continued to cast a protective veil that advantaged the handmade over the machine-made through a fiscal and regulatory mix of subsidies, tax benefits, concessions, differential excise duties and the reservation of certain categories of production specifically

[12] 3rd Five Year Plan. Chapter 25:8. Village and Small Industries. http://planningcommission.gov.in/plans/planrel/fiveyr/index1.html.

[13] 1st Five Year Plan (1956–1960). Chapter 25.9. Small Industries and Handicrafts. This led to the establishment of the Handicrafts and Handlooms Export Corporation in 1962 to trade and promote crafts and to encourage private sector exporting activities.

[14] 6th Five Year Plan document (1980–1985). Chapter 1. Development Perspectives. Preface. http://planningcommission.gov.in/plans/planrel/fiveyr/index6.html.

[15] https://www.epch.in/index.php?option=com_content&view=article&id=76&Itemid=181. The membership of HEPC rose from 35 in 1985–1986 to 8656 in 2015–2016.

for the handmade.[16] The results of all these measures were apparent with a year-on-year increase in sales. However by the mid-1980s there was growing criticism of handloom policy initiatives that disadvantaged the mechanized production of textiles, today while largely dismantled, the differential pricing for yarn for the handloom sector continues as does the reservation, though much truncated, of certain product lines that remain reserved solely for handloom production.[17] These measures serve to bolster a huge sector of skill, tradition and employment from the onslaught of technology. Efforts to change policy in this area have met with stiff resistance from the weaving eco-sphere.

The planning process took into account not only a sector-wise assessment and evaluation of performance parameters but in addition, it set objectives for each sector within the larger developmental goals for the economy as a whole. By the 1980s the responsibility for the crafts and handloom sector had shifted from the Industry Ministry to the Ministry of Textiles and was administered under the aegis of the Office of the Development Commissioner Handlooms and Handicrafts, respectively. Within this framework government policy till the 7th Five year plan period (1985–1990) was broadly a continuance of the strategies established in the foundational decades.

The policy objective set in place with the 1st plan that aimed at making craft goods available to a wide geographical spread of consumers while cutting out the middle-man was translated into a direct-marketing effort set up by government-sponsored bodies that led to a huge expansion of sale outlets, craft emporia's and handloom shops. This policy initiative provided "an assured market"[18] for a sector that the planners felt was delinked from consumers. The then iconic handicrafts and handloom store—the Central Cottage Industries Emporium (CCIE) headquartered in the capital city of New Delhi, set up in 1952 was the finest expression of this policy. By 1960 "Over 100 emporia

[16]The Fourth Plan 1969–1974 "Further, in order to protect small scale and traditional industries from undue competition, the existing reservations will be continued and modified in accordance with the requirements".

[17]Hank Yarn Packing Notification 1974 and the Handloom Reservation Act of 1985.

[18]3rd Five Year Plan. Chapter 25: Village and Small Industries. II. Review of Progress 11.7.

and sales depots have been set up."[19] This policy of pro-active retailing continued and was strengthened in the 1970s with the setting up of regional emporiums in prime spaces across the country. These emporiums sourced the best of the arts, textiles and crafts of different states and brought the products of rural India to the growing number of metropolitan consumers. In addition to these permanent establishments an on-going part of sales and direct-marketing policy remains in the large number of temporary craft exhibitions held across the country that remain a regular feature on the consumer calendar. In 1984, another noteworthy development was the foundation of a permanent exhibition space in New Delhi—Dilli Haath, not unlike a village weekly market where craftsperson's and weavers display their products on a rotational basis. This hugely successful model has been replicated across the country.

In 1991, a cross-sectoral discourse on the need for changing national economic priorities resulted in the opening up of the Indian economy with the initiation of policies of liberalization that expanded the role of private and foreign investment, reduced import tariffs and taxes, a greater emphasis on export, and other objectives that found reflection across sectors in the national plans. Shifting goalpost now emphasized entrepreneurship, industrialization and an urban orientation. This was reflected in the direction of craft and handloom policy that now laid greater stress on the role of private players, reducing the role of government in direct-marketing, a continuing recognition of the role of NGOs in implementing policy on-the-ground,[20] a renewed accent on export, on capability-building, restructuring, public–private partnership and product development.

This marked shift in policy has now advantaged the urban and the mechanized over the rural and the handmade. With changing development priorities the craft sector by the start of the twenty-first century was relegated to the backwaters reflected in the phrase used by politicians and policy makers to describe it as a "sunset industry" viewed now

[19] 3rd Five Year Plan II. Review of Progress 11.12.

[20] 8th Five Year Plan document (1992–1997). Volume ii. 6.10.4.

through as being out of sync with the times rather than as a muscular economic activity contributing to GDP. While continuing to acknowledge the sectors cultural underpinning and its huge employment potential in rural areas it faced declining budgetary allocations in the national accounts. The overall direction of policy has since remained the same.

Beyond the Economic

The policy approach, in addition, went beyond the economic and livelihood aspects of the craft to support the creation of systems and frameworks that invested not just in the infrastructure and institutions but in addition in projects and programs linked to aspects from design, culture and heritage to IPR. These initiatives had a far-reaching and enduring impact, both directly and in unintended directions, on the economic, social, cultural and creative aspects of craft development.

Among the many initiatives was the recognition of the crucial importance of design and product development to the crafts that led to the establishment of Regional Design Development Centers in 1956[21] and the Weavers' Service Centers,[22] the Indian Institutes of Handloom Technology,[23] the National Center for Textile Design and other organizations that built the framework that were supportive of the sector. In 1961, the National Institute of Design (NID)[24] at Ahmedabad was established while the National Institute of Fashion and Technology came into being in 1986.[25] These institutions and the many others they spawned changed forever the design landscape in India and the outcome of this foresight was the many designers working with the crafts and serving as a bridge, mediating between rural craftspeople and their

[21]The first 4 were established between 1956 and 1960 in the 2nd Five year plan period.

[22]5 Weaver's service centers were set up at Bombay, Madras, Varanasi, Calcutta and Kancheepuram between 1956 and 1960 in the 2nd Five year plan period. There are now 28 Weavers service centers across the country.

[23]There are now 10 Institutes of Handloom Technology across India.

[24]There are now three additional NIDs with more planned in the future.

[25]There are now 16 NIFT's located at different centers across India.

evolving urban markets. This connection and interaction has strengthened and multiplied over the decades as is apparent from the increasing emphasis on design and product development.

Research and documentation of the crafts found a place in each plan document. The over 150 surveys that formed part of the 1961 population census, the research reports and document financially underwritten by the government, the handloom and handicraft census were all a part of this effort. A small though important start in 2012 has been the inclusion of artisans in the National Economic Census this beginning it is hoped would be followed by a Satellite Account specific to the handmade to build more robust data for the sector.

In 1965 the policy of honoring and awarding recognition to the living Masters of the traditional arts, crafts and textiles for their outstanding contribution to craftsmanship were introduced. Coveted by practitioners over a thousand craftspeople have received the honor since.[26] This practice has subsequently been extended beyond government to become an established manner of recognition by other institutions and organizations thus extending the range widely across the crafts.

A museum space dedicated to the crafts was inaugurated in New Delhi in 1972. The National Handicrafts and Handloom Museum colloquially known as the Crafts Museum houses over 50,000 objects of folk and tribal art, crafts and textiles, a museum shop, an open air craft area where craftsperson's demonstrate their skills and sell their products directly to museum visitors. The museum's approach celebrates the knowledge systems of living tradition and remains the go-to-place for those with interests in the crafts.

In the 1980s in a period before ethnic became chic cultural diplomacy introduced Indian crafts to the global market. The Festivals of India, held in Britain, USA, Russia, Japan and France were a major series of high profile events and exhibitions, a cooperative effort

[26]126 Ship gurus and over 1000 National awards have been given by the Ministry of Textiles to handicraft and handloom weavers since 1965.

between the Government of India and the host country.[27] Drawing attention to the many manifestations of Indian culture the wide-ranging presentations included exhibitions of contemporary crafts and textiles with live demonstrations of skills that focused on the continuity of tradition. "…and as Mrs. (Indira) Gandhi, the then Prime Minister said 'it had succeeded beyond our wildest hopes.' It did not serve just as a 'show window' for India but had actively created interest in India."[28] The retail stores, "Sona" or the golden one, set up by HHEC in the 1980s in New York and Paris brought the best of Indian crafts to a global market.[29] These short-lived festivals though extending to just about a decade sparked an interest in Indian crafts this gap in the market was soon to be filled in very effectively by private entrepreneurs, NGOs and exporters who responded to a globalizing worlds demand, repositioning handcrafted products not just for the world but a growing middle-class market within India itself.

In the same way the stress on collaborating with NGOs that continued to be emphasized over the plan periods resulted in a muscular and effective civil society that has served to push the interests of the sector while increasingly acting as a watchdog and taking issue through advocacy on a number of issues that impact it and its practitioners.[30]

The introduction of the Geographical Indications of Goods Act (GI), a sui generis intellectual property right legislation introduced in India in 1999 is applicable and extends its protection to products of traditional knowledge that are associated with or deriving from local cultural traditions.[31] Of all the GI's granted to date over 60% of the total are in the

---

[27]The first festival was held in 1982 in the United Kingdom. Soon to be followed by others over the decade.

[28]Doshi, Saryu. 1983. Continuity and Change: Festival of India in Great Britain Introduction. Marg.

[29]Retail stores of the Handicrafts and Handlooms Export Corporation.

[30]7th Five Year Plan Volume 2. Village and Small Industries Chapter… Handicrafts: Review. 4.36. 'The involvement of voluntary agencies would be encouraged'.

[31]The GI Act was notified on 15th September, 2003. It is defined as "*A geographical indication (GI) is a name or sign used on certain products which corresponds to a specific geographical location or origin (e.g. a town, region, or country). The use of a GI may act as a certification that the product possesses certain qualities, is made according to traditional methods, or enjoys a certain reputation, due to its geographical origin*".

area of traditional arts, crafts and handlooms. A noteworthy number as IPR protection is being taken seriously as part of government policy.[32]

Policy efforts in the crafts have extended to cultural diplomacy with products of craftsmanship being used as gifts for all visiting dignitaries and heads of states besides forming part of the interior décor of Indian High Commissions and Embassies the world over. Furthermore, as part of cultural diplomacy craftspersons travel overseas to showcase their skills as part of official programs. A further policy push has been the inclusion in 2015 of Jaipur, the capital city of Rajasthan, in the UNESCO Creative Cities Network as the first creative city of craft in India, joining 16 other cities in the list. In addition the nomination of the craft of traditional brass and copper utensils of the Thatheras of Jandiala Guru in Punjab as one of the 12 Indian nominations on to the representative list of the UNESCO intangible cultural heritage convention is noteworthy.

Policy Prescriptions

While much has been achieved the sector continues to be beleaguered by issues that range from access to finance, raw material availability, market access, upgrading of skills to attrition in its numbers as the young prefer other options of employment. This coupled with inroads of technologies including that of 3D printing to unknown challenges that lie in the future requires the adoption of strategic policy instruments to equip and empower craftspeople for the times to come. Craftspeople across India have over the millennia demonstrated their ability to evolve, adapt and creatively innovate new times we now need forward-thinking proactive policy that will secure for them a strong foothold and a lasting position in the future.

Craft policy in India is not just the monopoly of the Ministry of Textiles, it is impacted by policies from other branches of the executive

[32]Sethi, Ritu. Deconstructing GI to Create Value for the Handmade. http://www.craftrevival.org/voiceDetails.asp?Code=219.

as its vast eco-sphere includes not just the practitioners and transmitters, differing modes of production and skills, a huge variety of raw material, a large number of women, tribal and folk oral knowledge systems, but aspects relating to tourism, heritage, culture, design, innovation and creativity. Thus at the last count, 17 different Ministries have policies that impact the sector.

The time has come for policy makers to give recognition to the multi-sectoral aspects of this invaluable cultural asset and economic force by synergizing the approach through holistic policy prescriptions that are bolstered by a push to build a robust economic data base for the sector.

The world over, Cultural and creative industries (CCI) like the crafts are increasingly becoming recognized as drivers of meaningful development. A World Bank report states that CCI "…can be part of the solution, fostering social inclusion, climate action, and income generating activities."[33]

India has been an active discussant on CCI recognized in the 11th five year plan laid out a comprehensive and pathbreaking road map "… there are certain sectors wherein presence and contribution of culture and creativity is much more dominant and visible….Even though there may be difficulties in bringing various segments of CCI under a single umbrella, it should not be difficult to lay down a co-ordination and consultation mechanism to ensure an integrated policy and planning for the entire sector. Importance of this sector needs to be highlighted due to its great potential for growth and employment generation. …. they are more effective in building employment and human capital than agriculture, IT or large industry. According to an estimate, in India, Agriculture employs 37–40% of the workforce; Culture and Creative Industries, 45–48%; all other industries together employ around 17–20%."[34]

[33]The World Bank Group, Cultural Heritage: An Asset for Urban Development and Poverty Reduction. http://siteresources.worldbank.org/INTCHD/Resources/430063-1250192845352/CHandslums_Oct.pdf.

[34]Report of the working Group on Art and Culture for XI Five-Year Plan and Proposals for XI Five-Year Plan (2007–2012) & Annual Plan (2007–2008). 5. Cultural and Creative Industries.

Additionally, a recognition of the role that the crafts play in fulfilling India's global commitments on climate change and the 2015 UN Sustainable Development Goals (SDGs) needs to be translated into action. Of the 17 SDG, ten are directly or indirectly connected to the crafts.

These need to be prioritized into policy.

References

Cultural Heritage: An Asset for Development and Poverty … . n.d. Retrieved from http://siteresources.worldbank.org/INTCHD/Resources/430063-1250192845352/CHandslums_Oct.pdf.

Planning Commission, Government of India: Five Year Plans. n.d. Retrieved from http://planningcommission.gov.in/plans/planrel/fiveyr/index1.html.

Planning Commission. 1950–1956. *1st Five Year Plan*. New Delhi: Government of India.

Planning Commission. 1956–1961. *Second Five Year Plan*. New Delhi: Government India.

Planning Commission. 1961–1966. *Third Five Year Plan*. New Delhi: Government of India.

Planning Commission. 1969–1974. *Fourth Five Year Plan*. New Delhi: Government of India.

Planning Commission. 1980–1985. *Sixth Five Year Plan*. New Delhi: Government of India.

Planning Commission. 1985–1990. *Seventh Plan*. New Delhi: Government of India.

Planning Commission. 1992–1997. *Eighth Plan Five Year Plan*. New Delhi: Government of India.

Sethi, R. 2010, April. Deconstructing GI1 to Create Value for the Handmade. Retrieved from http://www.craftrevival.org/voiceDetails.asp?Code=219.

Sethi, R. 2012. Catalysing Craft: Women Who Shaped the Way. *India International Centre Quarterly* 39 (3/4): 168–185.

The Planning Commission, Government of India. 2005. *The Taskforce for Creative and Cultural Industries*. New Delhi: Government of India.

Crafts Policies in Japan

Kazuko Goto

Introduction

Cultural economics has typically focused on the arts rather than crafts, but what is the difference between the two? Both have cultural and economic dimensions: Artists are involved in the arts, and artisans in crafts. What, then, is the difference between artists and artisans? Art is assumed to be important for creativity and innovation, but what role do crafts play in the knowledge economy? Looking at the case of Japan, this paper will reassess the structure of craftsmanship and explore the possible integration of cultural and economic policies for crafts to address the question of how crafts can be sustained culturally and economically in the globalized market.

K. Goto (✉)
Setsunan University, Osaka, Japan
e-mail: k-goto@econ.setsunan.ac.jp

A. Mignosa and P. Kotipalli (eds.), *A Cultural Economic Analysis of Craft*,
https://doi.org/10.1007/978-3-030-02164-1_10

Craftsmanship in Japan

There was no Japanese word for "art" (*Bijutsu*) until the introduction of Western philosophy when the country was opened up. There was, however, a word for "crafts," (*Kougei*) which included both the concept of arts and crafts. Both of the characters used to construct this word refer to skills acquired through long training (Mori 2009). There was no hierarchy between arts and crafts; they were not differentiated. Highly aesthetic paintings were drawn on screens and paper sliding doors in homes.

After the opening of Japan in 1868, the government started to display traditional Japanese crafts at international expositions. It was difficult to introduce the concept of arts. It took almost thirty years. Finally, paintings, artistic crafts, and sculpture were defined as fine arts. Then, crafts were divided into two categories: artistic crafts and industrial crafts. However, the border between them was vague.

Crafts were important products for export in Japan at the beginning of the Meiji era (1868~). Therefore, design was necessary to make crafts sophisticated. Painters of Japanese paintings (*Nihonga*) provided designs for dying, pottery, and textiles in Kyoto, where these traditional crafts have a long history. Craftsmen improved their skills with those designs. For painters, who lost their patrons with the collapse of the social ranks of Samurai and Court-noble, providing design was a good opportunity to earn money (Yoshinobu and Daicho 2018).

At the Vienna World's Fair in 1873, Japanese traditional crafts were admired. However, when the boom of Japonism was gone, Japanese crafts displayed at the Paris World's Fair in 1878 were strongly criticized. The critics said that they were industrial products rather than arts, they were also criticized for having old-fashioned designs (Mori 2009).

One reason behind this criticism might be that the concept of fine arts in Japan was not fully established and so the crafts displayed were assumed to be industrial products. Japanese people did not have enough knowledge of Western art history or fine art techniques. As a result, it was difficult to show creativity of crafts in the Western context of art history. Through these experiences, the government changed its cultural policy to catch up with "Western fine arts". Artists started to learn Western techniques and Western styles of art, which are quite different from Japanese paintings. Two kinds of paintings—Western-style paintings and Japanese-style paintings including Japanese prints—have, since, coexisted in Japan.

Nevertheless, in Japan, the concept of crafts was well developed. Artistic crafts were separated from crafts, and economic crafts and manufacturing were separated. At the beginning of the Meiji Era (1868~), Japan was a backward country in terms of manufacturing. Technology was not yet developed and most products were made by hand using simple tools. However, after the introduction of technology, crafts were divided into economic crafts and artistic crafts. Artistic crafts are aesthetic creations, whereas economic crafts are functional. The prices of artistic crafts are high. On the contrary, the prices of economic crafts are relatively low. Products of economic crafts were used for everyday life. They still have beauty: the "beauty of use." If economic crafts would lack design and beauty, they would not survive in the competitive global market where consumer tastes are highly developed.

Crafts include both cultural and economic aspects, and have been promoted by both cultural and industrial policies. From the viewpoint of Japanese cultural policy, crafts represent tangible and intangible cultural heritage. From the viewpoint of industrial and economic policy, crafts represent industries that are clustered within a particular region. When it comes to the use of intellectual property rights, copyright is applied to artistic craftworks, because they involve originality. In contrast, trademarks are applied to ordinary crafts and designs that are made through mass production. In general, copyright protects fine arts and trademark protects applied arts. However, Japanese courts have stated that copyright can sometimes be applied to ordinary crafts because their aesthetics demonstrate originality.

Cultural Policy for Tangible and Intangible Cultural Heritage

The Agency for Cultural Affairs under the Ministry of Education, Culture, Sports, Science and Technology manages cultural heritage policy. The Agency treats important craftworks as tangible cultural heritages, and craft-related skills as intangible cultural heritages. The Agency for Cultural Affairs encourages the cultural aspects of crafts.

Japan closed its borders from 1639 to 1854. When Japan reopened its borders, paintings and craftworks began flowing out of Japan. The government recognized that it was necessary to keep important paintings and craftworks in Japan and to establish a national identity. To recognize important cultural heritage, the government examined an enormous number of paintings and craftworks found in temples and shrines. The Cultural Heritage Preservation Law for Temples and Shrines was established in 1897, since then paintings and craftworks with historical and artistic value have been preserved as tangible cultural heritages.

Japan started to adopt Western culture after it opened up. The government tried to catch up with Western countries in terms of economic development, while simultaneously introducing Western civilization, social systems, and culture. Art was one part of this, so the government tried to establish the concept of art and art schools in Japan.

Japan thus imported artistic concepts from Western countries. However, arts and crafts were assigned equal rankings. For example, the Faculty of Fine Arts at the Tokyo University of Art included departments for painting, sculpture, architecture, aesthetics, art history, and crafts, indicating that crafts were considered a fine art.

The Comprehensive Law for Cultural Heritage Preservation was established in 1950. This law integrated previous laws related to tangible cultural heritage with new ones for the preservation of intangible cultural heritage. A notable feature of this new cultural heritage policy was that it established the concept of intangible cultural heritage before even UNESCO did.

Tangible cultural heritage includes buildings and artistic craftworks. Artistic craftworks include paintings, sculptures, calligraphy, classical books, and archaeological and historical resources. Intangible heritage is defined as skills of traditional performing arts and traditional crafts. The policy stresses the importance of skills. Intangible heritage policy targets skills of "traditional crafts," not crafts in general. Intangible heritage should have historical and aesthetic value.

The reason why intangible heritage policy includes crafts was that manufacturing developed but the traditional skills of crafts began disappearing. For example, paper manufacturing developed using technology, whereas Japanese handmade paper made from plant fibers diminished. However, Japanese handmade paper has distinguished historical and cultural value. Thus, it became a target of preservation. The traditional skills of pottery, dying, Japanese lacquerware, metalworking, wood and bamboo crafts, and doll making are addressed as intangible heritage.

Cultural policy aims at maintaining the historical and cultural value of crafts. Craft skills are passed on as intangible cultural heritages. In 1954, the Living National Heritage was established. A Living National Treasure is a person who carries important traditional skills from the past to the future. Living national treasures represent the apex of the hierarchy of craftspersons, and contribute to establishing a "brand" for their craftworks. A person recognized as a Living National Treasure receives $20,000 per year for educating young craftsmen in order to pass on traditional skills. The payment of $20,000 is not an award, it must be used for education. The number of Living National Treasures of Crafts was 176 in 2017.

Cominelli and Greffe (2013) argue that the principle behind the Living National Treasure system is the transmission of skills. This is true. However, the number of recognized Living National Treasure is very limited because of the limited budget of the Agency for Cultural Affairs in Japan.

Craftworks produced by living national treasures can be sold at high prices, because they have high cultural value and a powerful brand image. In contrast, craftworks by young craftspersons are sold at very low prices. However, there can be a gap between the demand and supply of craftworks by skilled craftspersons. Because of the higher prices of the products made by skilled craftspersons and limited demand for that.

The Living National Treasure is an effective means of passing on craft skills to future generations in Japan. However, these skills depend on the endurance of the crafts industry. If the crafts industry is not sustainable, it will be difficult for such skills to survive.

Higher Education System for Crafts

The Tokyo High School of Crafts was established to develop education in crafts in 1921. After World War II, it was absorbed into the Faculty of Engineering of Chiba National University in 1951, where it became a part of industrial design. On the other hand, Tokyo University of the Arts has a tradition of researching and teaching artistic crafts. Therefore, the crafts education after World War II seems to be divided into artistic crafts and industrial design. The border between them, which is economic crafts, was neglected in Tokyo. The Tokyo High School of Crafts had played an important role in developing economic crafts (Mori 2009). In contrast, Kanazawa College of Arts was established to supply craftsmen in the region in 1946. Kyoto Institute of Technology was established in 1948 to research and teach crafts (Mori 2009). Both Kanazawa and Kyoto have a long tradition of crafts.

Many schools for teaching specific techniques for crafts are supported by regional and local governments. However, these are not colleges or universities. They are rather practically oriented.

Targeting crafts involves a certain amount of overlap between Japan's cultural and economic policies. However, the two policies are handled by different ministries. The economic policy focuses on the private aspects of crafts, including intellectual property, clustering, distribution, and industrial organization.

Economic and Industrial Policies for Crafts

The Law for the Promotion of Traditional Craft Industries was established in 1974. The Ministry of Economy, Trade and Industry (METI) is entrusted with the promotion of craft industries. The rationale for the promotion of the traditional crafts industries is that they can enrich people's lives and stimulate regional economic development. This might seem to overlap with the duties of the Agency for Cultural Affairs, but the two organizations have differing policy aims: The Agency for Cultural Affairs focuses on the cultural aspect of craft, while METI focuses on the economic and industrial aspects of crafts and promotes regional traditional craft industries and their trade.

The Law for the Promotion of Traditional Craft Industries addresses 225 traditional craft goods produced in specific districts. The law promotes only crafts considered as traditional, but a given craft can be a target of both intangible cultural heritage policy and the industrial policy of METI, so there can be overlap.

To be designated as a traditional craft under the law, goods must meet five conditions:

1. The craftwork is used in everyday life.
2. Main production processes affecting quality must be performed by hand.
3. The craftwork is produced by traditional skills and expertise passed on for more than one hundred years.
4. Primary materials have been used for more than one hundred years.
5. The crafts industry should be concentrated in a specific regional district.

How Are Craft Skills Passed on?

Two elements are critical to sustaining traditional craft industries: inheritance of skills and developing craft industry regions. The Association for the Promotion of Traditional Craft Industries cooperates with METI, local governments, and regional craft unions, and certifies traditional craftspersons. Certification requires at least twelve years of work experience in a district specialized in a specific craft industry, and passing an examination.

However, productivity in traditional craft industries is relatively low. Consumption of traditional craftworks is decreasing, due to lifestyle changes that do not accommodate traditional crafts products. It is thus difficult for craftspersons to earn enough money, making it difficult to attract successors to learn and later pass on traditional craft skills. Traditional craftspersons passing the examination are only certified, not licensed, and are not guaranteed a minimum wage.

Table 1 Number of certified craftspersons by age, as of 2010

Age	Number	Percentage (%)
30–39	98	2.2
40–49	424	9.5
50–59	916	20.6
60–69	1483	33.4
70–79	1178	26.5
80+	342	7.7

Source Goto (2013)

However, recognized craftspersons can became independent entrepreneurs because certification recognizes their skills, increasing their trustworthiness. Craftspersons are thus motivated to obtain certification, so the recognition system aids the passing on of craftspersons' skills and expertise (Table 1).

These numbers show that most craftspersons are 60 years old or older, and there are relatively few young craftspersons. In 2010 there were 4441 certified craftspersons, including 569 women. Young women are increasingly interested in craftwork and undergoing training. This is a good sign for the sustainability of crafts.

How Do Traditional Craft Districts Survive?

Traditional craft industries tend to cluster, and craft districts play important roles and functions. The characteristics of craft districts include the following:

1. Skills can be passed on within the district. Expertise and knowledge spread within the district, encouraging innovation.
2. Small companies cooperate and compete in these districts, and the resulting "flexible specialization" helps to adjust to consumer demands.
3. Districts can establish a brand.
4. Traditional craft districts comprise craftspersons, small- and medium-sized companies, and wholesalers.

METI subsidizes 225 production unions and associations for traditional craft goods in their production districts. Notably, individual craftspersons do not receive METI subsidies. The aim of METI subsidies include the following:

1. Education of craft skills aimed at developing successors for traditional crafts,
2. Archiving of skills,
3. Research on acquiring materials for traditional crafts,
4. Marketing to increase demand for traditional crafts,
5. Creating new designs.

Subsidies help craft districts, but unequally. District autonomy is important. For instance, Yamada (2013) investigated pottery districts in Japan,[1] including Arita, a pottery district established more than four hundred years ago. Arita is the name of both a city and its district, which includes 230 companies and families that own the kilns and produce porcelain ware. The Kakiemon kiln and the Imaemon kiln are particularly famous and influential. Kakiemon Sakaida is a personal name passed on from father to son, as is Imaemon Imaizumi. Kakiemon Sakaida XIV has been designated as living national treasure and Imaemon Imaizumi XIV is now designated as living national treasure. The Kakiemon kiln has been recognized for its skills in producing milk-white porcelain as an important intangible cultural heritage. The Imaemon kiln is noted for its blue glaze and decorations in red, yellow, and green.

Yamada (2013) also analyzed the history and the industrial organization of the Arita pottery region, and found that three types of kiln coexist. The first type is large kilns that have adopted mass production systems using machines and division of labor. The second is midsized kilns like Imaemon and Kakiemon. The third is independent, small kilns. Two large, well-capitalized kilns play important roles in

[1]Yamada, K. (2013). *Business System and Entrepreneurship in the Traditional Pottery Production Center*. Tokyo: Yuhikaku.

maintaining the pottery region and promoting Arita pottery exports. They produce high-quality, daily-use pottery, establishing the brand of the district and providing an economic baseline for the Arita pottery district. Yamada (2013) considers these two major kilns as anchors for the Arita district. Craftspersons learn skills through on-the-job training at the big kilns, and some become independent after acquiring their skills.

In contrast, the Kakiemon and Imaemon kilns present original porcelain styles and designs. These kilns employ skilled artists and craftspersons who produce artistic pottery and high-quality, daily-use products. These skilled craftspersons generally work at the same kiln until they will retire. These kilns pass on skills, and strengthen the brand image of Arita-ware. The Kakiemon and Imaemon kilns focus on different markets, allowing them to coexist in the region.

Industrial and economic policies are working upon the autonomy of traditional industrial districts. Traditional craft districts organize associations that accept subsidies and distribute products. If the districts lack autonomy and an atmosphere of innovation, their survival becomes difficult.

Difficulties of Traditional Craft Industries

Despite the policies in place, the output of traditional crafts has decreased since 1975. The output of traditional crafts in 2009 was a quarter of what it was in 1975. The number of enterprises and employees has also decreased dramatically. The output of traditional textiles decreased rapidly, whereas the output of traditional pottery and traditional Japanese lacquerware increased until the beginning of the 1990s and then decreased, showing a slower decrease compared to traditional textiles.

METI points out three problems. The first is a decrease in demand due to lifestyle changes that do not accommodate traditional crafts products. The second is low productivity because traditional crafts products are made by hand and traditional materials and skills are expensive. Furthermore, complicated production processes take time and the scale of enterprises is small. The third problem is a decrease in the number of craftsmen, especially in the younger generation.[2]

METI points out that there has also been a decline in the natural and original materials and tools that traditional crafts require. This makes it difficult for traditional craft industries to persist. Also, the majority of Japanese consumers do not value traditional craft products. METI started promoting creative industries in 2011, and traditional craft industries are being integrated into creative industries. METI and the Association for Traditional Craft Products have furthermore started to promote product exports.

The "Cool Japan" Strategy

An example of this is the strategy called "Cool Japan" that the Japanese government established in 2010. It is a promotion strategy aiming at improving the image of Japan to stimulate export and tourism. Under the Cool Japan strategy, METI promotes creative industries such as fashion, animation, food culture, and traditional crafts. The Cool Japan Association was established in 2013 with the aim of developing overseas demand and markets for Japanese creative products. The government has invested 58.6 billion yen and private companies have invested 10.7 billion yen in the Association. The Cool Japan Association invests in various projects aimed at developing overseas markets for creative goods.

The full effects of the Cool Japan strategy remain unclear, but the number of tourists from abroad is rapidly increasing; while 8.61 million tourists visited Japan in 2010, 24.04 million came in 2016.

The Cool Japan strategy focuses on young individual craftspersons who are seeking new opportunities. Young craftspersons and designers work together to produce new products related to traditional crafts.

---

[2]METI. (2011). Dentouteki kougeihin sangyo wo meguru genjyou to kongo no shinkousesaku ni tsuite. http://www.meti.go.jp/committee/summary/0002466???/006_06_00.pdf. Accessed 11 Dec 2017.

However, the results are sometimes criticized as featuring immature skills and superficial products.

The Cool Japan strategy focuses on establishing Japan's brand image and developing overseas markets and the distribution of creative products. However, traditional craft industries cluster, and skilled craftspersons work in those districts. Craft districts have their own production system, so if a strategy does not fit the production system or does not work for skilled craftspersons, the impact of that strategy will be limited.

Conclusion

This paper illustrated intangible heritage policy and industrial policy for crafts in Japan. Intangible heritage policies, with the Living National Treasure system, are important for preserving traditional craft skills. However, the number of Living National Treasure is limited. Moreover, products made by Living National Treasure are extremely expensive. They are distinguished artistic crafts rather than crafts for daily use. Japan's economic policy aims to preserve traditional crafts for daily use and promote clustering of crafts. Nevertheless, the output of traditional crafts has decreased since the policy was established. Hence, the Cool Japan strategy was launched to overcome the limits of the previous policies by creating a brand image and stimulating exports, integrating craft industries and creative industries. The effects of this new policy remain unclear. To support the skilled craftspersons and to stimulate innovation based on the intrinsic value of craftworks made by original materials and expertise are keys for creativity and sustainability of crafts. Whether the Cool Japan strategy can achieve this condition is yet known.

Two policy proposals can be made. First, the economic (industrial) policy for traditional crafts should promote collaboration between kilns and trading companies located near kilns. Crafts are a part of creative industries, which are a combination of creativity and business. Second, the industrial policy for traditional crafts should take into account new perspectives, such as the indication of geographical origin and intellectual property. However, a lack of successors for skills is a serious problem. Young people do not seem attracted by crafts. However, there are some encouraging signs. For example, a textile company in Kyoto city is collaborating with distinguished foreign fashion companies. They use the traditional textile made of silk for interior designs. To extend the uses of the textile, the textile company invented new techniques to weave wider textile. A young successor challenges to create new market.

References

Cominelli, F., and X. Greffe. 2013. Why and How Intangible Cultural Heritage Should Be Safeguarded. In *A Handbook on the Economics of Cultural Heritage*, ed. I. Lizzo and A. Mignosa, 402–417. Cheltenham: Edward Elgar.

Goto, K. 2013. *Economics of Creative Industries, Contract, Copyright and Tax Incentives*. Tokyo: Yuhikaku.

METI. 2011. Dentouteki kougeihin sangyo wo meguru genjyou to kongo no shinkousesaku ni tsuite. http://www.meti.go.jp/committee/summary/0002466/006_06_00.pdf. Accessed 11 Dec 2017.

Mori, H. 2009. *Nihon kougei no kindai*. Tokyo: Yoshikawa Kobunkan.

Yamada, K. 2013. *Business System and Entrepreneurship in the Traditional Pottery Production Center*. Tokyo: Yuhikaku.

Yoshinobu, H., and T. Daicho (eds.). 2018. *The 150th Anniversary of the Meiji Period; Making and Designing Meiji Arts and Crafts*. Kyoto: The National Museum of Modern Art.

Crafts in the Netherlands: From an Economic to a Value-Based Perspective

Marleen Hofland-Mol and Marion Poortvliet

Introduction

The Dutch pride themselves on being prudent, internationally oriented and innovative. In such a mindset, the (creative) crafts did not appear to be something to be worthy of serious attention. At least that was the case during the neo-liberal phase of Dutch society from the eighties up until recently, say 2010. The market forces were considered to be compelling and they dictated that the crafts were of the old economy and lacked the innovation and productivity gain that the new economy required. At the same time, the art world downplayed craftsmanship as a quality. As a consequence, politicians were keen to dismantle the minimal infrastructure that was in place to support the crafts; educational

M. Hofland-Mol (✉)
Albeda College, Rotterdam, The Netherlands
e-mail: m.hofland@albeda.nl

M. Poortvliet
Utrecht University, Utrecht, The Netherlands
e-mail: marion@craftscouncil.nl

A. Mignosa and P. Kotipalli (eds.), *A Cultural Economic Analysis of Craft*,
https://doi.org/10.1007/978-3-030-02164-1_11

institutions, which focused on teaching specific crafts, lost resources and attention and some were forced to close down. In the meantime, the Dutch did not seem to care about their crafts. Delfts blue, the icon of Dutch crafts, was made for foreign tourists; the Dutch had lost interest, as they did for so many of their traditional crafts.

Around 2010, the Dutch society appears to change its mind about the crafts. The secretary of education expressed new interest in the crafts, a platform on the crafts was established consisting of several prominent Dutch people, in 2013 the Museum Boijmans Van Beuningen dedicated a large exhibition Hand Made to the crafts, and in 2012 the Dutch crafts council was founded. Companies and professionals adopt the term "craftsmanship" in their public stance, thus expressing the public appreciation of skilled work.

It is early to tell whether the Dutch are prepared to embrace the crafts as an important quality in their society. The signs are positive, at least for those who care about crafts and craftsmanship in the Netherlands. In this chapter, we assess the state of craftsmanship in the Netherlands. Our focus is on what is defined in the introduction as creative craftsmanship and pay some attention to cutting edge craftsmanship. Accordingly, we leave aside regular craftsmanship even though it makes up the lion share of the craft sector in the Netherlands. The reason we do so is that the story of the creative crafts sector is the most telling when it comes to an assessment of the crafts in the Netherlands.

The Situation of the Crafts in the Netherlands

The concept of "crafts economy" (SER 2013, p. 13) was introduced in the Netherlands in 2009 by the industrial board of crafts, Hoofdbedrijfschap Ambachten (HBA). In doing so the board intended to raise awareness about the importance of crafts for the Dutch economy. This strategy seems to have worked as in 2013 the Dutch Social Economic Council SER (2013) was asked to advice the Dutch ministry of Economics, as well as the ministries of Social Affairs and Employment and Education, Culture and Science on the crafts economy in the Netherlands. In order to do so, they developed a working definition on the concept of crafts. According to their report, a profession or activity in the crafts sector should include a combination of the following elements:

- Competent, manual and skilled creation;
- Predominantly educated through practice;
- With proficiency as main value;
- Practiced as an economic activity. (SER 2013, p. 12).

De Kort and Van Hulle (2015) give a useful overview of the field of crafts in the Netherland. They use nine clusters and differentiate them into thirty-six former used HBA-branches. As a result, the field of crafts is more sharply demarcated with the various professions being bundled into specific clusters (Table 1).

Up to this point, it can be argued that there is no consensus on what specifically the creative crafts sector in the Netherlands entails. UNCTAD and UNPD (2010) confirm that defining and categorizing the arts and crafts is a complicated task. Their study recognizes the need for a common understanding as the arts and crafts sector plays a crucial

Table 1 Crafts economy, clusters and model professions

Cluster crafts economy	Model professions
Outfitting/finishing	Plasterers, painters and decorators
Construction	Carpenters, pavers, glazers and roofers
Creative industry/communication	Designers (interior, clothing, products, websites), jewellers and ceramists
Building maintenance crafts	Chimney sweepers and window cleaners
Health and beauty care	Hairdressers, beauticians, dental technicians, opticians and hearing care professionals
Installation/electrical engineering	Plumbers, electrical engineers, ICT-mechanic and telecom mechanics
Metal, wood and other production crafts	Welders, toolmakers, furnishers, sewers, hat and shoemakers, tailors and saddle makers
Repayment crafts	Car, bicycle and airplane mechanics
Nutrition	Butchers, bakers and fishmongers

Source Kort, J. de and R. van Hulle (2015)

part in the economy even though the field is frequently overlooked and cut off from public policies. At the request of the HBA and the SVGB, the Foundation for Vocational Training for Healthcare and Crafts (now the SBB), a group of cultural economist tried to place creative craftsmanship in the Netherlands in the international context. Klamer et al. (2013) define the various disciplines of arts and crafts sector further. They distinguish unskilled handwork and craftsmanship. To attain craftsmanship, training and constant practice are necessary conditions. They furthermore distinguish "utilitarian crafts" and "creative crafts" where the first serve a concrete and practical purpose and the second engage in the production of "unique objects, each with a distinctive quality and expressing the creativity of the maker" (idem, p. 11).

Figure 1 visualizes the different types of crafts creating a comprehensive context of the crafts field. Both the UNCTAD and UNPD (2010) and Klamer et al. (2013) incorporate the design category in their framework. In the latter study, this results in the concept of "cutting edge crafts". This is where contemporary crafts, arts and design come together. Craftspeople belonging to this group explore new grounds,

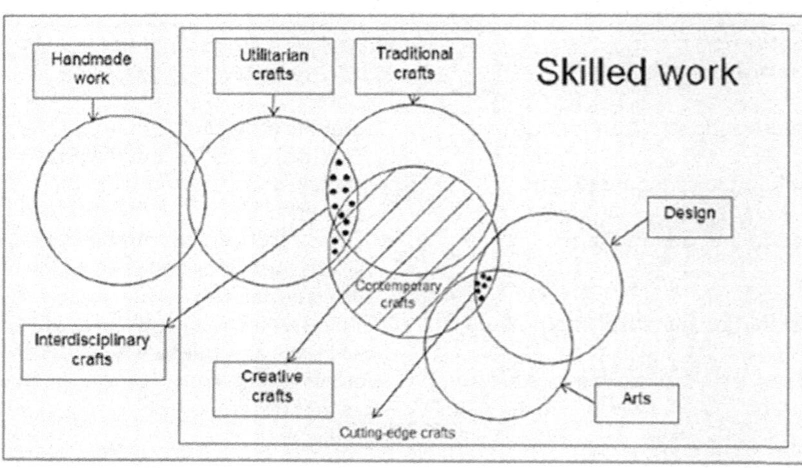

Fig. 1 The definition of utilitarian crafts versus other crafts and skills (*Source* Klamer et al. 2013)

develop new practices and form a new range of artefacts. This description could apply to designers or artists (Klamer 2013).

Knowing how to frame the various concepts of craftsmanship in the Netherlands what can we say about the contribution of creative crafts to the country's economy? First, professional knowledge and knowledge about technical innovations are increasingly important for the production of innovative products. The crafts economy is, therefore, perceived to be a creative sector and part of the knowledge economy which has been growing over the last twenty years (SER 2013). Second, crafts are of great importance for innovation and growth in other parts of the economy providing specialized components and fabrics. Third, one of the most outstanding qualities of craftsmen is their ability to provide individual custom-made products, like handmade wedding rings. The expectation is that the demand for well-crafted goods will grow, as people with increasing incomes and social status will desire goods and services of distinctive and authentic quality, and will be willing to pay the price. In creative craft branches like wooden furniture and ceramics growth is expected as the interest for these products shifts from functional, mass production to expressive, experience products and services (SOS Vakmanschap 2012). Fourth, crafts business are important for social cohesion as they provide work and local products. Research shows that "crafts shops" contribute in a positive way to the quality of life because locals meet each other in those creative places (PBL 2010). And lastly, besides the social and economic values mentioned above, the cultural value of specific craftsmanship needs to be mentioned as well. The diversity of craftsmanship is of enormous cultural value. As is the restoration and preservation of cultural heritage where specialized craftsmanship is essential. This contributes to the image of the Netherlands and has its influence on tourism and the location climate.

The crafts are an important economic sector. The Dutch crafts economy, broadly defined to include utilitarian and creative crafts, offered work to 815,636 persons in 2013. This equals 728,124 FTE (fulltime equivalent) and 10% of the working labour force. The labour is performed in 42,000 enterprises. This corresponds to approximately 30% of all companies in the country. These enterprises have a total turnover of roughly 165 billion euros and contribute 60 billion to the Gross National Product.

The average age in the sector is 41 year, which is the identical level as the average age in the Dutch labour market overall. Employees in the Dutch crafts sector earn €26,100, net on average per year per FTE, a little less than the average net income per FTE in the Dutch labour market of €28,000, per year (De Kort and Van Hulle 2015).

The crafts are part of the cluster creative industry and communication. De Kort and Van Hulle (2015) studied this cluster and identified the following characteristics. The cluster is perceived as being entrepreneurial, highly educated and growing. 96% of the work force has completed an MBO education. Between 2008 and 2013 the employment grew by 9%. However, one has to take into account that the production of movies, the development of software, architects and advertising agency all are taken into account in the cluster of the creative industry and communication. Whereas creative crafts like the manufacturing of clothes, shoes, bags and furniture are counted as belonging to the cluster metal, wood and other production crafts.

And whilst the cluster creative industry and communication appears to be entrepreneurial and innovative, other studies argue that the Dutch arts and crafts sector is in need of more entrepreneurship (De Kok et al. 2009; Janssen and Gankema 2012; Klamer et al. 2013). The SER (2013) suggests in its report that entrepreneurship and craftsmanship has to go hand in hand. In practice, the craft micro-entrepreneur finds it hard and demanding to combine craftsmanship and entrepreneurship on a daily basis. Furthermore, as merely craftsmanship is not enough the SER mentions a set of factors which are relevant to become successful in the arts and crafts field, such as being creative and innovative in addition to commercial thinking. Moreover, the awareness of new technological trends and materials is perceived as lacking, even though it is seen as an essential part of the craftsman's toolkit.

Policies in Place and the Role of Institutions

The Netherlands is a corporatist country. That means that the Dutch congregate, collaborate and form societies and councils when possible. When the Dutch feel threatened, they seek others to collaborate.

Guilds have given way to semi-governmental organizations. Several such organizations were founded to provide collaborative settings for the craft sector. For instance, the HBA is a semi-public organization that organizes and represents the crafts sector. Although a far cry from the intricate infrastructure of the German crafts sector, the HBA gave the Dutch crafts a common voice.

However, the neo-liberal mindset that overtook Dutch politics and bureaucracies in the eighties led to the dismantling of corporatist institutions, including the HBA which was abolished in 2015. The idea was apparently that the crafts better be left to the market.

In recent years several private initiatives seem to attest to a revaluation of the crafts in the Netherlands. Amongst these is the foundation of the Crafts Council Netherlands (CCN), intended to be a driver, concept developer and a platform for an infrastructure that connects and sustains the craft heritage with the enhancement of the "culture and economy of making" (Over CNN n.d. CNN). A grass root organization, the Nederlandse Gilde van Goudsmeden (the Dutch guild of goldsmiths), experienced a sharp increase in members from 2010 until 2015. These developments seem to indicate an increased awareness of the importance of crafts in the Netherlands.

Likewise, the Dutch government does value its creative industries. However, with the transfer of craft industries to low-wages countries, the production of artefacts disappeared resulting in a dramatic decrease in assignments for designers. They could not realize their ideas no longer resulting in designers taking matters in their own hands: designs were produced on their own account, independent of any industry. This development resulted in the formation of Dutch Design around 1990. The designers thus organized production under their own management and promoted their own label: Droog Design. The production of the artefacts was done in small editions abroad, where specialized workshop could offer high-quality craftsmanship for reasonable prices.

At the end of the twentieth century, this development takes another turn as designers turn against the existing production methods as they allegedly stand in the way of innovation. They start-up their own workshops and produce in-house. Currently, Dutch designers, together with the industry, create innovative making processes and products where not only the design or concept but also the material forms are the point of departure. Successful "maker-designers" create value due to their way of working. As a result, the market for local products is growing. And due to their pioneering role in the innovation process the Dutch government has pointed out the creative industry as one of the nine top sectors to invest in, in order to secure and improve the quality of living (Advies Topteam Creatieve Industrie 2011). With the ambition to "become the most creative economy of Europe in 2020" (p. 1) the Dutch government recognizes the need for nourishing creative entrepreneurial desire in education programmes. This is not shown when policies enhancing the creative crafts are concerned, hampering the sector as a whole but most importantly on crucial areas as innovation, entrepreneurship and education. An obvious example is the high VAT tariff of 21% which is used on crafted products when they are produced in series and not being recognized as artefacts, which gives the maker the right to use the significantly lower tariff of 6%.

In addition to the minor role of institutions and the government a deeper cause of the decline of the creative crafts in the Netherlands is the lack of appreciation for creating with the hands. This low level of appreciation seems to be deeply rooted in the Dutch society where merchant and recently cognitive skills are especially valued. This is quite different from other countries like for example Japan where masters in crafts are highly appreciated and where crafts are valued by the government. The same goes for countries that surround the Netherlands. Germany, especially, is able to sustain a culture of making and of craftsmanship, with a distinct respect for the unique human capacity to make, to create (Klamer et al. 2013).

Education System

We can argue that from 1950 onwards a large number of creative crafts like textile technics, leather works, glass blowing and ceramics have not been performed on a professional level in the Netherlands any longer. The manufacturing industry was re-allocated to low-wage countries and with this development, the transmission of creative techniques disappeared. Moreover, without economic relevance there did not seem to be grounds to teach crafts skills. As what is the use of teaching weaving if one cannot become a weaver anymore?

To understand the development and characteristics of the Dutch education programmes on arts and crafts, a clear perspective of the education structure in the Netherlands is essential. The Dutch education system consist of 8 years of primary education followed by 4, 5, or 6 years of secondary education and 2–6 years of higher education (depending on the type and sort of education). Table 2 gives a schematic overview of the qualification system in the Netherlands.

With the exception of one Associate Degree course of two years, all arts and crafts education programmes are level 3, vocational training, but mainly level 4, specialist training, so-called senior secondary vocational education programmes. For both programmes learning in a professional practice environment, like an atelier or workshop, forms an essential part of the programme varying from 20 up to 60% of the

Table 2 The Dutch qualification in relation to the European qualification system

EQF	NLQF	Dutch qualification	
8	8	Doctorate	
7	7	Master	
6	6	Bachelor	
5	5	Associate Degree	
4	4+	VWO (University preparatory education)	
4	4	MBO 4 (senior secondary vocational education and training)	HAVO (senior general secondary education)
3	3	MBO 3 (senior secondary vocational education and training)	
2	2	MBO 2 (senior secondary vocational education and training)	VMBO 2 (preparatory secondary vocational education)
1	1	MBO 1 (senior secondary vocational education and training)	VMBO 1 (preparatory secondary vocational education)

education time (Nuffic 2014). The qualification and examination terms of vocational education programmes are identical nationwide and developed by the Cooperation Organization for Vocational Education, Training and the Labour Market (Over-SBB n.d. SBB) in cooperation with the business field. The SBB has a legal duty to maintain the educations qualification structures as well as accredit and coach work place companies. Furthermore, they are the advisor for both the Dutch Ministry of Economic Affairs along with the Ministry of Education, Culture and Science on vocational education and the labour market. Moreover, different from bachelor and university studies in the Netherlands, the SBB will only consider starting an educational programme when there is a demand from the occupational field.

There are ten education institutes offering programmes under the umbrella of "creative craftsman" in arts and crafts in the Netherlands of which two are Regional Education Centres (ROC's) and three vocational schools (vakschool). With their regional function the ROC's offer a wide variety of mainly general education programmes at various locations depending on the regional needs and population. Vocational schools, like the Wood and Furniture College (HMC) or Sint Lucas, are small education institutes offering programmes in a specific field. In her research for the SBB, Voncken (2014) concludes that one of the main features of sustainable craftsmanship is the quality of the educational institutes. However, quality often seems to be compromised in the struggle for survival. This makes finding sustainable, long-term solutions difficult. Table 3 provides an overview of all level 4 Dutch education institutes providing arts and crafts education programmes.

The study of De Kort and Van Hulle (2015) shows that about 70% of the people working in the craft industry have an intermediate professional diploma (in Dutch "MBO", level four). Almost 13% have a bachelor. As Van der Wel and Schuring (2009) show, in line with the descriptors defined in the European Qualifications Framework (European Commission n.d. EGF), level four students acquire a range of skills to create solutions for specific problems in a certain field. Still, "demonstrating mastery and innovation in order to solve complex and unpredictable problems in a specialise field of work or study" (European Commission n.d. EGF) are skills developed in a bachelor,

Table 3 Overview of the institutes offering level 4 arts and crafts education programmes in the Netherlands

Educational institute	Arts and crafts programmes	Categorization
Zadkine (Vakschool Schoonhoven)	Creative craftsman (gold- and silversmithing)	ROC
Sint Lucas	Creative craftsman (ceramics, glass, leather and textile)	Vakschool
Hout en Meubilering College (HMC)	Wood and furniture Creative craftsman (wood, leather and textile)	Vakschool
Cibap	Creative craftsman (wood and textile)	Vakschool
Friesland College	Creative craftsman (wood, ceramics and textile)	ROC
Koning Willem I College	Wood and furniture	ROC
ROC Deltion College	Wood and furniture	ROC
ROC Midden Nederland	Wood and furniture	ROC
ROC Twente	Wood and furniture	ROC
Summa College	Wood and furniture	ROC

Source www.beroepinbeeld.nl

level 6, course. This is important as the vast majority of Dutch arts and crafts students merely follow a level four programme, occasionally followed by a level 5 Arts and Crafts programme (Nuffic 2014). If creative crafts students would like to widen their horizon they should consider enrolling in a bachelor course arts or design at several Dutch academies. A study by Janssen and Gankema (2012) suggested that the lack of a bachelor arts and crafts programme in the Netherlands results in some programmes offering a level 4+ course. In their education manifesto, the Crafts Council England (2014) calls for the promotion of world-class higher education and research in crafts. Klamer et al. (2013) propose an extension for multiple creative crafts education disciplines to include a master title in order to promote these fields and to develop the sharing of skills and knowledge.

We distinguish two directions in the Dutch creative crafts education field. First, there is the training for "creative craftsman" at the middle professional level (MBO in Dutch) that prepares students to become independent specialists and entrepreneurs who design, make and sell artefacts.

In these programmes, students learn new digital technics next to traditional skills to develop traditional and innovative products. They become identifiable craftspeople like goldsmith or furniture maker. The other direction is design. Art and design academies, that succeeded craftwork schools, are part of the higher education, level six programmes. The last fifty years these schools have changed from product and discipline minded to educating creative makers and thinkers according to societal themes like sustainability, healthcare and social amenities. Some institutions, like Sint Lucas and the Design Academy Eindhoven, have succeeded in fruitful collaborations. Their focus is on design and less on making. Students who graduate are designers and lack a clear professional identity.

Identification of Issues and Shortcomings and Possible Future Policy Directions

One might say the creative crafts evolve around the pillars: economy, culture, society and education. Until the start of the twentieth century, the Dutch seemed to emphasize economic value and therefore were downplaying the importance of the creative craft sector. However, along with the rise of grass root initiatives like the Dutch Crafts Council, the Dutch Guild of Goldsmiths and renowned crafts museums like the Textile Museum in Tilburg, a new awareness of a more value-based approach appears to emerge. In such an approach it is not only economic values but also social and cultural values that get the attention. It is the recognition of both the artefact as well as the skills of the master and their importance for Dutch culture and quality of life as a whole.

To achieve this all four mentioned pillars need to be connected and valued equally. There seems to be a need for cooperation, which is a complicated task as the arts and crafts sector is fragmented with numerous niches. Moreover, the creative crafts worker finds balancing craftsmanship and entrepreneurship especially demanding. However, with a grounded definition on creative crafts, and "cutting edge crafts" (Klamer et al. 2013) in particular, the various crafts could be specified and placed in an international perspective as suggested by the UNTAD and UNPD (2010). This way polices to reinforce the Dutch arts and crafts could be set into place. For example, a more crafts friendly VAT-policy or the reintroduction of a compulsory contribution for all creative crafts workers would reassure investments in overarching issues and research.

Furthermore, the pillar of education needs overall enforcement. There is a need for specialized craft skills and knowledge. Even though the need for crafts education has been put on the agenda there is no balanced and integrated education programme. Opportunities to learn about craft and making need to be offered throughout all stages of education. Furthermore, a workshop is needed not only for the crafts worker, but also a laboratory where scientists and designers can do research. Next to this a master title will contribute to the creative crafts economy making craft workers highly skilled, innovative, good promotors and teachers. Finally, introducing a master title at bachelor level might help improve the quality of creative crafts in Netherlands and making it cutting edge.

References

Advies Topteam Creatieve Industrie. 2011. Creatieve industrie in topvorm. Retrieved from Rijksoverheid https://www.rijksoverheid.nl/documenten/rapporten/2011/06/17/creatieve-industrie-in-topvorm.

Crafts Council England. 2014. *Our Future Is in the Making: An Education Manifesto for Craft and Making*. London: Crafts Council England.

de Kok, J.M.P., M. Mooibroek, F. Pleijster, and A.R.M. Wennekers. 2009. *Innovatief ondernemerschap in detailhandel, horeca en ambacht*. Zoetermeer: Economisch Instituut voor Midden-en kleinbedrijf (EIM).

de Kort, J., and R. van Hulle. 2015. *Structuuronderzoek ambachtseconomie 2015*. Delft: ABF Research.

European Commission. n.d. EQF. Retrieved May 21, 2017, from https://ec.europa.eu/ploteus/nl/node/1440.

Janssen, H., and H. Gankema. 2012. *De toekomst van het creatief vakmanschap. De Opleiding als motor voor duurzame innovaties in eeuwenoude ambachten*. 's-Hertogenbosch: KPC groep.

Klamer, A., T. Fjeldsted, K. Goto, L. Jiang, P. Kotipalli, and A. Mignosa. 2013. *Crafting Culture; Final Report*. Rotterdam: Stichting Economie en Cultuur.

Nuffic. 2014. *Het onderwijssysteem van Nederland beschreven*. The Hague: Nuffic.

Over CCN. n.d. In CNN. Retrieved March 18, 2018, from https://crafts-council.nl/en/over-ons/.

Over SBB. n.d. In SBB. Retrieved May 21, 2017, from https://www.s-bb.nl/over-sbb.

Planbureau voor leefomgeving. 2010. *Bedrijvigheid en leefbaarheid in stedelijke woonwijken*. Den Haag/Bilthoven: Planbureau voor leefomgeving (PBL).

Sociaal-Economische Raad. 2013. *Handmade in Holland*. Den Haag: Sociaal-Economische Raad (SER).

UNCTAD, and UNPD. 2010. Creative Economy Report: Creative Economy a Feasible Development Option. New York. Retrieved from http://www.unctad.org/en/docs/ditctab20103_en.pdf.

Vakmanschap, S.O.S. 2012. *Monitor SOS Vakmanschap – editie 2012*. Utrecht: SOS Vakmanschap.

Van der Wel, M., and F. Schuring. 2009. *Welk spoor kiest u? Waarderingskader voor het bevorderen van ondernemerschap*. The Hague: LEI Wageningen UR.

Voncken, E. 2014. *Schakels naar duurzaamheid*. Utrecht: Bureau Turf.

Crafts Policies in the UK

Julia Bennett

Introduction

Craft enriches our lives, pushing new boundaries in materials, technologies and skills to produce artistic and scientific achievements that give texture and meaning to the fabric of our lives, communities and neighbourhoods. As a core component of the UK's thriving creative industries, the craft economy employs 150,000 people and craft businesses add value, contributing £3.4bn to the UK economy each year (TBR 2014).

From master diamond cutters to makers who build film sets and props, from the centuries-old traditions of guilds to state-of-the-art digital fabrication, from the small batch production of designer makers to one-off glass sculptures, the UK's interest in craft is burgeoning. Craft skills are applied today in industries such as engineering, medicine, technology, architecture, fashion and design and in examples such

J. Bennett (✉)
Head of Research and Policy, Crafts Council, London, UK
e-mail: j_bennett@craftscouncil.org.uk

A. Mignosa and P. Kotipalli (eds.), *A Cultural Economic Analysis of Craft*,
https://doi.org/10.1007/978-3-030-02164-1_12

as using machine embroidery to engineer automotive components and medical implants. Participation in craft fosters wellbeing and nurtures our human desire to create.

Craft is practised in settings from homes to community centres to higher education post-doctoral research institutions, by one-person start-ups making ceramics in garden sheds to large-scale textiles companies exporting to international markets and by young children being introduced to techniques long honed by older generations.

The diversity of practice and discipline that is craft is also reflected in the matrix of policy and infrastructure levers that, with a huge variety of impacts, help, hinder—and sometimes are simply ignorant of—the growth in interest and the state of the craft economy. In this chapter, I will explore how those policy frameworks shape craft in the UK, examining how effective they are at responding to the current context of the sector and the extent to which policies foster the creative process, sustaining and developing its value to communities and to the economy.

The UK Context for Craft

Craft activity in the UK is situated within the parallel policy frameworks of culture, which focuses broadly on access and participation, and the creative industries, which is driven by the economic growth agenda. At the time of writing, the UK policy landscape was being dominated by the decision to leave the European Union. The Government's policy response to the resulting economic uncertainty and to the renewed constitutional debates in Scotland, in particular, included the publication of a Green Paper, *Building Our Industrial Strategy* (HM Government 2017). As I set out below, the strategy has the potential to offer support to the craft sector, impacting on craft innovation and on the potential talent pipeline of future makers.

The ability of the craft sector to influence the current debate is dependent on its voice. This has gradually grown stronger, following the 1997 UK Government's confirmation of craft's place in the definition of the creative industries (Department for Culture, Media and Sport 1998), which enabled the sector to insist on a role in policy development. Under devolution arrangements, each of the four nations now has its own Minister[1] responsible for the parallel creative and cultural policies that affect craft.[2] The statutory bodies of the Arts Councils (in England, Wales and Northern Ireland) and Creative Scotland provide leadership, support and some funding to the individual nations' development agencies, such as the Crafts Council, Craft NI and Craft Scotland, as well as to local organisations that support craft. In addition, the creation in 2011 of the Creative Industries Council, a government/industry cross-sector lead body, and in 2015 of the membership body, the Creative Industries Federation (the Crafts Council sits on both), has further strengthened the voice of the creative sector.

19.6% of the population in England participated in some kind of craft in 2015/2016, with 13.8% pursuing textiles (for example, embroidery, knitting and crochet), the most popular participatory art form (Department for Culture Media and Sport 2015/2016). Opportunities to engage in craft activities, from metalwork to 3D printing, ceramics to wearable technology, are available across the educational age range in state-funded provision, through social enterprises and private practice. The craft market is expressed through a multitude of small sales and fairs, alongside commissions, galleries, exhibitions and international exports and supported by a growth in the appetite for experiencing the personal and the authentic in handmade or small batch-produced artefacts.

---

[1]Rt Hon Matthew Hancock MP, Minister of State for Digital and Culture at the Department for Culture, Media and Sport (UK); Fiona Hyslop, MSP, Cabinet Secretary for Culture, Tourism and External Affairs (Scotland); Ken Skates AM, Cabinet Secretary for Economy and Infrastructure (Wales). At the time of writing the Northern Ireland Assembly has been dissolved and new ministers were still to be appointed.

[2]In March 2016 the UK Government published a White Paper (Department for Culture, Media and Sport 2016), setting out for the first time in fifty years the government's ambition and strategy for the cultural sectors in England. Scottish Government ministers are partners in a national Creative Learning Plan (Alba Chruthachail/Creative Scotland and Riaghaltas Na h-Alba/The Scottish Government 2013), and in 2015 the Welsh Government published Creative Learning through the Arts—an action plan for Wales (Llywodraeth Cymru/Welsh Government 2015), intended to improve attainment through creativity, to increase and improve arts experiences in schools, and to support teachers and arts practitioners in developing their skills.

The journey towards Brexit has prompted both anxiety in the craft sector (for example, in relation to future trade tariffs, customs duties and intellectual property rights) and optimism about future opportunities. The announcement of a snap general election in 2017 created further turbulence, as the Conservative Government sought to increase its mandate but the result left it with a weaker minority government. The Crafts Council surveyed the craft sector in July 2016 (Crafts Council 2016), one month after the referendum, and the findings reveal a mixed response to the prospect of Brexit, with concerns expressed but also a sense that with the right strategy, this could still be a moment of opportunity for the crafts sector.

The Industrial Strategy Green Paper set out for consultation the Government's vision of a 'stronger, fairer' prosperity in the UK (HM Government 2017: 3) and requested views about proposed interventions to support business. In essence, the Green Paper was a move towards a road map to prepare industry for a new trading environment. Broadly, the announcement was welcomed by the creative industries and by the Crafts Council because it recognised the achievements of the creative industries as one of seven sectors that 'have high productivity, competitive advantages at a global level, and growth potential' (HM Government 2017: 97). The creative industries have grown at 6% per annum since 1997 compared to a UK average of 4.3% and are now worth £84.1 billion per annum to the UK economy (Creative Industries Council 2016: 14). The strategy includes commitments to invest in research and development, mechanisms to encourage trade and inward investment and the introduction of a new system of technical education.[3]

The Crafts Council has argued in its response[4] to the consultation that the Green Paper offers a route to seize the opportunities of Industry

[3]To be known as T-Levels, a reform of vocational education qualifications that will sit alongside A-Levels, the advanced level qualifications usually taken at age 18 in more academic subjects.

[4]Crafts Council. 2017. Crafts Council Response the Building Our Industrial Strategy: Green Paper. http://www.craftscouncil.org.uk/content/files/17-04-11_Consultation_response_final.pdf. Accessed 24 May.

4.0 (also known as the Fourth Industrial Revolution).[5] Yet this opportunity will only be realised if the strategy heralds a systematic exploration of the fusion of craft and technology skills through encouragement and support of cross-sectoral innovation and collaboration. Strategic investment in research and development has the potential to move craft innovation from a position of a happy accident to one in which it acts as a driver for successful businesses. This is exemplified by Sarat Babu, a maker, engineer and materials scientist who founded a company that developed a diverse range of materials capable of changing their physical property and created synthetic tissue replacements for medical use. Such a company relies on innovation in the understanding and manipulation of materials to generate added value in the economy. As KPMG notes, 'Craft skills and knowledge have a strong economic impact and significant potential to drive further growth and innovation in other sectors' (2016).

The new system of technical education, announced alongside the Green Paper, is intended to create parity of esteem between vocational and academic education routes. The new Technical Levels (or T-Levels as they will be known) offer an opportunity to strengthen the status of vocational qualifications, seeking to emulate the existing Swiss/German 'dual system'. However, in order to become a respected and effective vocational route for craft, T-Levels will need to form part of a coherent, strategic approach to education and skills development linked through every stage of an individual's career. The evidence in the crafts sector in England in particular shows that this is often not the case and that craft and, indeed, creative education more generally, is facing a crisis that jeopardises the future of making. The Crafts Council highlighted these issues in an education manifesto for craft and making (Crafts Council 2014).[6] The Crafts Council's time-series research study (TBR 2016) investigates craft-related education and training in England 2007–2008 to 2014–2015. It presents a picture of a sector facing an unsustainable

[5]A term allegedly coined at the Hamburg Messe, Industry 4.0 integrates technologies from the Internet of Things with other technological advances in production and manufacturing systems.

[6]See also Creative Industries Federation (2015).

model for educating and training our current and future makers, fuelled in part by the perverse incentives of successive governments' performance frameworks that have resulted in a de-prioritisation of creative subjects in schools. In particular, the findings show that student numbers taking Art & Design and Design & Technology GCSEs[7] have fallen by 23% in this time period (compared to a fall in total GCSE student numbers of only 6%). Higher education courses in craft-related subjects have fallen by 50% and, even though student numbers in some disciplines such as textiles are holding up, the drop in course numbers is concerning. Textiles students are also disproportionately represented in the 66% growth over the same period in non-UK domiciled students. With the abolition of post-study student visas in 2012, there is now a greater risk of this talent leaving the UK.

The evidence also shows that the number of students taking entry-level[8] further education courses in craft-related education and training increased from 7290 in 2007/2008 to 49,890 in 2014/2015. The increase in cohort size is welcome, but only 8% of that number are progressing to Level 3 and Level 4 courses in the same subjects and it is therefore unlikely that many of the entry-level students will pursue careers in craft.

By contrast, the evidence shows a welcome rise in the number of people pursuing National Apprenticeships in craft under a scheme introduced in 2008 in which Government funding is available to pursue nationally advertised roles with employers.[9] However, numbers remain very small, with only 1900 Apprentices in England in 2014/2015, set against the numbers pursuing equivalent qualification levels at GCSE (277,500 in the same year), A Level (20,260) and in a range of other equivalent qualifications. In addition, most of this growth occurred in 2013/2014, reflecting a shift in funding policy to apprenticeships, away from other work-based learning routes. As a consequence, routes into craft are diversifying, potentially offsetting the declines in other

[7]General Certificate of Secondary Education, usually taken in England at age 16.

[8]Entry Level and Level 1.

[9]The entry process differs in each of the four UK nations.

education routes, but currently the numbers are very small. A further obstacle to apprenticeships, that is likely to be faced by microbusinesses, is the challenge of taking on a first employee, a barrier identified by Young (2013), which may be reducing potential growth in craft businesses. Anecdotal evidence suggests that the microbusiness sector, including craft, could be a more enthusiastic employer of apprentices if the application process was more transparent and if improved support were available to cluster and share an apprenticeship across several businesses.

In general, the education system and related careers advice still promote to students the notion of seeking a job, yet many of those minded to pursue a career in craft go on to work for themselves. Indeed, the UK craft economy can be characterised by growing numbers of sole traders/freelancers (88%, BOP Consulting 2012: 3) and microbusinesses. Recent studies (O'Leary 2014; HM Government 2016; RSA 2017 and Creative Industries Federation 2017) show an increasing trend in the UK economy towards self-employment and entrepreneurship. Some students in higher education are supported in this ambition, yet early findings from a collaborative Ph.D. between King's College London and the Crafts Council,[10] suggest that this is approached very differently by higher education institutions; in a comment in her Crafts Council blog, February 2017, Lauren England notes that some are 'staking a claim to the development of entrepreneurial skill sets and business acumen, while others do not (explicitly) engage with entrepreneurship at all'. Higher education institutions are incentivised to report on graduates' destinations, but the data do not reflect clearly the number of graduates who set up in businesses themselves.

Continuing professional development (CPD) is also vital to strengthen makers' skills in a competitive market and to explore new creative directions. Yet time spent on training and development is time away from making the product. Training, therefore, needs to be adapted and relevant to the particular needs of microbusinesses, with

[10]Crafts Council. 2017. "Crafting Professional Practice Through Higher Education". http://www.craftscouncil.org.uk/what-we-do/research-reports/. Accessed 24 May.

tailored programmatic support at an early stage to act as a springboard for those businesses. Respondents to a recent Crafts Council survey of makers' business development needs (undertaken to inform professional development programmes for craft professionals, offered by the Crafts Council now for nearly five decades) also identified marketing, finance, enterprise, intellectual property rights and export skills as a priority. The latter become more urgent in the light of Brexit. In its advocacy work to strengthen craft skills, the Crafts Council has endorsed parliamentary committee recommendations about re-examining tax regimes for freelancers working in the creative sector (HMSO 2013: 40) and has called for the introduction of new tax incentives both for freelancers' CPD and to encourage bigger businesses to invest, for example, in hand skills training in the textiles and fashion industries. The latter would be particularly valuable in areas in which new businesses are building on heritage craft industries, such as textiles in Yorkshire, shoemaking and leather work in Northampton and ceramics in Stoke-on-Trent. Those businesses are helping to shape local identity and have the potential to attract further investment. One example Amy Frearson noted in a Dezeen article on 26 March 2017, is the Wooltex factory in Yorkshire, one of several specialist textile mills around Europe in which textile manufacturer Kvadrat has invested. It is a strong example of inward investment into the UK for local production. However, the article reports that the biggest challenge now faced by Wooltex is 'attracting young people to train and work for them, and build up the knowledge needed to continue the craft'.

The employment and skills environment for craft can be seen to face a number of policy and practical obstacles. The issue of premises for craft businesses risks compounding these challenges. Makers have often located their studios in former industrial space, more readily able to accommodate a range of technologies and mess and where, traditionally, rents were cheaper. However, the impact of steep rises in urban property prices, particularly in southern England, is now compounded by a national increase in business rates.[11] The global recession of a decade

[11]Charged on most non-domestic properties. See https://www.gov.uk/introduction-to-business-rates/overview.

ago also led to property developers being given the right to create residential units out of former offices without seeking planning permission. This placed a premium on industrial space and led to unintended consequences for creatives, who were frequently priced out of potential studio space. Tom Fleming Creative Consultancy (2015) has evidenced the knowledge, industrial and network spillovers across Europe related to the presence of clusters of artists and cultural organisations, yet property developers often appear to be the main financial beneficiaries of this effect. Some of the impact on craft and creative businesses was mitigated through the protection of a small number of areas of high creativity from the suspension of the requirement for planning permission.[12] In spite of this measure, craft businesses are still being forced to relocate to more remote locations to find affordable rents. Investment in creative workspace is urgently needed, not only to secure the future of businesses but also in recognition of the wider impact on their sustainability. A recent case study of studios along the Ipswich Cambridge rail corridor (Smiths Row 2016) confirms that clustering involves the ability 'to access a combination of professional support and a space for networking and exchange with other artists, particularly those artists disadvantaged by lack of social mobility, rural isolation and financial or health barriers'. Now there is evidence that the fragile health of creative businesses is gradually being taken more seriously: the Greater London Authority regeneration committee recently recommended the creation of areas of small live/workspaces to be known as Creative Enterprise Zones (Greater London Authority 2016), offering a spark of hope to makers, as long as the zones include permission for the more industrial processes characteristic of some craft disciplines.

[12]Areas exempt from office to residential change of use permitted development right 2013.

Conclusion

The 2015 UK Government's Industrial Strategy offers an opportunity to reappraise support that is appropriate to the particular characteristics of the small but firmly rooted craft sector. Many craft sole-traders succeed in spite of the declining and fragmented routes into a craft career. Characterised by a culture of high entrepreneurship, it is a sector that is still only partially represented in national statistics, owing to exclusion of businesses (that often start out) operating under the threshold for Value-Added Tax,[13] one of the metrics by which economic activity is recorded. A commitment to greater investment in Research & Development activity to support collaboration across industrial sectors would represent a welcome catalyst to increase innovation in craft businesses and in the application of those craft skills to the benefit of the wider creative economy. Accompanied by a more strategic and coherent approach to the risk of market failures in education and training, together with measures to increase the availability of studio space, there is an opportunity for the climate of experimental creativity and commercial innovation, so typical of craft, to lead to greater engagement by audiences and participants, as well as fulfilling more effectively the sector's economic potential.

References

Alba Chruthachail/Creative Scotland and Riaghaltas Na h-Alba/The Scottish Government. 2013. *What Is Creativity—Scotland's Creative Learning Plan.* Scotland.

BOP Consulting. 2012. *Craft in an Age of Change.* London: Crafts Council.

Crafts Council. 2014. *Our Future Is in the Making: An Education Manifesto for Craft and Making.* London: Crafts Council.

Crafts Council. 2016. *Crafts Council EU Referendum Survey: Findings, Analysis and Next Steps.* London: Crafts Council.

[13]A general, broadly based consumption tax assessed on the value added to goods and services.

Creative Industries Council. 2016. *Create Together*. London: Creative Industries Council.

Creative Industries Federation. 2015. *Creative Education Agenda*. London: Creative Industries Federation.

Creative Industries Federation. 2017. *Creative Freelancers*. London: Creative Industries Federation.

Department for Culture, Media and Sport. 1998. *Creative Industries Mapping Documents 1998*. London: DCMS.

Department for Culture Media and Sport. 2015/2016. *Taking Part Survey*. London: DCMS.

Department for Culture, Media and Sport. 2016. *The Culture White Paper*. London: DCMS.

Greater London Authority. 2016. *Creative Placemaking: A New Approach to Culture and Regeneration?* London: GLA.

HM Government. 2016. *Julie Deane's Review of Self-Employment*. London: HMSO.

HM Government. 2017. *Building Our Industrial Strategy: Green Paper*. London: HMSO.

House of Commons Culture, Media and Sport Committee. 2013. *Supporting the Creative Economy*. London: HMSO.

KPMG. 2016. *Innovation Through Craft: Opportunities for Growth*. London: Crafts Council.

Llywodraeth Cymru/Welsh Government. 2015. *Creative Learning Through the Arts—An Action Plan for Wales*. Cardiff: Cyngor Celfyddydau Cymru Arts Council of Wales.

O'Leary, D. 2014. *Going It Alone*. London: Demos.

Smiths Row. 2016. *Defining Space: Making Studios Work, a Vision for Studio Provision Along the Ipswich—Cambridge Rail Corridor*. Bury St. Edmunds: Smiths Row.

RSA. 2017. *The Entrepreneurial Audit*. London: RSA.

TBR. 2014. *Measuring the Craft Economy*. London: Crafts Council.

TBR. 2016. *Studying Craft 16*. London: Crafts Council.

Tom Fleming Creative Consultancy. 2015. *Creative and Cultural Spillovers in Europe: Report on a Preliminary Evidence Review*. London: CCS.

Young, D. 2013. *Growing Your Business: A Report on Growing Micro Businesses*. London: Business, Innovation and Skills.

Craft: Economic Policies in the United States 1896–2016

M. J. R. Montoya

Introduction

The supportive ecosystem of craft economy has evolved dramatically in the past century. Part of these changes are due to the massive institutional and technological changes that took place during the twentieth century. In the United States, a paradigm shift in modes of production and the role the United States played in global affairs changed the way that art and craft was prioritized within the American economy. Moreover, as the creative and cultural economy has gained prominence as an indicator of economic vitality, so too have the ways that craft has been included in political discourse. The following provides a brief overview of the policies that corresponded with major social and economic shifts in the United States, beginning with the development of the first art and design schools and culminating in proposed regional and

M. J. R. Montoya (✉)
University of New Mexico, Albuquerque, NM, USA
e-mail: mrmonto@unm.edu

A. Mignosa and P. Kotipalli (eds.), *A Cultural Economic Analysis of Craft*,
https://doi.org/10.1007/978-3-030-02164-1_13

national policies that directly identify craft as an important economic driver.

The first policy tools to support art and craft and economy were vocational. The first design school in the United States, the Parsons School of Art and Design, was established in New York City in 1896.[1] In anticipation of the effects the Industrial Revolution would have on the American economy, Frank Parsons (then an instructor at the school) argued that demand for art and design would become an essential factor in industry. By 1936, the school developed a curricula aimed at feeding design expertise into many other industries. This prompted vocational training for agricultural workers through the Smith–Hughes Act of 1917. Together, art, craft, and design were included in the United States' economic agenda. Many of Parson's ideas about the connection between art and industry were the impetus for the inclusion of art into American vocational agendas and its consequent economic impact (Barlow 1967).

By the time the Great Depression struck the fabric of America's industrialized economy, policymakers needed to develop alternative ways of viewing economic productivity, particularly among a social demographic who had been alienated from years of industrial economic prosperity. Under the New Deal and the establishment of the Works Progress Administration (WPA) of 1939 art, craft, and design played an emerging role in a more diverse economic framework for the United States. With the establishment of the Division of Professional and Service Projects and Federal Projects Number One, the training and development of artists, engineers, architects, and musicians were both supported as viable vocations and were compensated through larger projects that stimulated demand for these vocations (Hapke 2009). This ushered in a new period of meaningful policy for craft in the United States. Potters and weavers were seen as not merely part of a luxury or leisure economy, but also as part of the way that disenfranchised workers could recover from the economic catastrophe of the previous decade—to the extent that the Vocational Training Act of 1963 significantly featured art and craft (Hyslop-Margison 2001). This opened up

[1]Then called The Chase School after founder and painter William Merritt Chase.

new possibilities within governance to include the arts and craft into policy agendas.

During the Civil Rights Era, the discourse on vocational training was not only focused on economic recovery and stability, but also on the inclusion of citizens who had been marginalized, persecuted, and segregated from civil society. It was in this era that the use of art and craft became a part of the productive qualities of civil discourse, including forms of civil protest and disobedience. Public art exploded during this era. Smaller organizations within cities and towns throughout America created public support networks that would later influence regional and national policy regarding art and craft (Ferree et al. 2004). It is during this period that the process of craft-making was of particular importance. As groups of people became invested in having a stronger voice in civil discourse, so too did the need to revisit traditions, lineage, and history. Craft was part of the language whereby history could be mobilized as a human right. As craftspeople actively engaged in work as part of social movements, process and product were distinctly understood as part of social progress. While the nation had not necessarily viewed craft as a very significant economic driver, there were several policymaking mechanisms in place to make that argument more strongly as voices within governance changed.

In 1965, the establishment of the National Endowment for the Arts (NEA), galvanized the role of arts as part of both economic and social processes. Now a part of the federal government, the NEA could interact with its bureaucratic counterparts. Although that discussion was not the most prominent part of federal policy, there was now a connective tissue that changed the way that art and craft could communicate with economic, legal, and political discussions happening at other levels of governance (Binkiewicz 2004). This empowered other parts of the national government, including the Library of Congress and the Smithsonian Institution to utilize its archival power to change the discourse on what public institutions could do to set other important agendas, including those related to the economic empowerment of marginalized American citizens (Karp and Kratz 2006). Several economists have suggested that the presence of strong institutional museum culture and formalized and evolving discussions on art and beauty are a key indicator of economic resilience (Hofstede 1988). It is here that the NEA becomes a pivotal policy instrument for the United States, particularly because it enables the arts to become a part of the umbrella discourse on art and craft in regional and local settings. As a grant-making institution and "thought leader" on issues of art, craft, and design excellence, it became a mediator of both product and process, which would lead to an era of local and state stimulation that eventually legitimized the cultural worker as an economic change maker.

As the NEA served as a clearing-house for art and craft policy, it also became the focal point of criticism of the role art and craft played in a larger policy context. In times of economic constraint or political turmoil, the NEA drew criticism about its importance and relevance. Several times the NEA has been subject to elimination or significant cuts from the United States budget. These discussions prompted activism from local and regional art and craft communities. For example, in 1981, when the Reagan administration considered abolishing the NEA, several unlikely allies, including conservative artists and businesspeople, argued its social and historic merits and reversed the decision to formally dismantle the NEA (Binkiewicz 2004). This would happen several times in its history, again in 1995 by Newt Gingrich's "Contract with America" policies and most recently in 2017 under the Trump Administration. It is these policy-driven attempts that reveal that not all policy in the United States progressively saw art and craft as priorities. It also helps inform the evolution of policy perspectives regarding art and craft over the century that led to what we now increasingly refer to as an era of cultural and creative enterprise. In order to stay relevant, art and craft work had to employ a different vocabulary.

During the period between the 1970s and the new millennium regional, state and local entities began supporting the work of craft workers through focused collaboration with arts and crafts councils and craft guilds. The American Craft Council (ACC), formed in 1943, prompted a larger transnational discussion by helping form the World Craft Council in 1964. Meanwhile, it organized the production of data and highlighted craft both regionally and locally within the United States. The New England Foundation for the Arts, for example, produced several important categorizations of the creative industries, including craft economy that helped further the economic agendas of craft within local and state governments. In 2009 and again 2012, the National Governors Association produced reports on the best practices related to creative and cultural work, and therein featured the craft economy and its role in producing viable and sustainable economic practices built on vetted policies. For example, Kentucky's decade long production of a craft marketing campaign and similar efforts in Colorado, Mississippi, and Michigan have been credited for providing both tax incentives and guild-oriented clusters to develop competitive advantages in international trade. Cumulatively, the NGA reports identified a myriad of policy and strategic recommendations that have been implemented in various ways at a state level throughout the United States. They may be summarized as follows:

- View Creative Industry as a State Economic Asset.
- Understand State's Cultural Industries—this includes organizing, measuring, and inventorying cultural assets in relation to changing economic conditions. Incorporate Efforts into Statewide Planning—which also includes creating visible events.
- Develop strategies to support the arts and culture sectors—this includes support for entrepreneurial ventures, providing technical assistance for startups, and providing business aid recovery efforts to mitigate risks in growing creative and cultural industries.
- Incorporating Arts into Community Development Plans—this includes providing training, "enterprise zones," and the development of "art spaces." These arts spaces include the reclamation of industrial spaces and the provision of tax incentives to repurpose existing spaces.
- Incorporate arts and crafts into tourism strategies—this includes support for branding, the promotion of distinct cultural products, and cultural events that emphasize craft.

These recommendations have led to the creation of tax incentives for craft workers, cultural economy innovation strategies that have featured craft workers more prominently, and the creation of "makers spaces" in urban planning that have added to the support mechanisms in place for craft workers. In terms of intellectual property, several organizations (including the ACC) have recommended IP protections for craft workers, particularly in light of emerging technologies such as 3D printing (Dratler 2005). One major precedent in IP discussions came from Native American rights to intellectual property, which culminated in the Indian Arts and Crafts Act of 1990 (IACA). The IACA was intended to be a truth-in-advertising campaign law that protected authentic Indian art from being attributed to an indigenous community, but has also raised problems concerning who is protected under the law and whether it actually protects indigenous art from being appropriated without proper compensation or credit (Minikowski 2017). By the turn of the millennium, art and craft policy manifested in a wide range of issues. Many of these policies have prompted much debate, but they also found ways to be included in other economic agendas.

It is here that the most comprehensive policy to date regarding craft has emerged. As the idea of cultural and creative entrepreneurship has saturated all levels of governmental discourse, new policies such as the Comprehensive Resources for Entrepreneurs in the Arts to Transform the Economy (the CREATE Act) of 2016 have been proposed. This law, proposed by Sen. Tom Udall of New Mexico (with a corresponding house bill by Rep. Debbie Dingell of Michigan), attempts to tie together efforts made at the regional and local level, while also addressing important issues regarding international trade and intellectual property. As industrial economies moved from the United States to developing economies, the United States focus on design and knowledge economy produced trade regulations, and intellectual property policies that directly impacted the role of creative economy. The CREATE act is the culmination of public recommendation that had been organized through the Department of Commerce, Department of Labor, Small Business Administration (SBA), Housing and Urban Development, and the NEA (AFA 2011).

The bill in its current form contains provisions as presented by Sen. Udall and co-author Robert Lynch:

- Direction that the U.S. SBA should work with micro-lenders, traditional lenders, and regulators to ensure that artists and entrepreneurs have access to micro-loans and that loan program criteria are not discriminatory toward arts-related businesses.
- Support for the development of SBA technical assistance programs targeted to meet the needs of the creative economy.
- A requirement that the Economic Development Administration and Rural Development Administration ensure that traditional economic development tools, such as incubators and grant programs, support the arts industry.
- Updates to the law to allow artists to claim tax deductions for charitable contributions based on the sale value of a piece of artwork, rather than the value of the materials used to create the artwork.
- The creation of an Artist Corps (similar to the AmeriCorps) within the Corporation for National and Community Service to help expand access to arts and arts education in communities.
- The creation of a demonstration project to promote creative and performing arts in local economic planning.
- Measures to expand cultural and educational opportunities for American students and families by encouraging foreign governments to lend artwork to U.S. museums and educational institutions and expediting the visa process for foreign visual and performing artists hosted by American organizations.

Should the bill become law, it will serve as the culmination of several key foundational aspects that evolved across U.S. policy in relation to art and craft economy. As new policies are introduced, they have had to account for new economic realities. For example, the interdependence of the United States on global matters has prompted American diplomacy to utilize craft as a mediator of cultural exchange, and in some cases, has highlighted issues of major geo-political importance (Feigenbaum 2001; AFA 2013). Issues of global conflict, human rights will also add to issues of economic interest, particularly connecting to work previously done through the Dodd–Frank Act on issues of value-chain equity and supply-train transparency (Barton 2017).

Consider momentarily that craft principles are increasingly part of the discourse on technological advancement and scientific research. Most recently in biomedical research, the use of Aymara (an indigenous community from Bolivia) weaving practice to develop new technologies to address heart disorders has gained the attention of policymakers within the National Institutes for Health, and new proposals for research and development funding may occur as a result (BBC 2015). The transnational nature of research, industrial supply chains, and big data have now made it impossible to not think about the need for non-linear ways to solve problems, including new people in those discussions, and creating pathways for different forms of economic resilience than previously considered. Not only has craft served as a powerful mediator of social and cultural inclusivity in politics and policy, it is now part of how we are challenging previously conceived notions of tradition, skill, and fairness. In the United States, that discussion is at a critical point of inflection, and it is likely that these discussions will evolve in relation to unlikely connections that have directly benefitted from a century-old foundation of policies that has confronted art and craft work as essential social and economic drivers.

References

Americans for the Arts. 2011. *Artist as Entrepreneur: Federal Guide Series for Arts Organizations*. Retrieved from http://www.americansforthearts.org/sites/default/files/pdf/2014/by_topic/funding-resources/Artist-As-Entrepreneur-Resource-Guide.pdf.

Americans for the Arts. 2013. *International Cultural Exchanges: Federal Guide Series for Arts Organizations*. Retrieved from http://www.americansforthearts.org/sites/default/files/pdf/2014/by_topic/funding-resources/August-2013-Updated-Version-of-International-Culture-Exchange-Resource-Guide.pdf.

Barlow, M.L. 1967. *History of Industrial Education in the United States*. Peoria: CA Bennett.

Barton, D. 2017. Refocusing Capitalism on the Long Term: Ownership and Trust Across the Investment Value Chain. *Oxford Review of Economic Policy* 33 (2): 188–200.

BBC. 2015. *The Bolivian Women Who Knit Parts for Hearts.* March 29. Retrieved from http://www.bbc.com/news/health-32076070.

Binkiewicz, D.M. 2004. *Federalizing the Muse: United States Arts Policy and the National Endowment for the Arts, 1965–1980.* Chapel Hill: University of North Carolina Press.

Dratler, J., Jr. 2005. *Licensing of Intellectual Property.* New York: Law Journal Press.

Feigenbaum, H.B. 2001. *Globalization and Cultural Diplomacy.* Art, Culture, & the National Agenda Issue Paper. New York: Center for Arts and Culture.

Ferree, M.M., R. Flacks, M. Ganz, D.B. Gould, R. Koopmans, C. Kurzman, and F. Polletta. 2004. *Rethinking Social Movements: Structure, Meaning, and Emotion.* Lanham: Rowman & Littlefield.

Hapke, L. 2009. *Labor's Canvas: American Working-Class History and the WPA Art of the 1930s.* Newcastle: Cambridge Scholars Publishing.

Hofstede, G., and M.H. Bond. 1988. The Confucius Connection: From Cultural Roots to Economic Growth. *Organizational Dynamics* 16 (4): 5–21.

Hyslop-Margison, E.J. 2001. An Assessment of the Historical Arguments in Vocational Education Reform. *Journal of Career and Technical Education* 17 (1): 23–30.

Karp, I., and K. Kratz. 2006. Introduction. In *Museum Frictions: Public Cultures/Global Transformations*, ed. Ivan Karp. Durham: Duke University Press.

Minikowski, A.W. 2017. The Creation of Tribal Cultural Hegemony Under the Indian Arts and Crafts Act and Native America Graves Protection and Repatriation Act. *NDL Rev.* 92: 397–533.

National Governor's Association. 2009. *National Governors Association Report on Art and Economy—Best Practices for Policy Implementation.* Retrieved from https://www.nga.org/files/live/sites/NGA/files/pdf/0901ARTSANDECONOMY.PDF.

National Governor's Association. 2012. *New Engines of Growth: Five Roles for Arts, Culture, and Design.* Retrieved from https://www.nga.org/files/live/sites/NGA/files/pdf/1204NEWENGINESOFGROWTH.PDF.

The Comprehensive Resources for Entrepreneurs in the Arts to Transform the Economy (CREATE Act). 2016. Retrieved from http://www.americansforthearts.org/sites/default/files/CREATE%20Act.pdf.

The Indian Arts and Crafts Act of 1990. *US Department of the Interior, Indian Arts and Crafts Board.* Retrieved March 24, 2017, from https://www.gpo.gov/fdsys/pkg/CFR-2001-title25-vol1/pdf/CFR-2001-title25-vol1-sec308-4.pdf.

Part III

Economic Issues

An Economic Assessment of Asian Crafts

Simon Ellis and Joseph Lo

Introduction

Asian crafts are distinctive for the materials that are used (e.g. bamboo), the skills that are applied (e.g. batik) and the modes of production (e.g. 'One Product per Village' schemes). All these stem from centuries of tradition, but in recent times have come under threat from a variety of forces (e.g. globalization, climate change, technological change). This article aims to characterize modern Asian craft production from an economic point of view.

The geographic scope of Asia and the Pacific[1] ranges from the most populous countries in the world (India and China each with more than

[1]We define this region based on UNESCO 'regions'.

S. Ellis (✉)
Montreal, Canada

J. Lo
Smithsonian Institution, Washington, DC, USA

A. Mignosa and P. Kotipalli (eds.), *A Cultural Economic Analysis of Craft*,
https://doi.org/10.1007/978-3-030-02164-1_14

1.3 billion inhabitants respectively) to the smallest island nations (e.g. Niue with less than two thousand inhabitants). The examples and the analysis we take are thus inevitably based on our personal experience as no one can know the craft of such a vast area.

Our analysis follows Fochingong and Lotsmart (2003) who identified a model of economic and social self-reliance, as well as Ruzek's (2014) discussion of the informal economy and 'eco-localism', but is based primarily on first hand evidence from national statistics and direct survey in the countries of Azerbaijan, Bhutan, China, Georgia,[2] Indonesia, Philippines and Thailand, with references to secondary work from other countries such as India and Japan. We argue that for many countries in Asia as compared to other regions of the world craft remains an activity that produces objects that have a key function/role in local economies in which local artisans use local materials and manage local ecosystems.

Artisans and Sustainable Development

The new global Sustainable Development Goals place great emphasis on local jobs, managing the local environment and even obliquely mention craft by suggesting the need for 'sustainable tourism that creates jobs and promotes local culture and products' (Goals 8 and 12).

The gathering of local raw materials is consistent with Ruzek's (2014) concept of eco-localism of informal industry. Gathering and collecting materials from the natural environment is only possible when the practice is informal as the supply is unreliable and inconsistent. For instance, according to those who participated in the study from Indonesia (Lo 2014), the supply of good quality volcanic ash for stone carving is scarce and the task is undertaken by the artisan him/herself. The carbon footprint from the sales of products is less than those in the formal economy, and the gathering of raw materials sustains a lesser

[2] The Caucasus area of Azerbaijan and Georgia is culturally between East and West, North and South and is included here as it has been a particular focus of work for one of us (Simon Ellis) since 2012.

impact on the environment because they are harvested locally without using motorized transport. Chinese ethnic minority artisans in Yunnan and Guizhou like those in Indonesia, use local materials in a sustainable manner (Lo 2011). For example, bamboo weavers reported that bamboo is a very fast growing plant and very common in their local environment. However, in recent years, because of lack of cultivation, Indonesian craft producers expressed concerns that some specialist plants are now difficult to access. To mitigate this problem, they have expressed an interest in cultivating these plants.

Philippine 'abaca' (hemp) production is a good example of local management of crops (Respicio 2014; Dept of Agriculture 2015). The outer layers of the plant are used for rope and paper production, but the innermost fibres are used to make fine woven textiles. Separation of these different layers cannot be achieved by machine, limiting volume production. Local management of the crop is needed to identify the best examples for textile production. The Bhutan national statistics and survey data show that 27% of households produce textiles, largely for home use (Askerud and Lo 2013).

Asian policies place considerable emphasis on local production of artisan products. Thailand crafts are best known for their 'one village one product' OTOP programme of support (Punyasavatsut 2008; Natsuda et al. 2011; Cheewatrakoolpong and McKenzie 2013). This model is a twentieth-century Japanese revival of a traditional Asian practice (Murayama 2012). Japan (Claymone 2010; Natsuda et al. 2011) and Vietnam (Ngoc 1994) have villages which are known for having produced a particular craft product e.g. pottery, or basketwork for centuries. Some villages, or communities, became recognized for supplying royal courts with their special products. For example the craft village, Baan Baht, in the centre of Bangkok, is said to have been established by King Rama I to supply traditional monastic bowls.

Yet despite the small local scale of craft enterprises the sector can make a large contribution to national economies. In Thailand over half of cultural employment can be defined as Visual Arts and Crafts according to the UNESCO Framework for Cultural Statistics (2009). If this was an industrial sector then it would be the eighth largest employment sector in the Thai economy with 1.1 million employees. Over 800,000 of these employees are from four specific groups—manufacturers of jewellery, wood, baskets and textiles.[3] Admittedly many of these workers may be more engaged in larger scale production but the sheer numbers involved give a strong sense of the vitality in the production of these items.

Local Markets

The eco-local production of Asian crafts is matched, for the vast majority of products, with a concentration of local sales in which products have a clear function in the local market. This contrasts with the situation in OECD countries in which crafts are largely 'ornaments' and tend to be sold to tourists from outside the local community.

There were 71,739 OTOP products registered in Thailand in 2012 (Fig. 1), half were clothes or utensils (e.g. bowls, ladles…), over one quarter were food or drink, and just over 10% were herbal often medicinal products. Each OTOP product is prepared in a manner specific to the village concerned.

Studies of the Thai OTOP scheme (Natsuda et al. 2011; Phadungkiati et al. 2011; Kanthachai 2013) emphasize that even with government help OTOP producers struggle to get beyond local markets. In an early study Cohen (2000: 198–209) found that out of the four lowland villages two developed their own innovations, and two relied on 'outside' commercial organizations or retailers for new forms of pottery. Wherry (2008: 119) notes that OTOP artisans at Ban Thawai refused government suggestions to work in revamped storefronts as they realized this would detract from their 'authenticity' as far as foreigners were concerned.

Surveys (Table 1) of artisans in rural Bhutan (Askerud and Lo 2013), China (Lo 2011), and Indonesia (Lo 2014) show that most products were sold 'at home', and the surveys for China and Indonesia report

[3]These figures were compiled by Simon Ellis during work on the cultural and creative economy in Thailand in 2012–2013 and are derived from the Thai Labour Force Survey.

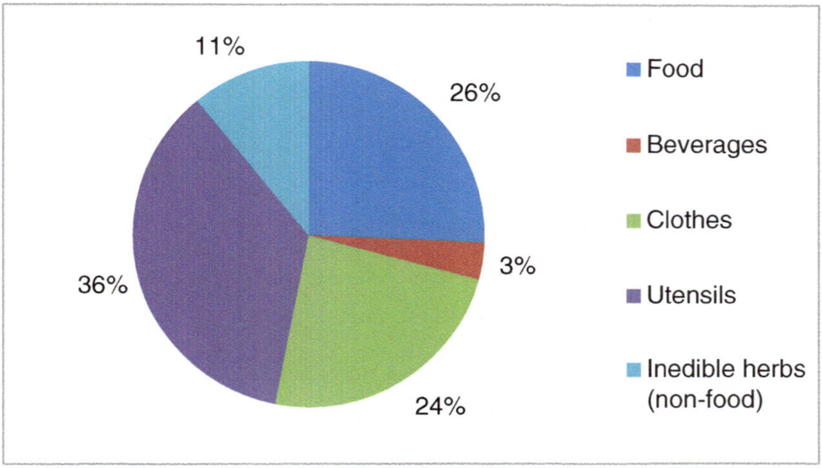

Fig. 1 OTOPs products registered 2012 by category (*Source* www.thaitambon.com)

Table 1 Sales points for craft items; most frequently cited by artisans

	China (%)	Indonesia (%)	Bhutan (%)
Home	76	37	70
Local market/Nearest town	71	31	22
Within the country/Major cities	29	0	24
International	14	0	0
Distribution based on orders	31	33	12

Source Bhutan (Askerud and Lo 2013), China (Lo 2011), and Indonesia (Lo 2014)

that over 80% of customers paid in cash. Of course the purchasers may have gone on to resell items elsewhere, but for the artisans themselves this was a local business.

The average reported longest distance for Chinese ethnic minority craft producers to sell their ware was 1219.75 miles while in Indonesia, the longest distance to sell their craft items was 12 miles. The average for the two surveys combined was 615.9 miles. This falls within Ruzek's (2014) proposed 1000-mile radius from production to market to be considered 'eco-localism' associated with a reduced carbon footprint and a sustainable production and distribution system.

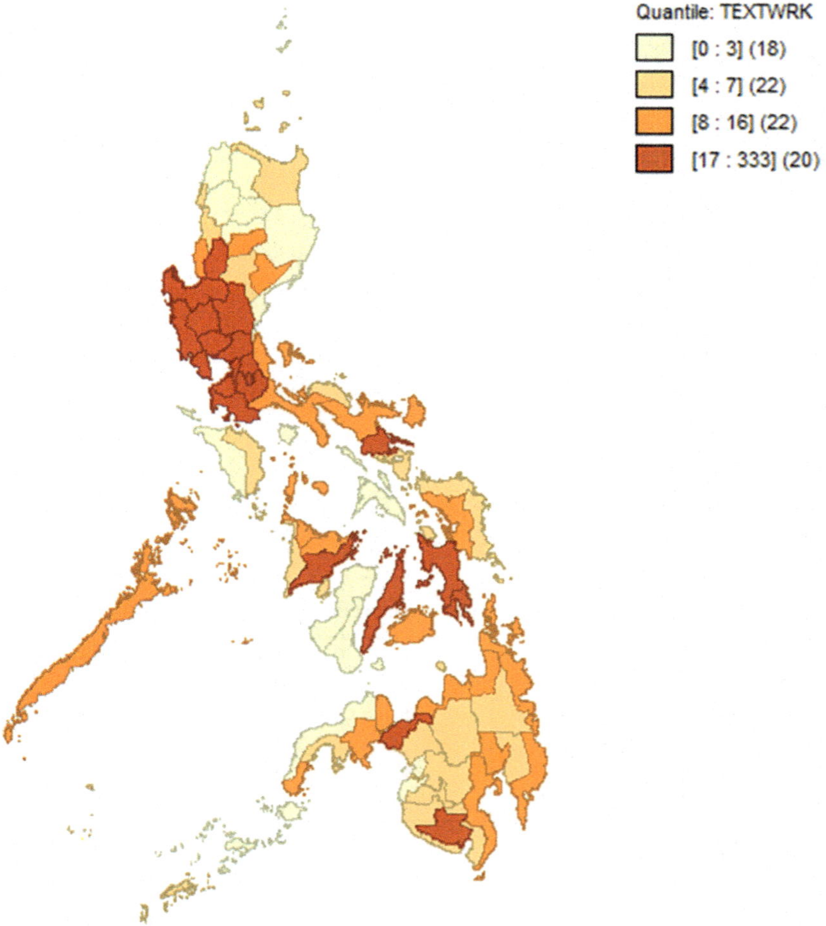

Fig. 2 Distribution of textile workers in the Philippines by province (*Source* PSA Labour Force Survey, April and July 2016)

In the Philippines local textile workers can be found in every part of the country (Fig. 2) and is not just an urban pursuit.

The link between local raw materials and local sales demonstrates that Asian craft production is driven by local demand. In this context craft objects are not 'ornaments' but usually fulfil functions relating to everyday life either in practical terms or as symbolic objects linked to local belief systems. This seems fundamentally different to craft objects in many OECD

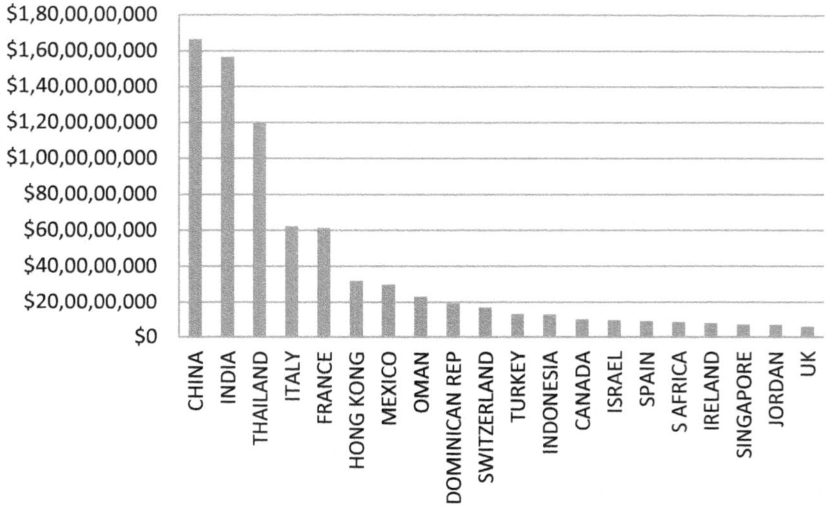

Fig. 3 Top 20 countries by value for jewellery imports into the USA (latest available year 2010–2013) (*Source* comtrade.un.org (2014))

countries which are seen as 'ornaments' or 'souvenirs'. Nonetheless, there is a growing appreciation of the skills and function of craft objects in more developed countries that is driven by a desire for quality products that are 'unique' rather than mass-produced (Echavaria 2013; Gibbs 2013).

Thailand competes with industrial giants India and China, for imports of jewellery into the USA (comtrade.un.org, Ellis 2014, 2015, Fig. 3). Admittedly the market is dominated by mass production, and assembly based on a range of standardized models rather than the work of individual craftsmen, but this evidence demonstrates that craft skills and local production can in some cases be scaled up to meet international markets. A similar process has for example taken place in Africa with basket production to supply US retail giants Macy's, Walmart and Whole Foods (Nkubana 2013). One basket is produced by one worker ensuring an individuality and 'craft' aspect to the final product no matter what the overall scale of production, and this is reinforced by a photo/label identifying the individual basket-maker.[4]

[4]Nkubana (2013) and personal communication to Simon Ellis.

Table 2 Sources of income for crafts producers, percentage of respondents

	China (%)	Indonesia (%)	Bhutan (%)	Average (%)
Sales of products	78	15	25	39
Support from family and friends	31	11	12	18
Personal savings	55	50	14	40
Income from other work	6	2	37	15
Loans from bank, credit unions or government	16	16	1	11

Source Bhutan (Askerud and Lo 2013), China (Lo 2011), and Indonesia (Lo 2014)

Entrepreneurship and Self Reliance

The association of Asian artisans with local economies and environments is strengthened by considering their financial models and sources of inspiration. Survey data (Table 2) suggest that external finance had very little place in supporting craft production.

Using the ten-year panel data from the Townsend Thai Project (townsend-thai.mit.edu). Nyshadham (2013: 10) has shown that village households which switched from agriculture to business throughout the period of the study were more likely to increase their income, than those who did not. Such 'entrepreneurial' households were more likely to have a younger head, to be larger, and to have a higher level of education (Nyshadham 2013: 11). Business start-ups as everywhere were fragile, and the longer a household was in business the less likely it was to fall back to agriculture as its main occupation (Nyshadham 2013: 16). While there was considerable churning the level of household business ownership was stable at 45% across the period of the survey (Nyshadham 2013: 12).

In the evaluation of micro-finance in Hyderabad, India, Banerjee etal.(2015) have argued that entrepreneurs used new loans for start-up, and following this were more likely to buy hard goods for private or business investment, while forgoing 'temptation' goods (e.g. alcohol, and tobacco). By contrast the Townsend Thai data suggests that entrepreneurs were more likely to take up loans *after* they had started their business than in the lead up to business launches (Nyshadham 2013). Cheewatrakoolpong and McKenzie (2013) report pace Townsend that OTOP producers without real estate still find great problems in finding loans to expand their businesses, though Natsuda et al. (2011) do confirm the Townsend data's suggestion by indicating that in Chiang Mai at least most OTOP producers started their business with their own money rather than a government loan.

Survey data suggest that while artisans think their income is lower than the average in their community it is actually above average. As discussed earlier (Table 2) artisans reported in the surveys that most payments were made in cash in the home, and few reported any difficulties in obtaining payment. The Philippine Labour Force Survey suggests that rural self-employed earn more in textiles than the rural self-employed in other sectors.

Thus while evidence on entrepreneurship is somewhat equivocal it suggests a high degree of self-sufficiency in which artisans obtained local cash payments and rarely relied on external financial support.

Innovation Without Education

Artisans in OECD countries are generally better educated than those in Asia. A survey of 32 OTOPs producers in Chiang Mai in 2009/2010 by Natsuda et al. (2011: 21) found that 53% were over 50 years old and thus would not have been exposed to the modern education system. By contrast a similar survey in Chiang Rai province found that OTOPs producers were generally women aged 41–50 with only elementary education (Kanthachai 2013), while the entrepreneurs in the Townsend dataset had an average age of 38 and 27% had completed primary education (Nyshadham 2013: 8). This profile is the same as that identified for Philippine hand weavers as discussed earlier. A survey of some 600 craftspeople in Jharkhand state, India, in 2009/2010 found that 28% were illiterate (PRUDA 2010: 47).

Figure 4 shows the education profile of artisans in other craft surveys compared with the relevant national populations. The Thai artisans

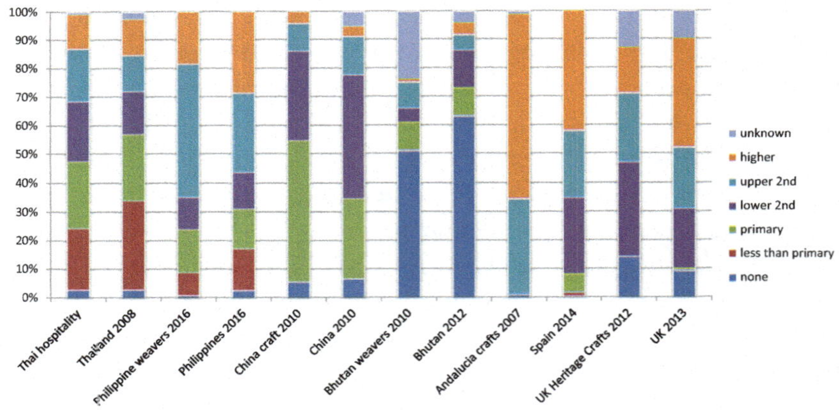

Fig. 4 Education profiles of artisans compared with the corresponding national population (*Source* Craft surveys (see Bibliography) and National Labour Force Surveys)

include both a substantial portion of graduates like the European examples, and a significant proportion of those with only primary education, more similar to the survey data (Askerud and Lo 2013; Lo 2011) in Bhutan and China.

In the surveys over half of crafts practitioners reported learning informally from family, friends and peers, only in China did a significant proportion (66%) of craft producers report taking part in any formal training. John Howkins (2007: 136) says that entrepreneurs 'use creativity to unlock the wealth that lies within themselves', or in the words of the villagers of the first One Village One Product (OVOP) centre at Oyama in Japan during the 1960s 'resources are limited, but wisdom is unlimited' (quoted by Natsuda et al. 2011: 6). Craft products demonstrate that innovation and creativity in products which demonstrate a mastery of complex skills do not require a university education. By contrast in OECD countries crafts producers tend to be people with artistic training who have turned to craft after a career or for whom craft is an activity to put alongside more lucrative employment. While education levels are rising in Asia as in all countries of the world Asian craft producers are still more likely to be inspired by their local community and environment than by the intellectual currents of higher education.

A Profile of Asian Craft Producers; Changing Demographics

Some elements of a profile of Asian craft producers have already emerged from the analysis above. They tend to live in rural locations, to be older, and to rely both for raw materials and sales on their local communities.

The gender mix for craft is highly dependent on the product. Rural Philippine textile workers emerge from the Labour Force Survey as mostly women over 50. The table below only shows a significant mix of both sexes in both China and Indonesia (Table 3).

It can be noticed that gender roles in most types of crafts are mixed, although there are still residuals of traditional roles in specific craft practices. This could suggest changing craft practices and currently, it is more flexible and open towards different genders involved in different types of craft practice.

Comparing the age range of the survey respondents (Table 4), it can be seen that artisans from China and Indonesia were older than those in Bhutan. Based on current trajectory of the age structure, the human resource for the industry is secured for the next 15–30 years (assuming that quality of work declines after 60 years old due to deterioration of eyesight, physical strength, etc.).

In terms of younger participants in the craft sector, the surveys found that there has been a decline. In Indonesia, only 9% of the workforce was under 30 years of age (Lo 2014). In Bhutan, although there was no information on the average age of weavers, the most active age for weavers was between 20 and 40 years of age while the largest concentration of weavers were between the ages of 25–29 (Askerud and Lo 2013). Notably 'relatively few young women weave which is unexpected… the young adults represent only 3–4 per cent of the weavers' (Askerud and Lo 2013: 11). In Thailand studies have suggested OTOPs workers

Table 3 Types of crafts and gender; Leishan and Longchuan counties, China and Borobodur, Indonesia

Types of craft	Leishan		Longchuan		Borobodur	
	Male (%)	Female (%)	Male (%)	Female (%)	Male (%)	Female (%)
Iron smithing (blades)			98	2		
Silver smithing (& Pewter)	98	2	84	16		
Embroidery		100		100		
Batik	47	53			67	33
Bamboo weaving			100		95	5
Wood work	100				100	
Pottery	100					
Stone carving	100					

Source Lo (2011, 2014)

Table 4 Average and dominant age of artisans

	China	Indonesia	Bhutan
Average age	37	44	-
Dominant age	31–45	31–45	25–29
Range (%)	51	56	21

Source Bhutan (Askerud and Lo 2013), China (Lo 2011), and Indonesia (Lo 2014)

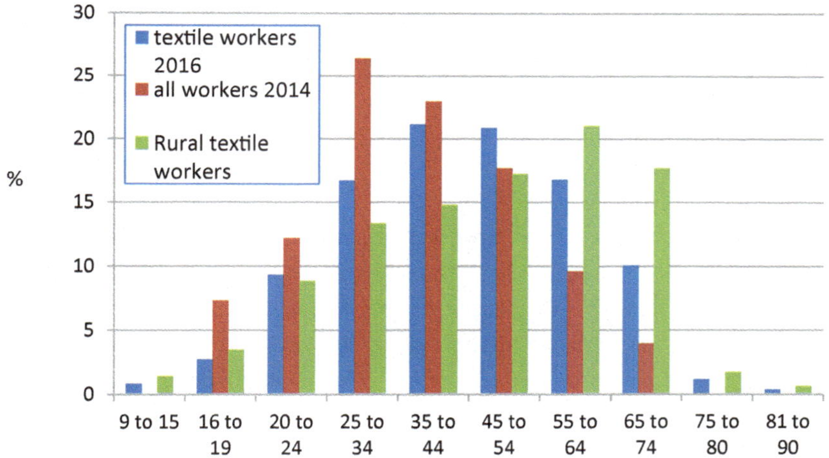

Fig. 5 The age profile of the Philippines workforce and textile workers compared (*Source* PSA Labour Force Survey, January and April 2016)

tend to be over 50 (Natsuda et al. 2011: 21; Kanthachai 2013), while the entrepreneurs in the Townsend dataset had an average age of 38 (Nyshadham 2013: 8).

In the Philippines the youngest textile workers are aged around 14 and the oldest in their 90s. The age profile of rural textile workers is particularly skewed towards those over 50 (Fig. 5). Informants state that younger children are used to 'knot' traditional fibre such as 'abaca' and 'pina' which are not spun like cotton (Respicio 2014). It can easily be imagined that old women in rural communities gain much status and independence in their communities through maintaining their great experience in weaving into old age. On the other hand as in many Asian craft traditions there is a growing risk that their skills will be lost to the younger generation.

In sum the age and sex of craft workers is closely linked to the production roles they have to play. While an older 'head of family' may be head of the business the whole family may have specific roles to play in the production process. This situation again emphasizes the way in which Asian craft production may still be closely linked to local ecological and social systems. Under modern social and economic pressures these divisions of labour may be under strain; so much so that certain crafts may be at risk of extinction if they do not adapt or receive government support.

Conclusion

National Statistics, surveys, and secondary sources all suggest that Asian craft production is based on local communities using local materials with local markets. Craftspeople throughout Asia have been recognized as Living Masters because of their great skill and yet many of them have little or no education. The economic contribution of craft can be very significant to local economies and can even make a significant contribution to national production.

A number of threats to Asian craft production can be recognized including scarcity of raw materials, and an ageing workforce. There are many pressures on craft producers to turn to cheap pastiches of cultural objects in order to sell them to tourists, but there are also signs that major North American and European retailers are recognizing a new demand for unique handmade products. Responding to this demand while maintaining functionality in the local economy may determine the future of craft production in many developing countries. If local communities in Asia are no longer able to maintain a link to functionality in local markets they too may see a broader move to ornamental, tourism-driven production and a loss of the skills base among today's older generation.

Acknowledgements and Note on Sources Simon Ellis worked on national statistics in Thailand 2012–2014 for UNESCO, and in the Philippines 2015–2017 for the Non-Timber Forest Product Group. This research involved direct collaboration with the national statistics offices of Thailand and the Philippines, as well as a Visiting Lectureship at Institute of Statistics, University of the Philippines at Diliman in April 2017.

Joseph Lo is currently a Curator for the Smithsonian Center for Folklife and Cultural Heritage. He was the lead technical officer for the implementation of craft surveys in Bhutan, China 2009/2010, and Indonesia 2014 for UNESCO and UNDP.

Bibliography

Algida. 2007. *Estudio de Mercado sobre Producciones Artesanales en los Territorios que component la acción conjunta de cooperación Artesanos Rurales Andaluces.* Rome: Junta de Andalucia & Partners.

Asia Development Bank and National Statistics Bureau of Bhutan. 2013. *Bhutan Living Standards Survey 2012.* Mandaluyong City: Asian Development Bank.

Askerud, P. 2010. *Bhutan Cultural Industries Sector Development; A Baseline Report 2009.* Thimphu: Ministry of Culture/Nat Bur Stats/UNDP.

Askerud, P., and J. Lo. 2013. *Bhutan Weavers Survey 2010.* Thimphu: Ministry of Culture/Nat Bur Stats.

Banerjee, A., E. Duflo, R. Glennerster, and C. Kinnian. 2015. The Miracle of Microfinance? Evidence from a Randomized Evaluation. *American Economic Journal: Applied Economics* 7 (1): 22–53.

Cheewatrakoolpong, K., and S. McKenzie. 2013. Specific Trade Facilitation Measures to Promote Export of Traditional Knowledge Based Goods—A Case Study of Mukdahan and Nakhon Phanom. ARTNeT Working Paper No. 123, Bangkok, ESCAP.

Claymone, Y. 2010. A Perspective on Culture and Technology Transfer of OTOP in Thailand: A Lesson from Japan. *International Journal of East Asian Studies* 15 (1): 111–118.

Cohen, E. 2000. *The Commercialized Crafts of Thailand: Hill Tribes and Lowland Villages.* Richmond: Curzon.

Curtis, F. 2003. Eco-localism and Sustainability. *Ecological Economics* 46 (1): 83–102.

Dept of Agriculture. 2015. *Abaca Value Chain Analysis Region V–Bicol Region.* Philippine Rural Development Program.

Echavarria, M. 2013. Craft as a Tool for Empowerment. In World Crafts Council ed. *Celebrating Crafts Kaivalam*, Chennai, pp. 45–48.

Ellis, S. 2014. Turning Craft into GDP in the Caucasus. In *Notion of Culture as a Force for Economic Growth—New Approach for South Caucasus*, ed. S. Ellis, 27–35. Tbilisi: GACC.

Ellis, S. 2015. *Measuring Traditional Skills (Taking Stock of What We Have Before We Lose It); Craft Statistics A Way Forward*. Washington, DC: Aspen Inst.

Fonchingong, C.C., and N.F. Lotsmart. 2003. The Concept of Self-Reliance in Community Development Initiatives in the Cameroon Grassfields. *Nordic Journal of African Studies* 12 (2): 196–219.

Galtung, J., et al. (eds.). 1980. *Self-Reliance: A Strategy for Development*. London: Bogle L'Ouverture Publications.

Gibbs, K. 2013. The Artisan Entrepreneur in the Global Market Economy. In *Notion of Culture as a Force for Economic Growth*, ed. S. Ellis, 95–98. Tbilisi: GACC.

Godfrey, P.C. 2008. What Is Economic Self-Reliance? *ESR Rev* 10: 4–8.

Howkins, J. 2007. *The Creative Economy*, 2nd ed. London: Penguin.

International Labour Organization. 2015. Transition from the Informal to the Formal Economy Recommendation, 2015 (No. 204): Recommendation Concerning the Transition from the Informal to the Formal Economy. 104th ILC Session, Geneva, Switzerland. Available at http://ilo.org/dyn/normlex/en/f?p=NORMLEXPUB:12100:0::NO::P12100_ILO_CODE:R204. Accessed 7 June 2017.

Jayachandran, S. 2006. Selling Labor Low: Wage Responses to Productivity Shocks in Developing Countries. *Journal of Political Economy* 114: 538–575.

Kanthachai, N. 2013. A Study of Development Strategies for OTOP in Chiang Rai. *SIU Journal of Management* 3 (1): 112–122.

Kenan. 2009. *Economic Contribution of Thailand's Creative Industries*. Kenan Institute Asia and Fiscal Policy Research Institute.

Kim, I., and I. Muhammad. 2013. Self-Reliance: Key to Sustainable Rural Development in Nigeria. *ARPN Journal of Science and Technology* 3 (6): 585–591.

Lo, J. 2011. *Chinese Ethnic Minorities Participatory Artisan Survey and Needs Assessment Report*. UNESCO/Chinese Arts and Crafts Assoc.

Lo, J. 2014. *Borobudur Cultural Mapping Report and Artisan Baseline Survey 2014*. Jakarta: UNESCO.

Murayama, H. (ed.). 2012. *Significance of the Regional One-Product Policy—How to Use the OVOP/OTOP Movements*. Thailand: Ritsumeikan University.

Natsuda, K., K. Igusa, A. Wiboonpongse, A. Cheamuangphan, S. Shingkharat, and J. Thoburn. 2011. One Village One Product—Rural Development Strategy in Asia: The Case of OTOP in Thailand. RCAPS Working Paper 11.3, Ritsumeikan University.

Ngoc, L.B. 1994. *Export Potential Assessment of Arts and Crafts in Vietnam.* Geneva: UNCTAD/VIetrade.

Nkubana. 2013. Power of the Handmade. In World Crafts Council ed *Celebrating Crafts Kaivalam*, Chennai, pp. 186–188.

Nyshadham, A. 2013. Learning About Comparative Advantage in Entrepreneurship: Evidence from Thailand. Available at townsend-thai.mit.edu. Accessed 26 May 2017.

OECD. 2011. *OECD Studies on SMEs and Entrepreneurship Thailand: Key Issues and Policies.* Paris: OECD.

Phadungkiati, L., K. Kusakabe, and P. Pongquan. 2011. Working for Money or Working for the Group? Community-Based Women's Rural Enterprises in Chainat Province Under the OTOP Project. *SIU Journal of Management* 1 (2): 39–72.

PRUDA. 2010. *Census of Handicraft Artisans.* Office of the Development Commissioner (Handicrafts), Ministry of Textiles, Government of India.

Punyasavatsut, C. 2008. SMEs in the Thai Manufacturing Industry: Linking with MNES. In *SME in Asia and Globalization*, ERIA Research Project Report 2007–2005, ed. H. Lim, 287–321.

Respicio, N. 2014. *Journey of a Thousand Shuttles; The Philippine Weaver.* Manila: NCCA.

Ruzek, W. 2014. The Informal Economy as a Catalyst for Sustainability. *Sustainability* 7 (1): 23–34.

Samphantharak, K., and R. Townsend. 2013. Risk and Return in Village Economies. Available at townsend-thai.mit.edu. Accessed 26 May 2017.

TBR. 2012. *Mapping Heritage Craft: The Economic Contribution of the Heritage Craft Sector in England.* London: Creative and Cultural Skills/BIS.

Tobgye, S.L. n.a. Education in Bhutan—Past, Present and Future: A Reflection. Available at http://www.judiciary.gov.bt/publication/education-CJB.pdf. Accessed 26 May 2017.

UIS. 2009. *2009 UNESCO Framework for Cultural Statistics.* Montreal: UNESCO Institute for Statistics.

UNESCO Bangkok. 2005. *The Jodhpur Initiatives: A Strategy for the 21st Century.* Bangkok: UNESCO Bangkok Regional Unit for Culture in Asia and the Pacific.

UNESCO Bangkok. 2007. *Statistics on Cultural Industries: Framework for the Elaboration of National Data Capacity Building Projects*. Bangkok: UNESCO Asia and Pacific Bureau for Education.

UN Thailand. 2011. *United Nations Partnership Framework Thailand 2012–6*. Bangkok: UN.

Wherry, F. 2008. *Global Markets and Local Crafts: Thailand and Costa Rica Compared*. Baltimore: John Hopkins.

A Cultural Economic Analysis of Crafts: A View from the Workshop of the World

John Ballyn

Most craft production has its roots in pre-industrial cultural heritage and tradition, finding or growing materials with which to make utilitarian products. Many tools and techniques used even today were developed or evolved thousands of years ago, often beyond historical record. Patterns, textures, dyes and finishing materials are also of ancient origin.

Yet crafts production has found a way to expand its manual production output to fit contemporary marketplace demands. India, for example, exported nearly US$ 3500 million worth of crafts to more than 13 nations during 2013–2014.[1] The Indian government has established a wide range of supporting bodies for handicrafts over the years, to provide skill training for artisans, undertake market studies, organise large

[1]Jahangir Ahmad Bhat and Pushpender Yadav. *Arabian Journal of Business and Management Review*: The Sector of Handicrafts and its Share in Indian Economy: Dec 2016. p. 4.

J. Ballyn (✉)
Independent Consultant, London, UK

A. Mignosa and P. Kotipalli (eds.), *A Cultural Economic Analysis of Craft*,
https://doi.org/10.1007/978-3-030-02164-1_15

trade fairs in India or participation in overseas fairs. There are agencies that design products and assist producers to make them.

P. R. China has perhaps 30% of the world's market for handicrafts.[2] Part of its success has been in the mechanisation of production, with development of simple machines to speed up production. Many artisans fill high volume orders simply by being organised into large centralised workforces. But the majority can still be small-scale units working as independent sub-contractors to entrepreneurs or customer agents, who consolidate individual artisan's output into shipments.

> Most of the products made in China are not considered as handicrafts, even though many are partially or fully handmade. China will produce anything that you will ask, better than anyone else, and at a better price, but these are not unique handicrafts like those being produced in other countries.[3]

In countries like India, China and the Philippines these supply chains are very well established and have considerable support from government departments specifically set up to facilitate exports, also providing artisans with subsidies/bonuses for those who export.

Another important factor is the rapid growth in both Chinese and Indian economies, which has meant that both nations have a growing number of their populations with the financial capability to buy modern crafts. So while there is a reciprocating exchange of crafts products between the two nations, both countries are also hoping to protect the sovereignty of their own producers. The definition of crafts and crafts production may also be challenged when quasi-industrial processes come into play.

For example: there were outcries in the Indian crafts community during 2011 when imports of industrially mass-produced sarees from

---

[2]Export Promotion Council for Handicrafts (EPCH) Brief Summary on Competitive study on Handicrafts Sector in China: EPCH.pdf. Available at http://www.epch.in/ChinaStudy/Summary.pdf.

[3]Professor Uma Suthersanen, Queen Mary University of London. Protection of Handicraft Goods and Traditional Cultural Expressions. p. 9. Available at 04_IP4GROWTH TM2_ Handicraft and Copyright Feb 2015_Suthersanen.pdf.

China apparently caused severe economic hardship to the handloom weavers of sarees in Varanasi, India.[4] It was not just that the Varanasi production rate was lower. More important was the fact that market demand for the cheaper Chinese sarees had a damaging impact on the output of finest quality sarees being made in India. The Indian middle-class market, like any other, wishes to buy the finest quality product; but does not necessarily have the money to buy them. The Chinese saw an opportunity and were successful until the government of India stepped into protect the Indian weaving community.

The challenges concerning design and product originality are very complicated, because crafts traditions of one region or country can be replicated in another. Macramé is thought to have originated among weavers in the Middle East during the thirteenthcentury.[5] Today it is possible to find macramé products being made by groups of women in almost every country in the world. In Kenya, famous for its carved wooden elephants, carved and painted wooden elephants originating in Sri Lanka have been offered for sale as authentic Kenyan crafts.[6] Basketry, from rattan, bamboo and grasses, is made with identical or similar weaving techniques wherever they are made in the world. This is because of the physical constraints imposed by the raw material, not because every technique has been copied from another region or country. Likewise, ceramic crafts have common making processes, and designs can be found in any magazine, or online websites.

Nobody actually knows how many crafts producers there are in the world, but the majority live in member nations of Africa, Asia and Latin America. For many, making crafts is a means of earning supplementary income in between working on the land; others earn enough from making crafts full time. A few manage to do well economically. Some are formally registered companies, NGOs, or operate under participatory

---

[4] *Hindustan Times*: Original Sin: Chinese Copies Ruin Banarasi Saris Weavers: January 5, 2011.

[5] Available at https://en.wikipedia.org/wiki/Macram%C3%A9. Accessed May 2017.

[6] The author, John Ballyn, made several visits to Kenya while living in Sri Lanka in the late 1980s. Here he found the Sri Lankan elephants in local Kenyan craft shops. The shop owners claimed that the products were made in Kenya.

management systems like co-operatives. But many are small and medium family enterprises; frequently operating in the informal sector.

To emphasise the challenges faced by the majority of the world's crafts producers it is necessary to look at the situation of modern western artisans. They are generally fully educated, and study in college for up to five years to gain a degree in their skill. They may go on to study for a Masters or Ph.D. in their subject. There are many support networks and institutions they can access, such as additional training courses in most aspects of business studies, with short-term and evening class courses being available in major cities. They might be able to obtain start-up funding when establishing workshops. Their output is usually low-volume, at most batch production of identical items.

There is access to IPP for the western artisan, with agencies such as Anti-Copying-In-Design (ACID),[7] founded in 1996 to provide advice and support to a wide range of entrepreneurs and artisans. ACID's purpose is stated on their website:

> ACID (Anti Copying In Design) is a membership trade organisation, set up as a round table action group in 1996, by designers for designers. ACID is committed to raising awareness & encouraging respect for IP within individual & corporate responsibility. By helping its members to understand and protect their rights, ACID is intent on stamping out intellectual property rights abuse.[8]

ACID's members pay a graduated fee, based upon the annual turnover of the member's business. For example, an enterprise with a turnover of less than UK£50,000 per year, would pay a basic annual membership fee of £140. For those with higher turnovers, such as between UK£250,000 and UK£500,000, the basic annual fee is £380.[9] The organisation publishes regular newsletters on current issues, collaborates

---

[7]ACID, Anti-Copying in Design is available at http://www.acid.uk.com/. Accessed May 2017.

[8]ACID, Anti-Copying in Design. http://www.acid.uk.com/what-is-acid.html. Accessed May 2017.

[9]ACID, Anti-Copying in Design. http://www.acid.uk.com/membership-fees.html. Accessed May 2017.

with mainstream creative media and also uses social networks to promote services and reinforce the importance of IPP. ACID maintains an IPP databank, which certifies the validity of any item registered there. There is provision of advice on IP matters, such as planning IP strategies for members' companies. ACID can help in finding mediators and provides free initial stages of legal assistance when challenging infringements. There are affiliations with EU, USA, ASEAN countries and P. R. China.

The world's main agency related to IP is the World Intellectual Property Organisation (WIPO),[10] which is a comprehensive provider of information for IPP. WIPO's web site says:

> WIPO is the global forum for intellectual property services, policy, information and cooperation. We are a self-funding agency of the United Nations, with 189 member states.
>
> Our mission is to lead the development of a balanced and effective international intellectual property (IP) system that enables innovation and creativity for the benefit of all. Our mandate, governing bodies and procedures are set out in the WIPO Convention, which established WIPO in 1967.[11]

WIPO has a wide range of publications about the application of IPP to the craft sector; available both in print and in downloadable .pdf format. There are also reports of workshops held in a number of countries,[12] exploring the challenges of making effective IPP systems for handicraft enterprises. WIPO has worked for many years to reach agreements about the types of protection available for handicrafts. The most commonly used include: Trademarks; Collective marks and certification

[10]World Intellectual Property Organisation (WIPO). http://www.wipo.int/portal/en/index.html. Accessed May 2017.

[11]World Intellectual Property Organisation (WIPO). http://www.wipo.int/about-wipo/en/. Accessed May 2017.

[12]World Intellectual Property Organisation (WIPO). Source: http://www.wipo.int/tools/en/gsearch.html?cx=016458537594905406506%3Ahmturfwvzzq&cof=FORID%3A11&q=Intellectual+property+protection+crafts. Accessed May 2017.

marks; Geographical Indications (GI).[13] Traditional Cultural Expression is another tool to protect heritage arts and crafts.[14]

While many artisans in Europe have told the author that the craft sector is not the best place to make a good living, it is certainly less precarious than for crafts producers living in developing or emerging economies. The levels of application of IPP in countries around the world are variable, but more importantly there are great differences between working as a crafts maker/artisan in the western world and being a crafts producer in a developing nation.

As mentioned above, many artisans in developing nations or emerging economies have less formal education, which can disadvantage them in competitive business environments. Most workers in small-scale informal sector crafts production learn their skills as children in the workshops of parents or other relatives. In recent years the Fair Trade movement has helped to improve working conditions for some artisans, but the vast majority are still at risk of exploitation. Small crafts enterprises have little economic security, being subject to the changes in market conditions. Many producers make large quantities of identical items using their hand technologies.

In certain instances markets may switch entirely away from one particular craft category, leaving the workers vulnerable. During the late 1970s, wood-block printers of Rajasthan, India enjoyed great success in the western markets, living very well, and supplying huge demand. At some point in the early to mid-1980s, the main fashions in western markets chose to move away from block-printed fabrics and started to use ikat textiles, a skill set not found in these particular Rajasthani block printing communities. The block printing communities suffered declining sales for several years because of a fashion change

---

[13]World Intellectual Property Organisation (WIPO). Source: Intellectual Property and Traditional Crafts. Wipo_pub_tk_5.pdf, p. 2. Accessed May 2017.

[14]Terri Janke. World Intellectual Property Organisation (WIPO) Case Studies on Intellectual Property and Traditional Cultural Expressions. 2003. Available at www.wipo.int/edocs/pubdocs/en/tk/781/wipo_pub_781.pdf. Accessed May 2017.

in the export market.[15] Because of this vulnerability through economics and market change, crafts workers dislike taking risks, having insufficient money to be able to sustain recovery from any mistakes.

Hundreds of thousands of crafts producers have little or no knowledge of basic business practices involved in running an efficient viable enterprise i.e. costing and pricing, quality control, marketing and promotion etc. They have an intuitive understanding of their domestic markets, raw materials, manufacturing, pricing, packaging and shipping procedures; but not necessarily as a strategic methodology in modern world markets. They can often use modern branded products in their homes, but do not appreciate that branding can be applied to their own enterprise.

They might watch satellite television, use mobile phones, own tablets or computer systems. Internet access is not necessarily beyond their reach, though electricity may be intermittent. With these modern information gathering tools they develop capabilities in exploring the market, looking for product ideas which they try to copy, and potential customers; with whom they may have difficulty in communication. In spite of their many disadvantages, all these crafts producers are very inquisitive about the realities of trading and enterprise management when they are given opportunities for discussion.

For many crafts producers around the world their main client is an entrepreneur, often described as a middleman. These middlemen have a variable reputation, but many of them are the only source of orders for handicraft communities. They often come from a major city where they have customers. They can control crafts producers' access to markets, domestic and export, wholesale and retail. The middleman provides product ideas to be made or copied, determines quality control and delivery schedules. Some provide advance payments to workers accepting an order. They often pay piece rates for making the products, a practice which applies much pressure on crafts workers. It is not

[15]Source: The author, John Ballyn, often worked in Rajasthan crafts workshops during the period 1979–1986, encountering block printers who spoke of the impact that the market shift to ikat had made on their income.

unknown for middlemen to take a design from one artisan and distribute it among several others, in order to reduce the price and increase the quantity. This artisan/middleman relationship is complex, having been intensely scrutinised over many years. While many middlemen can provide assistance to the producers with whom they work; these relationships are usually believed to be more beneficial to middleman than crafts producers.

In terms of creativity, crafts producers have not tended to develop new products as a business development strategy or an investment. Many new designs are simply traditional elements rearranged. Their ideas concerning what customers might prefer in terms of form, function and colour might bear no relation to the preferences currently in any marketplace. Crafts producers do not necessarily believe they can afford to regularly develop samples for which customers might not pay. Even though most Fair Trade customers do pay for samples provided, many commercial traders do not. Craftsmen and women are well aware that ideas they may have can be copied if designs are not carefully concealed from competitors. In spite of any controls, combined with the fairly relaxed nature of life in global crafts communities; there is always leakage of information. Never-ending strategic product development is one of the few actions crafts producers could use to counter IP infringement.

Few crafts producers outside the G7 countries[16] have sufficient detailed knowledge of Intellectual Property Protection (IPP) as a business activity. It might be difficult to access information for a multitude of reasons. Firstly, most current IPP activity is either handled nationally by IPP lawyers or agencies. These are often located in major cities, inconvenient for many crafts producers to locate. IPP legal language and arguments can be complex for crafts producers to understand. If the IPP agency is government owned, some craft makers might have diverse reasons for not wishing to become involved with it.

In order to appreciate how a craftsperson in a developing country or emerging economy might react to investigating potential of IPP for

[16]G7 countries include: Belgium, Canada, France, Germany, Italy, Japan, the Netherlands, Sweden, Switzerland, the United Kingdom and the United States.

his or her use; look at the web site for the UK Government web site Business and Self-Employed, and its section on Intellectual Property.[17] This is designed to be simple and straight-forward enough to be accessed by UK business personnel. There are 30+ headings to consider, many of them overlapping. There are activities and procedures to be followed. Before trying to register a design, one might have to check that it is indeed original and unique. In UK a government intellectual property office charges £25 to undertake a search of (a) national IP registers, (b) EU registers, and (c) WIPO registers to ensure that the product design being submitted is indeed unique.[18]

If all is well then illustrated submissions have to be prepared.[19] A craftsperson might have to obtain professional help in preparing material for submission. In the western context it is relatively easy for an artisan to prepare a submission themselves. In a rural town in a developing nation, it is likely to be complicated and probably expensive.

Registration fees for IPP will seem excessive to the individual crafts producer. In the UK government case above it costs UK£50 to apply for registration of one product, UK£150 for up to 50 products.[20] For most crafts there is no point in paying high registration fees for low-value products, which is one market being supplied by makers from less developed nations. Even for the western artisan registering product designs is complex and can be expensive. Licensing a registered product to another producer in the international craft sector level under consideration is a rarity.

Defending IP[21] is a prime reason for registering crafts products. If a product is being copied the maker is advised to talk to the copier.

---

[17]UK Government web site for Intellectual Property Matters. https://www.gov.uk/browse/business/intellectual-property. Accessed May 2017.

[18]UK Government web site for Intellectual Property Matters. https://www.gov.uk/register-a-design/check-if-you-can-register-your-design. Accessed May 2017.

[19]UK Government web site for Intellectual Property Matters. https://www.gov.uk/register-a-design/prepare-your-illustrations. Accessed May 2017.

[20]UK Government web site for Intellectual Property Matters. https://www.gov.uk/register-a-design/apply. Accessed May 2017.

[21]UK Government web site for Intellectual Property Matters. https://www.gov.uk/defend-your-intellectual-property. Accessed May 2017.

In many countries, the response would probably be laughter. Stepping up the action suggests using a mediator. Finding one in the typical craft community would be difficult. The final stage is taking legal action. In many countries lawyers' fees are beyond most Small and Medium Enterprise artisans.

Taking the UK model further, no IPP law firm shows a fee rate online, but an ordinary solicitor's fee rate can be seen below:

> What hourly rates do Solicitors charge?
>
> There is no straight answer to this. Across the many specialist areas of law, different scales apply, and the seniority of the solicitor needed for your case will have a significant effect on the final bill. Rates in the large cities are also significantly higher than elsewhere.
>
> Rarely do hourly rates dip below £100 per hour for the most junior of staff, while senior solicitors are usually charged at a rate over £200. You can see that it's vital to know both the hourly rate of the person dealing with your case – it certainly concentrates the mind when dealing with them.[22]

This seems to indicate that even a UK artisan could be challenged by having to find such fees. This tells us that (a) the product to be offered for IPP has to be significantly unique or special and (b) it has a market value worth protecting. For the majority of crafts producers this is not necessarily the case.

The UK government web site example is reasonably simple. The registration is easy and not excessively expensive. But infringement defence seems to be increasingly expensive as it moves along. The UK legal system functions because there is an apparent adherence to, and respect for, the law in the country. Crafts producers in many countries do not necessarily respect their legal system, because they see examples of the law being used against the disadvantaged. Then there is the money, the time lost, possible travel costs and time to find an IPP agent or

[22]Source: http://solicitorsfee.co.uk/solicitors-hourly-rates.html. Accessed May 2017.

lawyer. These costs are prohibitive to handicraft producers in a small or medium sized community.

In many countries it would take a lot of money and a long time to do anything in court. For most producers the existing system is very difficult to implement. If products range from U$5 to US25 per piece, they will probably have a market life of two to three years, before being replaced. In real life situations, it would be less frustrating if they set up a rolling product development strategy, providing customers with 10 or more new designs on a regular basis.

We have seen that of all the IPP types, there are some preferred in nations where crafts production is important. The WIPO publication "Marketing Crafts and Visual Arts: A Practical Guide" describes GI thus:

> A geographical indication is a sign used on goods that have a specific geographical origin and possess qualities or reputation that are due to their place of origin.[23]

Several countries have started to use non-agricultural GI to establish IPP for specific items.[24] Colombia has approximately 43 handicrafts registered under a GI system, which includes traditional hats, baskets and woodcarvings. The project also reports on damage to biodiversity, soil conditions, protection of traditional knowledge. Additional economic benefits to artisans have yet to materialise, as little information about importance of GI IPP has been disseminated to the crafts persons, nor is there sufficient government support to the communities in this regard.[25]

---

[23]International Trade Centre UNCTAD/WTO (ITC) and World Intellectual Property Organization (WIPO). *Marketing Crafts and Visual Arts: The Role of Intellectual Property: A Practical Guide*, Geneva: ITC/WIPO, 2003. xiii, 135 p., p. 10.

[24]Catherine Saez: Intellectual Property Watch: Panel: Protection of Handicrafts Gains Global Interest; Challenges Persist in the South: 09/12/2013: para 6.

[25]Johana Melgarejo Arzuza and Alessandra Giuliani: Tropentag 2014. Prague: Geographical Indications of Handicrafts: A Tool to Improve Livelihood and Protect Biodiversity in Remote Communities? p. 1.

In India, by 2012, some 220 products were registered under GI, 60% of which were handicrafts. The first craft product registered under GI was the Kashmir Pashmina in 2008.[26] Even though the registration is in place, both Nepal and China have launched or continue to run shawls of different quality known also as pashmina. Also there is no evidence of financial benefit to the Kashmiri crafts producers from GI registration, nor of any litigation originating from India challenging alleged infringements.

Mongolia has a large Cashmere wool industry producing raw wool and processed fibres. Since the reorganisation of the Mongolian Comecon economy to a global trading state, government has lost controls and organisation over nomadic life of herders. These movements impair the establishment of clear GI locations as reference. The whole cycle of operation lacks coordinated management to establish an IPP regimen that will eventually provide benefits to the herders.[27]

A variant of GI might also be a classification under Appellation of Origin:

> An appellation of origin is the geographical name of a country, region or locality, used to designate a product that originates there, and that has quality and characteristics that are due exclusively or essentially to the geographical environment, including human factors.
>
> Example: Bohemia crystal indicates that the product is manufactured in Bohemia, the Czech Republic, following the art traditions of the region.[28]

Collective marks and certification marks identify the source and quality of a product. For example:

---

[26] Sanjiv Singh, IGNOU New Delhi: Geographical Indication; A Case Study of Kashmir Pashmina (Shawls): 12 SanjivSingh.doc.pdf, p. 2.

[27] Nadja El Benni and Sophie Reviron, Swiss National Centre for Competence in Research: Trade Working Paper No 2009/15: Geographical Indications: Review of Seven Case-Studies World Wide: 2009: p. 19.

[28] International Trade Centre UNCTAD/WTO (ITC) and World Intellectual Property Organization (WIPO): *Marketing Crafts and Visual Arts: The Role of Intellectual Property: A Practical Guide*, Geneva: ITC/WIPO, 2003. xiii, 135 p., p. 10.

> Harris tweed is cloth that is hand-woven by the islanders of Lewis, Harris, Uist and Barra (Scotland) in their homes, using pure virgin wool that has been dyed and spun in the Outer Hebrides. The Certification Mark was first granted in 1909, registered in 1910, and stamping began in 1911. It ensures that all cloth certified with the Harris Tweed Orb symbol complies with this definition and is genuine Harris Tweed, the world's only commercially produced hand-woven tweed.[29]

Brands and Trademarks are not commonly used by crafts producers, simply because they have not learned that brands or trademarks have a value. The WIPO publication "Marketing Crafts and Visual Arts: a practical guide." describes these as:

> A brand or trademark is a sign or any combination of signs, capable of distinguishing a product or service from other products or services on the market. The main task of a trademark is to individuate a product or a service – consumers are able to distinguish between different goods with different marks precisely on the basis of the marks. Unlike other types of IP, the term of protection for trademarks is not limited; they can be renewed indefinitely by the owner.[30]

It would not be difficult for many crafts producers to establish themselves as a brand with a trademark. It requires some graphic design inputs, and the agreement of the enterprise. A trademark is part of an enterprise's identity, being used on business stationery and in promotions they undertake. Once registered it becomes protected from copying by competitors. If a producer group takes the path of registration, they must remember that consistent good quality is essential to their survival, because a trademark can be read as a symbol either good or bad quality for both company and product.

---

[29]Marketing Crafts and Visual Arts: The Role of Intellectual Property: A Practical Guide, Geneva: ITC/WIPO, 2003. xiii, 135 p. International Trade Centre UNCTAD/WTO (ITC) World Intellectual Property Organization (WIPO) 2003, p. 119.

[30]Ibid., p. 10.

Traditional Cultural Expression[31] has been used by Aborigine artists in Australia to protect their paintings from unauthorised use. In 1993, Banduk Marika, an Aboriginal artist from Yirrkala, Australia, successfully brought a case against a carpet company, Indofurn Pty Ltd, for copying a painting "Djanda and the Sacred Waterhole" and using it as a carpet design.[32]

The case of Terry Yumbulul V Reserve Bank of Australia raises an interesting situation, in that the Copyright laws of Australia do not recognise common ownership of heritage arts, so the use of commonly owned Aborigine images on Australian bank notes was found not to be a valid claim. This is possibly a flaw, because aboriginal peoples often regard all art as communal in origin, while the government does not. This case was lost.[33]

Major IPP agencies have not found it easy to address the needs of the majority of crafts producers because of the deep complexity of identifying, classifying and registering products, involving issues of historical priorities, ancient techniques, cultural issues and location. Agencies such as WIPO have been more involved with the whole IP spectrum around the world. Because crafts have not been a key priority for very long, some countries, like India, Colombia, and several others, are developing their own IPP systems using a combination of Certification of designs, Trademarks, Collective marks and GI.

Given the start by Colombia, India and other nations, what criteria should be considered when thinking of truly helping crafts producers protect their IP?

- The primary reason for IPP has to be the protection of cultural heritage, traditional skills and techniques, and artisan income in particular communities. By protecting cultural heritage there is likely to be continuity in employment. If support training is given in

[31]Emma Cohen: International Intellectual Property Institute: Intellectual Property Protection Options for Traditional Communities: 2012.

[32]Ms. Terri Janke. World Intellectual Property Organisation (WIPO), Minding Culture: Case Studies on Intellectual Property and Traditional Cultural Expressions: WIPO, 2003: p. 8.

[33]Professor Uma Suthersanen: Queen Mary University of London. Protection of Handicraft Goods and Traditional Cultural Expressions. p. 42. Available at 04_IP4GROWTH TM2_ Handicraft and Copyright Feb 2015_Suthersanen.pdf.

diversifying product development that suits contemporary markets, then the product base is strengthened. It will probably fall to national governments to establish or strengthen national IPP bodies and their affiliation to a global authority such as WIPO.

- National agencies, possibly independent of national government, should be easily accessible to crafts making communities or groups. Regional or even district IPP representation might be needed within countries, perhaps where there are a great number of crafts producers. These agencies need to build awareness of IPP as both a business tool as well as a protection to historical crafts skills. They could provide training to enterprises, promoting IPP as a community value.
- Some local craft producers could form their own groups, with affiliations to a national body. For example: Rattan furniture makers in Pangasinan Province in the Philippines; the woodworking crafts producers in Saharanpur, UP, India; traditional batik painters in Yogyakarta and furniture makers in Jepara, both in Central Java, Indonesia. In each location groups could be formed with a common interest in IPP for their own skills and locality.
- These self-forming groups might perhaps be fee-paying membership owned structures similar to ACID, UK, with scalable fees according to size or turnover of producer's group. They could operate using plain language, internet access, computer, tablet and mobile phone services to connect effectively with both local crafts producers as well as the national central IPP organisations. Local group management might be on a rotational basis, or electoral.
- IPP services should be supporting and educating artisans about reasons for protection, not necessarily protecting low-value products. Legal advice is necessary should a producer enquire about potential infringement or ownership disputes. In certain instances cases might need to be supported in court.
- National IPP agencies need to build awareness by introducing crafts producers to IPP issues through workshops; helping to establish best practice in implementation of IPP strategy for small enterprises.

References

ACID, Anti-Copying in Design. Available at http://www.acid.uk.com/. Accessed May 2017.

Arzuza, Johana Melgarejo, and Alessandra Giuliani. 2014. Tropentag 2014, Prague: Geographical Indications of Handicrafts: A Tool to Improve Livelihood and Protect Biodiversity in Remote Communities? p. 1.

Bhat, Jahangir Ahmad, and Pushpender Yadav. 2016. The Sector of Handicrafts and Its Share in Indian Economy. *Arabian Journal of Business and Management Review* S3: 4.

Cohen, Emma. 2012. Intellectual Property Protection Options for Traditional Communities. International Intellectual Property Institute.

El Benni, Nadja, and Sophie Reviron. 2009. Geographical Indications: Review of Seven Case-Studies World Wide. Trade Working Paper No 2009/15, Swiss National Centre for Competence in Research, p. 19.

Export Promotion Council for Handicrafts (EPCH). Brief Summary on Competitive Study on Handicrafts Sector in China: EPCH.pdf. Available at http://www.epch.in/ChinaStudy/Summary.pdf.

Hindustan Times. 2011. Original Sin: Chinese Copies Ruin Banarasi Saris Weavers. January 5.

International Trade Centre UNCTAD/WTO (ITC) and World Intellectual Property Organization (WIPO). 2003. *Marketing Crafts and Visual Arts: The Role of Intellectual Property: A Practical Guide*. Geneva: ITC/WIPO. xiii, 135 p., p. 10.

International Trade Centre UNCTAD/WTO (ITC). World Intellectual Property Organization (WIPO). 2003. *Marketing Crafts and Visual Arts: The Role of Intellectual Property: A Practical Guide*. Geneva: ITC/WIPO. xiii, 135 p., p. 119.

Janke, Terri. 2003. Case Studies on Intellectual Property and Traditional Cultural Expressions. World Intellectual Property Organisation (WIPO). Available at www.wipo.int/edocs/pubdocs/en/tk/781/wipo_pub_781.pdf. Accessed May 2017.

Saez, Catherine. Panel: Protection of Handicrafts Gains Global Interest; Challenges Persist in the South. Intellectual Property Watch, 09/12/2013, para 6.

Singh, Sanjiv. 2014. Geographical Indication; A Case Study of Kashmir Pashmina (Shawls). 12. IGNOU, New Delhi. SanjivSingh.doc.pdf, p. 2. November.

Suthersanen, Uma. 2015. Protection of Handicraft Goods and Traditional Cultural Expressions. Queen Mary University of London, p. 9. Available at 04_IP4GROWTH TM2_Handicraft and Copyright Feb 2015_Suthersanen.pdf. February.

World Intellectual Property Organisation (WIPO). http://www.wipo.int/portal/en/index.html. Accessed May 2017.

World Intellectual Property Organisation (WIPO). 2016. Source: Intellectual Property and Traditional Crafts. Wipo_pub_tk_5.pdf, p. 2. Accessed May 2017.

The Invisible Giant: Economics of Artisanal Activity in India

Ashoke Chatterjee

Artisans and those working with India's craft communities have been concerned that so little serious attention is given to the welfare of this gigantic sector of production and heritage, despite endless hype about past glories. Over decades, artisans have remained invisible in priorities of national planning and investment, pulled out of the wings only at times when culture needs show-casing. All this, despite acknowledgement even by Presidents that handcrafts are the nation's second largest source of livelihood, after agriculture. The sector's advantages go well beyond its scale of actual and potential employment, critical as these are today in the face of jobless growth. Crafts offer a brake on the miseries of migration into urban slums by providing non-agricultural rural livelihoods to people in their own locations. Demand at home and overseas for handmade quality is almost unlimited, a strength few industries can claim in the face of global uncertainties. As artisans largely comprise those still at the margins of Indian society—including

A. Chatterjee (✉)
Crafts Council of India, Chennai, India
e-mail: ashchat@prabhatedu.org

A. Mignosa and P. Kotipalli (eds.), *A Cultural Economic Analysis of Craft*,
https://doi.org/10.1007/978-3-030-02164-1_16

women, tribal communities and minorities—the sector provides an important safety-net, particularly in remote and deprived locations. In an era threatened by climate change, hand production offers a low carbon footprint and the promotion of local materials, while cultural and spiritual factors of identity and self-worth go beyond statistical calculations into the heart of India's civilizational values.

While no other industry embraces such a range of opportunities for equity and sustainable growth, there is also its legacy of history, stretching from the dawn of history to the struggle against colonial domination led by Mahatma Gandhi and Rabindranath Tagore. It is they who for the first time in human history, placed crafts at the centre of a movement for freedom. With Independence, artisans were positioned within a framework of centralized planning, another global first. Seventy years later, the contrast is striking. The sector today is characterized by a pervasive mood of neglect, loss and anxiety. Weaver suicides are one tragic indicator. Others include the failure of a long list of official schemes to reach those for whom they are intended, and 'reforms' that are insensitive to the structures and value of hand production. One example is a move not long ago by the ministry charged with the welfare of weavers to attach machines to handlooms on the pretext of lifting productivity. The 'reform' would have destroyed at one stroke what distinguishes Indian textiles from the rest of the world. It was defeated not because the notion was patently absurd, but because weavers all over the country threatened a revolt in what was an election year. The rush into measures that can be devastating to an industry characterized by its dispersal and inaccessibility to services is now exemplified by demonetization and a new General Sales Tax (GST) regime, the latest sources of havoc inflicted on a huge sector still invisible to those who should know.[1] Perhaps most remarkable is such ignorance in a nation that is heir to a Freedom struggle that made hand production its catalyst, and used its power to overthrow the mightiest empire in history.

[1]Taxing the Artisan, Jaya Jaitly. *Indian Express*, New Delhi, 02.09.2017.

The Power and Burden of Legacy

That legacy reflects a time in which the charkha spinning wheel, hand-spun and hand-woven khadi, village industries and the 'Buy Indian' swadeshi movement together expressed a conviction that crafts could provide both emancipation and self-reliance, translating freedom as social and individual well-being. With Independence came yet another demonstration of the power of so-called cottage industries: first to manage the horrors of Partition by offering livelihood and dignity to women refugees traumatized by its violence, and then as craft exports for earning scarce foreign exchange that could help create infrastructure for India's industrialization. The centrality of hand production to the economic fabric was reflected in centralized national planning within which crafts were integrated, beginning in 1951 with India's First Five-Year Plan. India thus became the first emerging economy to position artisans and their crafts firmly within a development framework.

Craft production now demanded markets, particularly in urban centres. A response came from early pioneers in craft marketing: the iconic Central Cottage Industries Emporium in New Delhi, Contemporary Arts & Crafts in Bombay (now Mumbai), the Sona outlets established overseas by India's Handloom & Handicraft Export Corporation (HHEC), the national chains of Handloom House and Khadi Bhavans, and then in brands that included Cooptex, Fabindia, Shyam Ahuja and Anokhi—all helping to define a modernity that was Indian and yet global, offering hand production as a contemporary lifestyle that could communicate to new generations in new markets. Activists from civil society across the country created a vanguard of craft development institutions, and design entered the vocabulary of transformation.

Almost seven decades later, the Twelfth Five-Year Plan declared in 2012 that 'handloom and handicraft sectors have their roots in the *rich traditional, historical and cultural diversity that distinguishes India from the rest of the world*'[2] (author's emphasis). Yet that very year witnessed the absurd notion of motorized handlooms, indicative of powerless

[2] *Twelfth Five-Year Plan*, Planning Commission, Government of India, New Delhi, 20.12.2016.

artisans and the clout of lobbies for whom mechanization is the only acceptable modernity. With transformational shifts in economic, social and political contexts across the world, India's artisans and their crafts came to be regarded by some influential decision-makers as embarrassing hangovers of a past that needed to be discarded along with snake-charmers and maharajas. The term 'sunset industry' now came to be applied as justification for sinking past irrelevance so that India could achieve the image of a world power poised at the cutting edge of technology. To others, an India without its crafts was an unthinkable proposition.

Cultural Industries in a Globalized World

The dichotomy demanded understanding, and a search began for craft relevance in a world transformed by free-trade pressures. Craft activists were in the forefront, familiarizing themselves with an emerging concept of creative and cultural industries that the World Bank in 2000 introduced to help define legacies of heritage that could assist economies on the brink of globalization. Five years later, a UN/World Bank-sponsored gathering in historic Jodhpur would identify craft as the largest component of India's creative and cultural industries—a sector recognized today as an engine of growth and stability, and as perhaps the largest industry in the world, outstripping petroleum, and constituting some 3% of world GDP. At home, those who matter appeared not to be listening, even as one official report estimated that these industries were already engaging over 45% of India's workforce.[3]

A welcome signal for craft activists finally arrived, but not from India's Gandhian past, nor from this most recent international awakening. Instead, it came from recognition in the European Union (EU), by east Asian 'Tigers' and elsewhere that artisans and their crafts offer a seedbed of creativity and innovation that translate as huge competitive

[3]Report of the Working Group on Art & Culture, 11th Five Year Plan 2007–2012. Planning Commission, Government of India 2007.

advantages in the global marketplace, with a relevance that goes well beyond the handmade towards a pervasive culture of quality that can be indispensible to survival and success in competitive markets. Japan, Korea, Scandinavia and then China offered examples, further symbolized by an astonishing slogan that originated in the EU: 'The future is handmade'.[4] Indian activists contacted European colleagues: what did this slogan really mean? Surely the EU was not contemplating closing its factories and returning to cottage industries? The response was swift: the issue for Europe was not the abandoning of mechanization. It was the promotion of creativity and innovation, qualities non-negotiable in the context of global trade and stringent competition. Historically, these qualities are rooted in cultures of craftsmanship, which Europe had largely lost through its Industrial Revolution and all that followed. The EU could now take a lesson from Asian economies that had realized the critical need to protect craft cultures, not only as national pride but also to build domestic and export markets with a strong national identity: using a craft past to address a competitive future. India's unique advantage as the world's largest resource of craftsmanship was looked upon with envy, as well as with concern that an emerging Indian giant might unleash yet another wave of competition to rival that of Japan, China and Korea. While the dismissive 'sunset' syndrome at home made this unlikely, activists at home wondered what it would take to change attitudes.

The Challenge of Data

Advocacy efforts by the Crafts Council of India (CCI) and its partners quickly revealed that at the heart of this challenge was the absence of reliable data that could communicate the scale of artisanal contributions to the national economy. Without a convincing economic argument, other craft advantages would remain clouded, and the giant

[4]The Future Is Handmade: The Survival and Innovation of Crafts. *Prince Claus Fund Journal* #10A 2003, The Hague.

consigned to invisibility and rituals of periodic obeisance. The claimed status of India's second largest source of Indian livelihood after agriculture now required robust evidence. Official estimates of over 11M artisans (over 4.3M weavers in the handloom sector and almost 7M other craftspersons) have remained largely unchanged since India's Twelfth Five-Year Plan emerged in 2012. Other estimates have ranged from 73M to 200M, depending on how craft definitions are selected, and which craft processes are included. In 2015, yet another estimate reckoned that 250M artisans were organized into some 600,000 cooperatives across the country.[5]

Inevitably, the confusion over numbers and definitions has led to neglect within national systems of accounting, easing the way for a 'sunset' syndrome which quickly dismisses anything that cannot be measured with statistics. Dialogue with the Planning Commission and Ministry authorities indicated that this situation would continue unless a methodology emerged that could help define crafts and artisans with the clarity essential for national accounting. With encouragement of partners and central authorities, and with a small grant from the Tata Trusts, CCI undertook an exercise in craft pockets of Tamil Nadu and Gujarat to attempt the design of such a methodology. Following almost two years of field work with economist advisers, CCI's *Craft Economics & Impact Study* (CEIS) was brought back to the Planning Commission and others for critique in 2012.

CEIS findings then encouraged the Government of India to include artisans for the first time in the Economic Census 2013. As Census schedules were about to unroll, it was decided to adhere primarily to major crafts under the purview of the Ministry of Textiles, where Offices of the Development Commissioners for Handlooms and for Handicrafts are located. CCI partnered with the Central Statistics Office (CSO) of the Ministry of Statistics & Programme Implementation in an emergency effort to quickly train Census

[5]More Than Jobs, India Must Churn Out Job Creators, Ravi Venkatesan, *Sunday Times*, 15.03.2015.

managers and enumerators to understand and identify the selected crafts and artisans. The experience across India proved transformational, offering fresh insights and future directions. Earlier, it had been pointed out that the Economic Census 2013 would provide only broad indications of the sector, within the constraints of the 'economic establishments' as defined for Census purposes as well as a restricted list of handcrafts. These constraints were significant: many artisans fall outside the CSO/EC understanding of 'economic establishments' while crafts with major livelihood and output implications are outside the purview of the Ministry of Textiles. It was explained that EC2013 would be a beginning in a national effort at improving sector data, to be followed by a 'Satellite Account' specific to handmade industries, designed and conducted with an exclusive focus on hand production in its own right.

EC2013 findings are now under review, and its inclusion of artisans for the first time has proved a watershed. Findings have led to a number of issues under discussion by CCI and its partners with the CSO as well as with NITI Aayog that now replaces the Planning Commission in matters of economic overview. As a next step, it has been suggested that on the basis of data collected by CSO through the EC2013, CCI undertake sample-surveys to investigate issues arising from the new data, helping to unpack issues critical to the design and implementation of the proposed 'Satellite Account'. NITI Aayog has offered research facilities to hasten field work, and CCI is now seeking expert advice in order to move forward in these directions. The tasks ahead include prioritizing data requirements so as to ensure the strong focus required to measure such a vast and diverse sector. A thorough study of all existing sources of craft data will be needed, to glean information and clues towards the 'Satellite Account' objective. Areas of clarification in EC2013 findings will need sharp definition so that the sample-survey strategy is made specific to handicraft and handloom characteristics of process, participation and output. Locations will need to be carefully selected to reflect the most critical characteristics, and partnerships forged to provide guidance and field support.

Guaranteeing Indian Livelihoods: An Emerging Crisis

Data on the sector's contributions to employment and national productivity have taken criticality in a current context of building employment opportunities for some 800M vulnerable Indians. The need for new jobs each year is estimated at between 10M and 15M, while a frightening prospect of 'jobless growth' grows as new technologies enter the mechanized sector. India loses an estimated 550 jobs a day, and there is a growing anxiety of overseas pressures within its 'sunrise' IT sector. Controversy surrounds official claims of over new jobs created annually, and increasing attention is now drawn to India's so-called 'informal sector' that still accounts for over 90% of the national workforce, including artisans. The Indian government has identified 4000 traditional product manufacturing clusters that include handlooms, handicrafts and other traditional products.[6] It is here that outreach is essential to provide the capacities young artisans now demand: entrepreneurship, language, e-commerce and marketing savvy and access to design and technology. If it is acknowledged that only low-technology, labour-intensive strategies will create jobs for rural millions, could an improved system of national accounting of artisans and their crafts offer silver bullets of knowledge, wisdom and investment opportunity? Could robust data help transfer millions into a mainstream of dignity and hope? If data alone cannot provide all the answers, could it at least reveal the strength and capacity of a giant waiting in the wings with extraordinary advantages? To these advantages can be added yet another: the giant's grasp in these challenging times of a pervasive word and an elusive concept, *sustainability*.

---

[6]Six Steps to Job Creation, Santosh Mehrotra, *The Hindu*, New Delhi, 14.10.2017.

The SDG Opportunity

Today, the UN's Sustainable Development Goals[7] (SDGs) are the global mandate for understanding and measuring progress as equitable and inclusive growth, and not just as per capita and GDP calculations. Few human activities can match as craft does the potential of such a charter, or embrace of so many of its goals: combating poverty, growth that is sustained and inclusive, full and productive employment that translates as decent work for all, gender equity, industrialization that fosters innovation, employment that reduces inequalities, sustainable communities that are safe and resilient, responsible patterns of consumption and production to protect the planet and those who live on it, action to combat climate change, and opportunities for global partnership. Twelve years down the road, in its need to bring crafts and artisans back into national consciousness, and with SDGs as a welcoming and enabling environment, India can return to the symposium it hosted in 2005 on creative communities. It had culminated in the *Jodhpur Consensus on Cultural Industries*,[8] recognizing crafts as 'a source of capital assets for economic, social and cultural development' and as 'a vital source for the cultural identities of communities and individuals which lead to further creativity and human development…What cultural industries have in common is that they create content, use creativity, skill and in some case intellectual property, to produce goods and services with social and cultural meaning'. Over a century ago, the visionaries who would lead India to freedom had advocated a similar path, taking its meaning into the heart of their historic struggle and then into free India's blueprint for growth. Today that direction retains relevance in an India and in a world so transformed since those times, reminding us of the stability, hope and quality that artisans and their crafts have gifted this country for centuries.

[7]Transforming Our World: The 2030 Agenda for Sustainable Development, UN General Assembly Document, New York, September 2015.

[8]Symposium: Asia-Pacific Creative Communities, Jodhpur (Rajasthan, India). UNESCO 2005.

References

Dadi, I. 2004. *The Future Is Handmade: The Survival and Innovation of Crafts*, vol. 10. The Hague, Netherlands: Prince Claus Fund.

Jaitly, J. 2017. Taxing the Artisan. *The Indian Express*, September 2.

Mehrotra. 2017. Six Steps to Job Creation. *The Hindu*, October 14.

Planning Commission. 2008. Report of the Steering Committee on Art & Culture for Eleventh Five Year Plan (2007–2012).

Planning Commission. (2012–2017). *Twelfth Five-Year Plan.* New Delhi: Government of India.

United Nations. 2015. Transforming Our World: The 2030 Agenda for Sustainable Development. *Resolution Adopted by the General Assembly.*

Venkatesan. 2015. More Than Jobs, India Must Churn Out Job Creators. *The Times of India*, March 15.

Measuring the Economics of Traditional Craft Production

Simon Ellis

Introduction

Craft or artisanal production is an elusive concept. Even leading specialists and artists disagree on its key qualities. On the one hand most people would agree that craft should be handmade. On the other hand many artisans use some form of machinery whether it is a powered loom, or a powered potter's wheel. It may be said that craft is produced by one person but there are enterprises or co-operatives involving hundreds of workers all of whom are producing unique products. Another key dimension is the use of 'natural' materials. In the case of textiles it can be hard for some kinds of garments to be based purely on 'natural fibres'. For textiles and paintings an issue is the use of modern 'chemical', as opposed to 'natural' dyes. Many specialists will accept a certain amount of use of 'chemical' colours, but some reject their use almost completely. Last but not least craft objects have to have some form of cultural association. This may be manifested in a particular

S. Ellis (✉)
Montreal, Canada

A. Mignosa and P. Kotipalli (eds.), *A Cultural Economic Analysis of Craft*,
https://doi.org/10.1007/978-3-030-02164-1_17

design, or particular materials. A craft product may have a particular form such as the Indian sari, but sometimes the cultural association may be less apparent, especially to someone from a different culture. An object which reflects most of these conditions; natural materials, handmade, strong cultural associations is often described as 'authentic' in other words a genuine expression of a particular culture or community. A much-simplified object with the same overall form but made from plastic or with over-simplified ornamentation will not be seen as 'authentic' and will probably not be considered 'craft' and is more likely to be seen as a mass-produced tourist souvenir or ornament.[1]

Given these complexities in definition it is not surprising that it becomes very difficult to establish a broad-based economic assessment of craft production. It may be impossible to place a consistent value on 'authenticity'. Value can vary considerably depending on the relative position of the valuer. A person from the same culture as the artist may value an item more highly than others if as an expert he considers it 'authentic', or he may value the item less than people from other cultures who may see the item as 'exotic' or styled in a way that particularly appeals to their aesthetic tradition. Globalisation risks downplaying 'authentic' characteristics and valuing those characteristics that appeal to North American and European tastes. Some 'masters' work may become 'visible' to collectors and highly valued, while others artisans work may be neglected.

This relativistic valuation of different cultural and aesthetic attributes is also accompanied as in some art markets by exchanges which happen outside the regular market system. Craft like other cultural and artistic products is often the subject of gifts, inside local communities families may exchange products in which each is skilled, e.g. pottery for blankets. In Asian countries it has been common for centuries for entire villages to specialise in particular products with exchanges between villages used to obtain a range of local products (see Ellis and Lo, Chapter 1). In the case of artists with an international reputation the art market has a clear view of their relative skills reflected in the relative value of art

[1]Some discussion of these difficult points can be found in UNESCO (2005: 3–18) and Borges (2011: 21–26).

auctions. In the case of craft there can be much dispute about the level of artistic input into a work and thus its 'true' value.

Traditional economists consider that many of these factors are resolved 'in the market', where seller and buyer approach the purchase with a large degree of shared information and agree a price based on the relative value of the item to both sides. Particular factors which cannot be accounted for in the transaction, perhaps including the very different cultural associations a craft object may have in different contexts are considered 'externalities' outside the immediate control of market forces.

This paper considers measurement largely from a national and international perspective. That is it adopts a more meso or macro-economic perspective. It focuses on economic data which can be presented at national level or higher. Geographically it is more concerned with development economics and tends to concentrate on craft production outside the OECD. Though many of the approaches it espouses can be applied in the OECD countries inevitably there are many more data sources, especially at a national and local level. It summarises a long-term personal initiative to improve the statistics and measurement of craft and artisan activities.

Classification and Approaches

One immediate approach that both economists and statisticians pursue is to introduce a systematic classification of products, workers and businesses. Such systematic classifications help standardise what is meant by craft and, at least make it clear which items are included in the figures and which items are not. In this sense even if the concept of craft production is unclear, the operationalisation of the concept in economic analysis is not. Furthermore adoption of such standards avoids items being counted twice. For example the standard forces authorities to decide whether leather belts should be included with leather shoes or with leather clothing. This is obviously a matter of whether one sets the standard as following leather-making as a production process or clothing as opposed to footwear.

The international bodies which create such standards do so through committees of experts from a range of different kinds of country worldwide, a mix of different continents, large and small countries, etc. The standard is then adopted by National Statistics Offices around the world. Items may be classified in different ways depending on the function of the classification. The two most important ones for craft are the International Standard Industrial Classification (ISIC) for industry/services, and the International Standard Classification of Occupations (ISCO) for types of job. The different approach and function of the two can be easily demonstrated. I work for a major jewellery manufacturer the company is classified ISIC 3211 'Manufacture of jewellery', but I am a chief financial officer so my job is an accountant. Thus I could be said to be working in a craft company/industry, but I am not a craftsman. If we are looking at the economic output of the jewellery sector we would normally include everyone working in that sector whatever their job. If we are counting the number of people making jewellery, as an accountant I would not normally be counted.

The UNESCO Framework for Cultural Statistics (UIS 2009) takes all the relevant statistical classifications and lists the statistical codes which are relevant for cultural activities including craft production. It includes the coding systems for production activity, occupations, products, exports & imports, consumption (household spending on cultural activities), time use (time spent on culture). For the non-specialist the most relevant classifications are jobs (ISCO) which we have already met above, and products. At national level the classification of products is not very well systematised and the most important international classifications of products concern exports and imports. This information is collected by customs offices around the world using the Harmonised System (HS) and the Standard International Trade Classification (SITC), and is concerned with physical goods, the 'type' of product, the weight and the value. When we are considering craft items this gives a natural preponderance to jewellery (HS code 7113 and subcodes) which through its use of precious stones and metals is both very dense and very valuable.

The classifications considered so far are all about production, but not consumption. Consumption can be judged through sales figures, but normally it is measured through surveys of household expenditure.

The international standard for this measure is the Classification of Individual Consumption by Purpose (COICOP). Unfortunately while the classification distinguishes activities such as spending on visits to performances it does not include any codes which might be specifically linked to crafts. Similarly the international classification for use in Time Use surveys (ICATUS) specifies performance, e.g. of music, in the home but has no craft related category.

In 2005 UNESCO proposed a classification of craft products based on material (UNESCO 2005). This has the benefit of clearly identifying when a product is made of 'natural' materials, and links the products back to the local environment. However the classification makes it hard to classify the many objects which are made of more than one material and does not classify objects by the more functional attributes with which the general user is more familiar. By adopting a classification purely by material it makes it hard to link the resulting data to national statistics thus divorcing the data from regular comparison with other sectors of the economy.

In general it is best to use some form of classification which aligns with national statistics. Only by aligning with national statistics will craft be seen within the context of the economy as a whole. National Statistics are also the basis for government policymaking. By aligning with national statistics craft studies are thus able to prove the importance of the craft when compared with other manufacturing sectors.

National Statistics—The Labour Force Survey and Household Expenditure

The Labour Force Survey (LFS) is conducted in the vast majority of countries. Conventionally it takes place every three months using a 'rolling' sample, which allows the data from each quarter to be aggregated into an annual total. Where the survey takes place every three months this can be important for craft production in developing countries as it may be a seasonal activity related to the agricultural cycle or tourist high season.

The LFS is the main source of information on the workforce and is conducted through households. This means that it is the best way to pick up data on household manufacture. Although the occupation classification ISCO does not allow a clear distinction to be made between machine-made and handmade production, by triangulating with other variables in the survey craft workers can be identified. Craft production in general is subsumed under major code 7—Craft and related Trade workers. Under this there are five two digits subcodes. The most relevant are 73—handicraft and painting, and 75 workers in wood and textile.

For example analysis of the Philippines LFS indicated that almost half of all rural textile workers were women over the age of 55. Such workers in rural areas are much more likely to be local artisans working from home, and most probably using hand rather than mechanised looms. Similar distinctions could be made for the production of furniture, jewellery, basketwork, and less clearly glass or ceramics (these last might include products such as, e.g. bricks).

The importance of women and often older women to craft production is commonly observed, but may sometimes be hidden or under-estimated in national statistics. Surveys such as the LFS often interview the 'head of household' who is usually a man. Male heads of household may minimise the contribution of other household members such as women and children. Villagers or members of minorities may fear government interference or prosecution for child labour or for unpaid taxes. The Philippine LFS 2016 records children as young as nine involved in textile production. Traditionally children work as 'knotters', tying together abaca or pina fibres, during lunch breaks or weekends (Respicio 2014).

Another key survey is the Household Expenditure Survey. This uses a standard set of categories for household spending which include a loose cultural and recreation activity group. Household expenditure surveys also tend to collect information on household income. I have long thought that this information could be used to calculate some element of income due to craft production, expecting that the non-agricultural income of rural households, especially as concerns female household members might be attributable to craft. However examination of individual data form the Philippine Family Income and Expenditure Survey 2009 only revealed a very small number of respondents citing manufacturing income as a supplement to agricultural income and the matter must remain conjectural pending further analysis.

Such surveys of household finance form the basis for national estimations of the level of poverty. Thus a further important point to test, if craft income is identifiable, would be the degree to which such income has raised families above the poverty line. This could then become the basis for argumentation of the degree to which craft production prevents poverty. It is for example a regular occurrence in craft surveys that artisans feel they are poorer than others, but in reality they have a higher income than other families in their communities. Workers in two Chinese craft surveys felt they earned less than other villagers, but in fact they earned four or five times more (Lo 2011: 7–9). Survey evidence from Bhutan (Askerud and Lo 2013: 18) suggests that weaving sales made up 15% of overall household income.

It is also likely that craft manufacturing activity is under-reported in general as such activity is often a secondary job. All forms of artist are often unable to have a steady income and resort to a more 'paying' job to finance their art. In this way although such artists may consider their art their primary job they are obliged to be included in the data for the 'more conventional' job through which they earn a living. In theory the LFS methodology, like that for Household income, records second jobs, but in practice few countries include the nature of second jobs in their database.

In sum household surveys as conducted by national statistics offices offer great potential for measuring the extent of craft activity and its economic impact, but the data need to be subject to careful and well-informed interpretation.

National Statistics—Business Surveys

Most countries conduct some form of business sample survey, but they are often only carried out irregularly every few years. Countries often also conduct Business Censuses which attempt to collect data on 100% of businesses in the country.

The classification of business activity (ISIC) is not as useful as the occupational classification in distinguishing craft from mass manufacture. This is because the survey is designed to produce data on a sectoral or industry basis. Moreover business survey data are commercially sensitive and so may not be made public in such detail that individual companies can be identified. The most relevant sectoral code is 3211—Manufacture of Jewellery, but this includes all jewellery such as mass-manufactured costume items.

Inevitably most craft businesses are small, the vast majority being independent artisans but including a significant number of worker co-operatives. Small businesses of less than 10 or 20 employees are problematic to survey. Firstly small micro-businesses have a short life, quickly starting up and quickly failing, and making it difficult to obtain a clear up to date picture of activity. Secondly, partly because of this, but also because micro-businesses have less need for formal registration in many countries, it can be very difficult for statistical agencies to draw up a sample from an ever-changing and difficult to identify strata of small businesses. In the face of these problems national statistics offices may choose either to 'over sample' small businesses to increase the reliability of the results, or to set a threshold to the size of businesses being surveyed. This threshold is usually between 5 and 20 employees depending on the degree to which data are available in the country concerned.

Another particular problem in developing countries, but relevant in a different way in OECD countries is the informal economy. In developing countries the majority of business may be conducted 'informally', to avoid government administrative costs (including tax) and sometimes involving many transactions 'in kind' (direct exchanges of goods, e.g. pots for food without money being involved). Craft exchanges are often not subject to monetary payments from the humblest village transactions, to the highest level where art objects may be 'loaned' to a museum.

National Statistics—Exports and Imports

Data on exports and imports of manufactured products are collected at the national level by the Customs and Revenue of the country concerned and at the international level by UNCTAD which publishes them on comtrade.un.org. The codings are quite detailed allowing considerable differentiation between different types of product. They are normally published at 4–5 digits but can be issued at up to 8 digits (e.g. Indonesia). Some of these codes do more or less distinguish handmade from machine-made products as well as those using natural as opposed to man-made materials. The most useful export code for craft is HS7113—Precious metal jewellery, which because it involves precious metal is perhaps more likely to be handmade.

Triangulation of business survey data, exports, and other economic data on production activities may allow further precision of craft production at national level. For example it may be possible to adjust the data to remove any mass manufacturers. Local information may help to eliminate the production of a particular town known as a base for major companies of, e.g. furniture manufacture, while equally production of certain villages (e.g. in Asia Ellis and Lo in this volume) may be known as craft.

Craft Surveys

National statistics allow one to see craft within the overall economy but the classification problems in distinguishing craft from machine-made production activities prevent one seeing the full circumstances surrounding the artisans in their home environment.

To address this requirement it is common to carry out a dedicated craft survey. Often this is intended to be a 100% 'audit' of all craftsmen working in the target area (country, region, and district). This can be hard to achieve as firstly crafts producers are not obliged to register with any central agency and secondly craft production is often a secondary activity which may not be easily identified by someone outside the local community. Few surveys thus achieve a 100% record of all crafts people in the target area, but equally it may be hard to know to what extent the respondents are a representative sample of such an elusive group of craft producers.

In the case of Georgia (Shanshiashvili 2013) a small group of interviewers spent some time talking to local town halls to identify local artisans and where they lived before proceeding to find them in their homes. It was however still difficult to be certain that all producers, including those who only distributed their products in the local community, had been identified. By contrast the 2010 Bhutan weavers' survey was carried out by the National Statistics Bureau (Askerud and Lo 2013). The 2007 Living Standards Measurement Survey has determined that 27% of all households in Bhutan carried out weaving, and so the survey sample was constructed to capture a similarly representative group of households. It should be noted that both Bhutan and Georgia are small countries and sample building in larger countries for a small scale activity such as craft can be much more complex.

An examination of available craft surveys across the world (Ellis 2014) identifies a range of common topics

- The demographic character of the crafts person and their household, including level of education and well-being
- Skills; how the crafts expert learnt their skills, years of experience (how old is the business?) other relevant skills (e.g. literacy), and how the master will pass on skills to the next generation including apprenticeships
- Membership of trade associations and other community groups
- Finance; issues of savings and loans, costs and pricing, income and profit
- The production process; hours worked, help from family friends and employees, sources of raw material, use of tools and machinery, sources of design, the nature of the workplace (home or business premises)
- Products; use of materials, non-craft production
- Distribution and marketing; sales points and how to get goods to them, participation in exhibitions fairs etc., sources of advertising and publicity especially ICTs and social media
- Problems that crafts people face.

The production process is often the core of the survey and thus the most developed section. Questions commonly cover

- Sources of raw material, how they are acquired, and sustainability (location, time spent)
- Source of design; friends family, other craftsmen, galleries

- Hours per week/month spent in production
- Number of 'helpers', employees, apprentices, and their status
- Workplace; home, dedicated building, open air, market
- Age of business, usually number of years.

However almost all craft surveys use slightly different approaches to each of these topics. This reduces their effectiveness in several different ways

- Successive studies in the same country or in different parts of the same country are not comparable
- Studies are not comparable between one country and another
- Each study spends resources developing its own methodology, 'reinventing the wheel', which could otherwise be used elsewhere to the benefit of the sector
- Issues of common interest to all artisans such as obtaining credit, or quality certification, are not addressed in a comprehensive manner which will allow active discussion based on a common understanding and definitions
- The overall strength of the sector is under-estimated because studies have difficulty in estimating how complete and representative they are.

There are a number of elements in a dedicated craft survey that lend themselves to economic assessments. Perhaps the most important of these approaches is the value chain analysis, which attempts to measure the value added over inputs at each stage of the production process. Input costs can include the cost of harvesting/collecting raw materials such as crops, wood, clay etc., as well as their transportation to the production site.

Value Chain Analysis

An interesting approach which has often been applied to production closely associated with artisans is value chain analysis. While the principle behind this is simple, its application has been rather 'mixed'.

The principle of the approach is to see how much value is added 'sales price—costs of inputs (raw materials, labour, distribution etc.)' at each stage of a product's 'journey' from the raw materials through to the retail sale. Such an approach meshes well survey data on precise manufacturing and distribution conditions with broader statistical data about prices, markets, sales, and indeed exports.

The difficulty is that most studies start with SME commercial manufacturing operations and follow through to global sales. The objective of such studies is often to examine the impact of globalisation in a particular sector especially textiles (Gereffi and Memedovic 2003; Milstein and Co 2008; Fernandez-Stark et al. 2011; Ruffer 2008; IDE-JETRO 2013; Martin 2013), while others concern bamboo (Greijmans et al. 2007), baskets (Belleza, undated).[2] This methodology has been standardised by UNIDO (2013). However for our purposes it is essential to apply the method from the point where raw materials are harvested in the field (indeed ideally one might consider starting with the purchase of seed to grow those materials and the inputs needed for it to ripen). Moreover where such studies of artisans have taken place they seem then to go no further up the value chain than handing over the products to the wholesaler (Greijmans et al. 2007). These value chain studies of craft also tend to be applied as much to the social as the economic aspects of the production process (Belleza, undated; Vietrade, undated; Aspen Institute 2017). This social approach to value chain analysis might highlight the symbolic exchanges of goods within local villages. Clearly such 'social' studies are important and produce valuable information. Reliable cost estimates of an annual rural production cycle from seed to garment are hard to estimate (Samphantharak and Townsend 2010, 2013) but are an extremely important technique for estimating the potential earnings of poor rural producers if the value chain was more slanted in their favour.

[2]For example many were undertaken after the collapse of the international textile agreement in 2005.

Problems in Household Accounting

The Townsend Thai Project (townsend-thai.mit.edu/) where project papers cited here can be found) has identified a number of problems with household accounting in rural villages in developing countries which are relevant to craft production. The Townsend Thai project is a panel survey of several Thai villages in central (Ayutthaya, Lopburi) and northern Thailand which has been run every year since 1997, by a team led by Prof Robert Townsend. Its main research function is economic modelling of rural livelihoods. It has collected a limited range of occupational data (Nyshadham 2013: 9). Survey questions tended to be directed at the head of the household which might lead to minimising of female roles in craft activity. The survey asked about one primary occupation without collecting the average hours worked (Nyshadham 2013: 26). This risks minimising the role of craft which can be a secondary occupation, or may be seen as such even when household members spend a great deal of time in craft production and sales. The survey has also come across several problems in assessing household income including fluctuating inventories, and flows which cross different accounting periods (Samphantharak and Townsend 2012: 11). It was also difficult to apportion utilities and other services to domestic or business purposes (Samphantharak and Townsend 2012: 16–17).

The Townsend data provides great detail on household economic decision-making and entrepreneurialism. For example Nyshadham (2013: 10) has shown that households which switched from agriculture to business throughout the period of the study were more likely to increase their income, than those who did not. Such 'entrepreneurial' households were more likely to have a younger head, to be larger, and to have a higher level of education (Nyshadham 2013: 11). Business start-ups as everywhere were fragile, and the longer a household was in business the less likely it was to fall back to agriculture as its main occupation (Nyshadham 2013: 16). While there was considerable churning the level of household business ownership was stable at 45% across the period of the survey (Nyshadham 2013: 12).

It has been reported elsewhere in this volume that studies by Townsend and others identified a mixed picture of the effectiveness of micro-finance (Ellis and Lo below). It is at least unclear the degree to which rural artisans are able to obtain credit to initiate or expand their businesses. Beyond this there are issues about how such loans are treated in household accounting.

Townsend also suggests the need for greater understanding about how assets are considered by rural households. He suggests that over the period 1999–2005 'positive investment events' in household assets were extremely rare (Samphantharak and Townsend 2010: Table 6.2). He notes that sales of assets, more specifically product inventory, should be seen as income, because many sales of assets are related to product life cycles or changes in demand (Samphantharak and Townsend 2010: 58–59). Thus it might be suggested that rural craftsmen like those studied in this volume for Asia (Ellis and Lo below) hold onto craft production not as assets but as delayed income awaiting opportunities or clients. Such assets, e.g. textiles or furniture could be 'used' as assets within the household pending such opportunities.

These delays between one activity and another affect other accounting processes too. Frequently inputs for production processes are acquired many months before their actual use (Samphantharak and Townsend 2010: 63–64). For example seasonal acquisition of raw material, e.g. wood may happen months before the agricultural cycle allows the freeing up of labour to turn it into furniture. Equally clothing may be manufactured and even worn for some time before being sold to others (Samphantharak and Townsend 2010: 36–37). There is thus a challenge to craft surveys and value chain analysis to track an input to production to output process which may last over many months and which may not even be obvious to the artisans themselves.

Samphantharak and Townsend (2010: 64–65) note that barter exchange or 'in-kind transfers' help mitigate cash shortages and maintain liquidity for households. Gifts have recognised cultural associations ever since Marcel Mauss' classic 1923 study. Remittances similarly can boost incomes without any explicit return to the giver though they also may lead to an expected 'social' return to the giver in terms of enhanced status. For craft producers such exchanges may on the one hand be seen as 'commissions' for particular pieces, the basis for family obligations in production, or as openings for further sales. All these returns however are not guaranteed and may only be realised in the longer term.

Another accounting problem concerns the unpaid activities of members of the household. Thus in traditional Philippine textile production men strip the abaca and children knot the fibres together. Such contributions to craft production may not be accounted for in surveys and national statistics and income may then be attributed to the Head of household rather than to the family business as a whole use (e.g. Samphantharak and Townsend 2010: 99–100).[3]

Conclusion—A Framework for Measuring Craft Production

It has commonly been stated that craft activities cannot be clearly identified in economic and labour market statistics. This paper has demonstrated that this is wrong. The following steps are likely to produce firm evidence for craft/artisan activity in any country.

Firstly statistics should be extracted from the Business Survey or National Accounts, for production activities, and from the LFS in terms of occupations. Relevant data should be obtained in as much detail as possible, preferably four digits or more for both sectors (ISIC) and occupation (ISCO). Some filtering of the data is then necessary in conjunction with local expertise. In the case of the Philippines it has been shown that textile workers who were rural or self-employed could be identified as artisans using handlooms and local fibres at home. It has been suggested that another determining factor of artisan production is likely to be self-employed or small companies (less than five employees).

This filtering is likely to result in an under-estimate of craft activity; for example some artisan co-operatives may include over one hundred producers each making their own individual products but it will be

[3]It should be noted that the Philippine LFS records children as young as seven or nine years old 'working' in textiles.

sufficient to highlight certain key information, e.g. in the Philippines over half of all artisan textile workers are women over 55.

Further analysis may be able to identify other important economic data such as the extent to which supplementary income from craft production keeps people out of poverty, or the percentage of value added retained by the original producer compared to that retained by the distributor or the retailer.

Secondly use of a dedicated survey of artisans will considerably enhance the depth of understanding of the different elements of production in terms of the hours taken in gathering raw materials, production time, transportation to market, and opportunity costs relative to other occupations such as agriculture.

If surveys use the same definitions as national statistics, especially the occupation description using ISCO, then benchmarking between surveys and national statistics should be possible. While a dedicated survey can learn an enormous amount about producers (e.g. where they learnt their skills, whether they are passing them on to the next generation) it cannot outline the strategic place of craft production within the national economy. It is only through national statistics collected across the economy that we can say, for example that artisan production is the eighth largest sector in Thailand employing more people than the Transport sector.

Bibliography

Askerud, P. 2010. *Bhutan Cultural Industries Sector Development: A Baseline Report 2009*. Thimphu: Ministry of Culture/Nat Bur Stats/UNDP.

Askerud, P., and J. Lo. 2013. *Bhutan Weavers Survey 2010*. Thimphu: Ministry of Culture/Nat Bur Stats.

Aspen Institute. 2017. Artisan Innovation Workshop Facilitator's Guid. Alliance for Artisan Enterprise.

Banerjee, A., E. Duflo, R. Glennerster, and C. Kinnian. 2015. The Miracle of Microfinance? Evidence from a Randomized Evaluation. *American Economic Journal: Applied Economics* 7 (1): 22–53.

Belleza Global Consulting. Undated. Turkana Basket Value-Chain Feasibility Study and Implementation Plan. USAid.

Borges, A. 2011. *Design and Craft: The Brazilian Path*. Sao Paulo: Terceiro Nome.

Cheewatrakoolpong, K., and S. McKenzie. 2013. Specific Trade Facilitation Measures to Promote Export of Traditional Knowledge Based Goods—A Case Study of Mukdahan and Nakhon Phanom. ARTNeT Working Paper No. 123, Bangkok, ESCAP.

Claymone, Y. 2010. A Perspective on Culture and Technology Transfer of OTOP in Thailand: A Lesson from Japan. *International Journal of East Asian Studies* 15: 111–118.

Cohen, E. 2000. *The Commercialized Crafts of Thailand: Hill Tribes and Lowland Villages*. Richmond: Curzon.

Echavarria, M. 2013. Craft as a Tool for Empowerment. In *Celebrating Crafts Kaivalan*, ed. World Crafts Council, 45–48, Chennai.

Ellis, S. 2013. Crafts; Bridging Creativity and Economy. In *Celebrating Crafts Kaivalan*, ed. World Crafts Council, 49–52, Chennai.

Ellis, S. 2014. Turning Craft into GDP in the Caucasus. In *Notion of Culture as a Force for Economic Growth—New Approach for South Caucasus*, ed. S. Ellis, 27–35. Tbilisi: GACC.

Ellis, S. 2015. *Measuring Traditional Skills (Taking Stock of What We Have Before We Lose It): Craft Statistics a Way Forward*. Aspen Institute.

Fernandez-Stark, K., S. Frederick, and G. Gerefi. 2011. *The Apparel Global Value Chain Economic Upgrading and Workforce Development*. Durham: Duke University.

Gereffi, G., and O. Memedovic. 2003. *The Global Apparel Value Chain: What Prospects for Upgrading by Developing Countries*. Vienna: UNIDO.

Gibbs, K. 2013. The Artisan Entrepreneur in the Global Market Economy. In *Notion of Culture as a Force for Economic Growth*, ed. S. Ellis, 95–98. Tbilisi: GACC.

Greijmans, M., O. Boualay, and J. Banzon. 2007. *Houaphanh Bamboo Value Chain Analysis Identifying SNV's Potential Advisory Services for the Development of the Bamboo Value Chain*. The Hague: SNV Netherlands Development Organization.

Howkins, J. 2007. *The Creative Economy*, 2nd ed. London: Penguin.

IDE-JETRO. 2013. *Aid for Trade and Value Chains in Textiles and Apparel*. Paris and Geneva: OECD and WTO.

Jayachandran, S. 2006. Selling Labor Low: Wage Responses to Productivity Shocks in Developing Countries. *Journal of Political Economy* 114: 538–575.

Kanthachai, N. 2013. A Study of Development Strategies for OTOP in Chiang Rai. *SIU Journal of Management* 3 (1): 112–122.

Keane, J., and D. Willem te Velde. 2008. *The Role of Textile and Clothing Industries in Growth and Development Strategies*. London: ODI.

Kenan. 2009. Economic Contribution of Thailand's Creative Industries. Kenan Institute Asia and Fiscal Policy Research Institute.

Lo, J. 2011. Chinese Ethnic Minorities Participatory Artisan Survey and Needs Assessment Report. UNESCO/Chinese Arts and Crafts Assoc.

Martin, M. 2013. *Creating Sustainable Apparel Value Chains a Primer on Industry Transformation*. Geneva: Impact Economy.

Mauss, M. 1923. Essai sur le don forme et raison de l'échange dans les sociétés archaïques. *L'Année sociologique (1896/1897–1924/1925)* 1: 30–186.

Milstein and Co. 2008. A Canadian Approach to the Apparel Global Value Chain. Industry Canada.

Natsuda, K., K. Igusa, A. Wiboonpongse, A. Cheamuangphan, S. Shingkharat, and J. Thoburn. 2011. One Village One Product—Rural Development Strategy in Asia: The Case of OTOP in Thailand. RCAPS Working Paper 11.3, Ritsumeikan University.

Nyshadham, A. 2013. Learning About Comparative Advantage in Entrepreneurship: Evidence from Thailand.

OECD. 2005. *Oslo Manual: Guidelines for Collecting and Interpreting Innovation Data*. Paris: OECD.

OECD. 2011. *OECD Studies on SMEs and Entrepreneurship Thailand: Key Issues and Policies*. Paris: OECD.

Phadungkiati, L., K. Kusakabe, and P. Pongquan. 2011. Working for Money or Working for the Group? Community-Based Women's Rural Enterprises in Chainat Province Under the OTOP Project. *SIU Journal of Management* 1 (2): 39–72.

Punyasavatsut, C. 2008. SMEs in the Thai Manufacturing Industry: Linking with MNES. In *SME in Asia and Globalization*, ed. H. Lim, 287–321, ERIA Research Project Report 2007–5.

Respicio, N. 2014. *Journey of a Thousand Shuttles: The Philippine Weaver*. Manila: NCCA.

Ruffer, J. 2008. China Textile in Global Value Chain. In *Chinese Firms in the Era of Globalisation*, ed. J-F. Huchet and W. Wang, 6ff. Beijing: China Development Press.

Samphantharak, K., and R. Townsend. 2010. *Households as Corporate Firms*. Cambridge: Cambridge University Press.

Samphantharak, K., and R. M. Townsend. 2012. Measuring the Return on Household Enterprise: What Matters Most for Whom? *Journal of Development Economics* 98 (1): 58–70.

Samphantharak, K., and R. Townsend. 2013. Risk and Return in Village Economies.

Shanshiashvili, A. 2013. Craft Sector in Georgia: Existing Resources Challenges and Recommendations for Further Development. In *Notion of Culture as a Force for Economic Growth—New Approach for Sough Caucasus*, ed. S. Ellis, 108–114. Tbilisi: GACC.

TBR et al. 2012. *Mapping Heritage Craft: The Economic Contribution of the Heritage Craft Sector in England*. London: Creative and Cultural Skills/BIS.

UIS. 2009. *2009 UNESCO Framework for Cultural Statistics*. Montreal: UNESCO Institute for Statistics.

UNESCO. 2005. *Designers Meet Artisans: A Practical Guide*. Paris: Craft Revival Trust/Artesanias de Colombia.

UNIDO. 2013. Greening Value Chains for Sustainable Handicrafts Production in Viet Nam.

UN Stats Commission Friends of the Chair. 2012. Guidelines on Integrated Economic Statistics. New York.

UN Thailand. 2011. *United Nations Partnership Framework Thailand 2012–6*. Bangkok: UN.

Vietrade. Undated. Export Potential of Arts and Crafts in Vietnam.

Wherry, F. 2008. *Global Markets and Local Crafts: Thailand and Costa Rica Compared*. Baltimore: John Hopkins.

Part IV

Future Development

The Importance of Craft Culture

Arjo Klamer

Craftsmanship Is Easy to Overlook

They had just rehearsed a part of the performance later that week. We gathered in an adjacent room to discuss their future strategy. "They" are the members of the top choir of The Netherlands. They had asked me to develop their entrepreneurial skills in anticipation of challenges ahead. A major challenge was the imminent withdrawal of the main financier, the Dutch public broadcast company. That day the topic was their mission. What is the choir good for? To which important purposes does it contribute?

After some introductory remarks they discussed their purposes in small workgroups. The output was varied but we could condense the suggestions to a few categories. As far as the members of the choir were concerned, their choir was especially important for the excellent practice of symphonic music in the Netherlands and abroad, supporting world class orchestras such as the Concertgebouw orchestra. They also saw a

A. Klamer (✉)
Erasmus University, Rotterdam, The Netherlands
e-mail: klamer@eshcc.eur.nl

A. Mignosa and P. Kotipalli (eds.), *A Cultural Economic Analysis of Craft*,
https://doi.org/10.1007/978-3-030-02164-1_18

contribution to the cultural identity of the Netherlands, as the choir stands for its rich and strong tradition in classical music. In addition, they saw their importance for the local town, Hilversum, where they practice and where quite a few of them live, and for the large numbers of amateur choirs in the Netherlands. All these goals made sense and would need to be expressed in conversations with stakeholders.

However, they were missing an important goal. When I told them so, they did not get it. I gave a hint: how about yourself? They still did not get it. "Why is the choir important for you, the singers?" One member offered: "the choir allows me to do my thing." Another mentioned his salary. "What is that good for?" People resisted this option with the argument that the singing is most important to them. Slowly they were getting to the goal that most professional organizations tend to overlook and that is "skillful work" or "craftsmanship." Singing is a craft, so I proposed to them, the singers; it requires endless practice to hone their skills. They have to take care of their bodies, their vocal chords in particular, study, learn a great deal about the music they sing, and practice some more. Singing is what their life is about, at least to a great extent. The choir enables them to develop their skills and to exercise their craft.

Accordingly, developing and sustaining the craftsmanship of classical singing is an important purpose of the choir. The choir members were visibly touched by this insight. It was an eye-opener.

The anecdote illuminates the blind eye towards the crafts and craftsmanship. People do not see it, even if you put their nose on top of it. House painters may be readier to recognize their own craftsmanship, but artists who paint may resist the classification. Surgeons and dentists usually react with some surprise when they realize that they practice a craft: they do not think of themselves as craftspeople. Neither do the singers till they are told so.

The Framing of Standard Economics Is Misleading

As Mignosa and Kotipalli already argued in the opening chapter of this book, the sense making that standard economics provides, leaves a blind eye towards the crafts. With its focus on financial transactions and monetary quantities it does not stimulate a serious look at the world of the crafts, at least not for its economic relevance. Even though several preceding contributions have pointed at the economic relevance of the crafts for economies such as the Indian one, providing plenty of jobs and a significant share in total production, industrialization and automatization will, so the economically trained surmises, render the crafts a dying sector, interesting only for heritage's sake. The sector is presumably dying because (a) machines and robots render manual labor obsolete and (b) crafted products become too expensive for the taste of the mass of consumers

However, even in the standard economic frame, the crafts should remain a factor to take seriously. Knowledge and creative economies continue to need plenty of handwork (Banks 2010). Societies that neglect the maintenance and further development of manual skills, are finding out that they need to import such skills. The preceding chapters provide various examples of such a need.

Even so, there are other, more comprehensive reasons to reappraise the crafts. In order to see a future with a substantive role for the crafts a broader perspective is called for, a perspective that encompasses the standard economic story but does a great deal more. It is a story that makes sense of craftsmanship, and of the existence of a choir, in a world that will increasingly care about qualities of all kinds. We need to make sense of the qualities that the crafts represent and stimulate.

Crafts as Shared Practices: Applying the Value-Based Approach

In *Doing the Right Things: A Value Based Economy* (2017) I develop a perspective that switches the current emphasis on quantities to one focusing on qualities. The presumption is that people, organizations and states act with the intent to realize things that are important to them. The answer to the question "what is important to you?" specifies your values, or qualities that you care about. Those you want to realize, or to valorize.

Valorisation usually goes by the way of acquiring or producing goods of all kinds. They include the private goods that economists like to consider, such as computers, bread, and houses. Those goods people need to realize "knowledge" maybe (that is what the authors of this book used their computer for), nutritious meals shared with colleagues, and a home. Private goods people usually buy in order to attain property rights. "Knowledge," "meals," and "homes" are shared goods: you cannot own them by yourselves but share them with others (cf. Chapter 6, *Doing the Right Thing*). They are the more important goods (yet are not accounted for in the standard economic story).

Shared goods are best understood as shared practices. A home involves a wide range of activities with members chipping in or contributing. Scholars contribute to "knowledge" by researching, conversing and writing and so do others who read their work and try to appropriate its content. Knowledge is not so much something you "have" but comes about in what you "do". (Note that a shared practice is different from a common as defined by Elinor Ostrom 1990; a common is a resource accessible to whomever whereas a shared practice requires meaningful contributions to share it. A shared practice is exclusive; a common is not.)

When we transport these concepts to the case of the choir we quickly recognize the choir as a shared practice to which all kinds of people contribute, including the director, the orchestras, the organizers, the financiers, the audiences, and above all, the singers. The singers contribute their craft, i.e. their skill to sing classical music. That craft is a practice, too. They study, rehearse: they practice singing. As researchers of the crafts (like Sennett 2009; Cavalli 2017; Luckman 2015; Crawford 2009) have reported, choir singers practice their craft "because it is important to them." They supposedly gain most satisfaction from excelling in their craft, doing the best they can. Recognition in the form of applause and financial reward is secondary. At least, that is what choir singers tend to say. If so, the practice becomes a praxis, having as a purpose the practice itself (cf. Chapter 7, *Doing the Right Thing*). The value is then intrinsic (a financial reward would be an extrinsic value).

Accordingly, the value-based approach encourages us to see craftsmanship as a practice with itself as a purpose, embedded in a shared practice that constitutes a craft. Starting with the practice of craft, we are encouraged to look beyond the transaction in which "consumers" buy craft products from the "producers," as we would in a standard economic account, and consider the context in which a craft comes about.

Like in the case of classical music, craft products need an environment that charges them with values, that gives them qualities that those involved can appreciate. Individual craftspeople will be unable to generate such an environment. The Japanese kimono maker, the Italian pottery baker, the German roof worker, they all depend on a context, a shared practice, in which all kinds of people participate. It is that practice that gives meaning to what they make and renders the qualities of their work recognizable, especially for fellow craftsperson.

"Consumers" participate in the shared practice that is a craft as well. Craft products enable their buyers and users to do something useful, like clothing themselves, pouring tea, or decorating their room. The standard story is that people buy a product for its utilitarian value. But in the case of crafts more is at stake. People come to listen to the choir because they know its excellent reputation and may be curious for its interpretation of the music that is on the program. They bring their knowledge and experience to the concert and participate more than that they consume. A Japanese woman will opt to buy an expensive kimono because she finds its quality important. She values the material, the design, and the craftsmanship of the makers. That is, she needs to know about the practice that is kimono making. She may know something about the materials used and can distinguish what are good designs and excellent colorings. She may even know something about the workshops and the craftspeople that make kimono's. Being interested in the practice, learning about it and probably talking about it with others, she participates in the practice as well. Likewise, an Italian values well-crafted pottery, and an exquisitely prepared meal. A German sets great store by well-executed machine work, carpentry or roof work. In all instances the quality matters. The users of craft products have an acquired taste and may use it to distinguish themselves in their social setting (cf. Bourdieu 1979). In that sense consumers are producers as well, as they coproduce the practice of craft together with the craftspeople and all those others involved (Ostrom 1996).

Turning to the practice of craftsmanship we do not just observe people producing products for the market by way of their manual skill, but also recognize their craftsmanship as a practice by way of which they realize something important to them. The reward, therefore, does not come only in the form of a payment by a buyer, but also as satisfaction of a job well done (cf. Sennett 2009; Crawford 2009). It is the quality of the work that matters. Singers choose singing as their thing and are willing to sacrifice a great deal (like lots of time, family life, higher incomes) to practice their singing. (Some of us scholars must identify with that kind of commitment.) The Japanese man who designs kimonos, a skill that took years of training, draws satisfaction from an improvement to a design even if the average kimono wearer would not be able to notice it. It is the constant drive to perfection or excellence as Cavalli calls it (Cavalli 2017) that fulfills the life of a true craftsperson. In the terms of the value-based approach we would say that craftspeople valorize an important value by practicing their craft.

Shared Practices Are Embedded in and Made Meaningful by a Culture

Broadening the perspective generates a richer, and more value-laden picture of the world of crafts than a standard economic account. We clearly see how the world of crafts is focused on qualities of various kinds, like the qualities of products, of work but also of the environment in which producers and their co-producers (consumers in the standard account) operate and that renders their activities meaningful. Kotipalli (2018) and Jiang (2018) who applied the value-based approach in their study of the crafts in respectively India and China, felt therefore the need to use the notion of culture to make sense of the influence of the environment on the crafts.

As I have laid out elsewhere (Klamer 2017: 8–9), culture has three meanings. "Culture in the anthropological sense (C1) connotes the stories, history, expectations, artifacts, symbols, identities and values that a group of people shares, and with which they distinguish themselves from other people" (ibid.: 8). C2 is the German notion of Kultur and "connotes civilization, usually expressed in the accumulated achievements of people in a certain region over a long period of time in the arts, sciences, technology, politics and social customs" (ibid.: 8). The third meaning of culture (C3) refers to "the arts, sometimes including architecture, design and certain crafts" (ibid.: 8). The latter are sense-making activities. (I would now include scientific and religious practices as well political, movie, and media practices.) Like the arts, the crafts can add meanings to people's lives, like a sense of what is esthetical, or a sense of tradition, of artistic and manual skills, or of the quality of design, of material, or a sense of mysterious qualities of the world we inhabit.

The notion of culture, and especially that of C1, makes us aware of the existence of what we now call a crafts culture. People who participate in a certain craft practice, as producers, critics, middlemen, and "users," share a culture in the sense of shared values, traditions, and experiences. The notion of culture also alerts us that cultures vary. When, say, the Japanese or the Germans share a craft culture, we imply that they distinguish themselves with that culture from each other and from all other people. Kotipalli and Jiang also appeal to craft culture in its second meaning, as they recognize in current craft practices clear traces of Indian, respectively Chinese traditions. Working the handloom has in an Indian setting a religious meaning, as westerners were able to witness in pictures of Gandhi at a handloom while fighting for Indian independence. Likewise, Chinese see in their porcelain a rich history and the achievement of great craftsmanship. Such practices, therefore, qualify as intangible heritage according to the UNESCO (2000). Culture in the third sense (C3) makes us pay attention to the meanings that the crafts create, sustain and preserve. Dressing up in a special kimono is charged with meanings to a Japanese woman, as is the acquisition of an age-old porcelain vase for a Chinese. Dutch people cherish the craftsmanship of millers as they remind them of their age-old struggle with water in their delta, and Germans are proud of the quality of handwork in their country because it supports their identity as a skillful people producing solid, sturdy and reliable products.

So What?

Recognizing the shared practices that constitute crafts and the cultural context provides a richer and more truthful picture of the crafts. The question is what follows.

One important consequence is that conventional policy instruments will not suffice when policy makers want to stimulate the crafts in their country. It is not enough to direct more resources to the crafts, improve the infrastructure with all kinds of organizations in order to promote and organize the crafts, and invest in the education of the crafts. Such measurements might be useful but they are unlikely very effective. If we are right with the value-based approach, changes in practices are called for and in the end a change in culture. Instrumental policies tend to be inadequate to bring about such changes. Usually those changes happen because of internal social changes or social changes brought about in confrontations with other cultures. The Dutch, who have neglected their crafts in this century, may get a wake-up call when they become aware of the craft cultures in Japan and Italy, notice the rich infrastructure that their eastern neighbors (the Germans, that is) have maintained for their handwork, and are getting nervous when they notice the efforts that Chinese and Indian governments undertake to bolster their crafts. As Appiah argues, a sense of honor may change the tide and bring about what he calls moral revolutions (Appiah 2010).

Accordingly, politicians seeking changes first of all want to engage in sense-making policies, alerting their constituents to the need to revalue qualities of products, to reappraise craftsmanship, and to care about the traditions of craftsmanship. They may do so by highlighting best practices elsewhere, to commission studies like this one, and to honor great crafts people.

The value-based approach has relevant consequences for craftspeople as well. They may realize that their work is not just about making quality products, or singing well, but that it is a practice that requires the involvement, participation, and contribution of multiple others. The choir does not just want to sell more tickets to their concerts but wants to get those who buy tickets to participate, and to contribute by, for example, talking about the concert to others. They will understand that the value of their practice increases when more people understand what they are doing and are able to appreciate the qualities of what they are doing. That is why they need to tell their stories, share with others what making quality products involves, so that people develop a distinctive taste.

People in general may come to realize that by getting involved in craft practices they are able to valorize something that is important to them, like being part of a rich tradition, or being able to share their knowledge and appreciation with others, and thus gain a social standing. Having a beautiful cupboard in the kitchen which is made by a well-known craftsman, may give a lifelong sense of satisfaction far more than a mass-produced species that is purchased for little money in a big store would do. A well-crafted product comes with a story. That story can be worth a great deal (as the children will realize when they are dividing the heirloom of their deceased parents).

There are also consequences for scholarship. If we are right with the value-based approach, and shared practices, culture and qualities are relevant when making sense of the crafts, economists will need to make substantive changes in their approach and their conceptual framework. Markets are not as straightforward as they seem to be now; the world does not revolve around market transactions and the prices that get established in them (cf. Jiang 2018), financial quantities are a poor approximation of what counts, and consumers do a great deal more than maximizing utility functions under financial constraints. Conventional sociological and cultural accounts fall short, too. It is not enough to study social settings, networks, and cultures; we need to understand what it takes to valorize what is important to people, including qualities and values.

This work on the crafts is a beginning of all these changes. Experience tells us that the turnaround will take several decades. That is how slow cultures change.

References

Appiah, Kwame Anthony. 2010. *The Honor Code: How Moral Revolutions Happen*. New York: W.W. Norton.

Banks, Mark. 2010. Craft Labour and Creative Industries. *International Journal of Cultural Policy* 16 (3): 305–321.

Bourdieu, Pierre. 1984/1979. *Distinction: A Social Critique of the Judgement of Taste*. London: Routledge.

Cavalli, Alberto. 2017. *The Master's Touch: Essential Elements of Artisanal Excellence*. Venice: Marsilio.
Crawford, Matthew B. 2009. *Shop Class as Soulcraft: An Inquiry into the Value of Work*. New York: Penguin Press.
Hargreaves McIntyre, Morris. 2010. *Consuming Craft: The Contemporary Craft Market in a Changing Economy*. London: Crafts Council.
Hillman Chartrand, Harry. 1989. The Crafts in a Post-modern Market. *Journal of Design History* 2 (2/3): 93–105.
Jiang, Lili. 2018. *Valuing Craftsmanship: In Particular the Crafting of Chinese Porcelain and Dutch Delft Blue*. Rotterdam: Erasmus University.
Klamer, Arjo. 2017. *Doing the Right Thing: A Value Based Economy*. London: Ubiquity Press.
Kotipalli, Priyatej. 2018. *Values of Craft: The Indian Case*. Rotterdam: Erasmus University.
Luckman, Susan. 2015. *Craft and the Creative Economy*. New York: Palgrave Macmillan.
Ostrom, Elinor. 1990. *Governing the Commons: The Evolution of Institutions for Collective Action*. Cambridge: Cambridge University Press.
Ostrom, Elinor. 1996. Crossing the Great Divide: Coproduction, Synergy and Development. *World Development* 24 (6): 1073–1087.
Sennett, Richard. 2009. *The Craftsman*. New York: Penguin Press.
UNESCO. 2000. *Evaluation of UNESCO's Programme for Crafts Promotion 1990–1998*. Paris: UNESCO.

Design and Craft: The Practitioners' View

Lucia Giuliano

Introduction

Talking about craftsmanship and design begs the question of how to define a craftsperson in this day and age, and what craft has become in the extremely complex world we live in, where many established meanings have been turned upside down. How can we pinpoint the notion of craftsmanship when the dividing lines between manual work, technology, machines and different occupations, not to mention the local and global arenas, and real and virtual space, blur and overlap constantly, giving rise to a contemporary scenario which is hybrid and chaotic?

And what does design mean in such a world? We can take this as our starting point, but there are no simple answers and the discipline of design also tends to escape definitions. Indeed, if we asked ten design professionals to define their field we would end up with ten different definitions.

L. Giuliano (✉)
Abadir. Design and Visual Arts Academy, Catania, Italy
e-mail: l.giuliano@abadir.net

A. Mignosa and P. Kotipalli (eds.), *A Cultural Economic Analysis of Craft*,
https://doi.org/10.1007/978-3-030-02164-1_19

They would all agree that design means "to make projects", but designing what, how, to whose brief, for what users, and to what end?

If we put this question to a historian, we would receive a fairly specific answer: design came about in Britain in the late 1800s with the advent of the Industrial Revolution, namely when mass production called for a new set of skills: those of the designer, appointed to create working designs for manufacturing in line, with the constraints of the production process and the existing technology, and responding to the demands of the market.

The need to design for the mass market differentiated the figure of the craftsman, who continued to work manually in his workshop, from that of the designer, who worked for companies and mass production lines, respecting the characteristic "*form follows function*" approach of industry. Design (designers in the service of industrial production) and craftsmanship became two radically different ways of producing material wares, in terms of both modus operandi and meaning.

Yet if we put the same question to a critic, the definition of design would lose these precise, clear outlines, especially when it comes to the modern day world.

As Alice Rawsthorn (2013) writes in her book *Hello World: Where Design Meets Life*: "Design is a complex, often elusive phenomenon that has changed dramatically over time by adopting different guises, meanings and objectives in different contexts, but its elemental role is to act as an agent of change, which can help us to make sense of what is happening around us, and to turn it into an advantage" (Ibidem, p. 9).

Quoting Lazlo Moholy-Nagy, who asserted that "designing is not a profession, but an attitude", Rawsthorn enlarges the confines of design, making it into a sort of world-changing superpower: today's designers might design a corporate strategy, a software programme, a lifestyle, a chair, a service, a community, a company process, an event or a teapot. As Moore puts it: "[…] a designer can be a flouncy stylist of clothes, or interiors, or someone in a laboratory coat, or, if you are a creationist, God" (Moore 2013).

For design schools this is not an insignificant concern, and each school inevitably attempts to forge its own approach, by breaking this complex panorama down into multiple "specialities" (product design, interior design, exhibition design, service design, etc.) or trying to convey this sense of multiplicity to its students by imparting both technical and manual skills, and developing the "intellectual" capabilities of budding designers, who as such, should be in possession of cross-cutting competences that enable them to operate in different contexts, interacting with different professionals.

In this regard, namely the designer's ability to work with other professionals to create high quality products, the late nineteenth century saw the advent of the Arts & Crafts movement, which took a stand against the decline in standards caused by the inferior quality of industrial products. This movement celebrated manual work and viewed artisanal craftsmanship as the highest expression of human skill. William Morris, one of its key exponents, undoubtedly used machines to produce the fabrics and furniture sold by Morris, Marshall & Co., but insisted that "*man is not in the service of the machine: it is the machine that must serve man, just as products should be designed to offer quality to man, not just be easy for a machine to produce*" (Le Muse, *Enciclopedia di tutte le arti*, 1964). In Morris's company the craftsman, designer and architect worked together to produce high quality products, despite the fact that "*this celebration of artisanal work, with the high costs it entailed, meant that the resulting products were only affordable to the elite and prevented the crafts from being integrated into industry*" (Treccani 2018).

To return to the relationship between craft and design today, and more specifically the production of tangible goods, designers must be capable of using their hands. They do so, not so much to produce goods themselves, but because they need to understand the process in order to have a meaningful dialogue with the actual makers of the products. The latter are those with in-depth knowledge of materials and how they behave, those working in workshops, laboratories and factories, and those selling and promoting the products.

In the "expanded" context that characterises the contemporary era, it is interesting to pick up on the archaic definition of craftsman offered by Richard Sennet (2008), who explores the Greek term for artisan and unites the idea of "public" with that of production.

> The archaic craftsman occupied a social slice roughly equivalent to a middle class. The demioergoi included, in addition to skilled manual workers like potters, also doctors and lower magistrates, and professional singers and heralds who served in ancient times as news broadcasters. [...] It was in the middle of this archaic society that the hymn to Hephaestus honored as civilizers those who combined head and hand. (Sennet 2008: 29–30)

The craftsman/demiurge of the ancient world described by Sennet (2008) appears to have something in common with the designer of today evoked by Rawsthorn (2013). He/she is a figure with a strong social role, capable of both intellectual and manual work, an agent of change who lends form and meaning to the physical world and more, capable of activating processes that change the way we live. In the contemporary scenario artisans continue to be the bearers of both tangible resources (techniques, materials, manual skills) and intangible assets (traditions, culture and history) that are closely connected to specific places, and therefore markedly local in nature. Designers, therefore, could, or should, act as the new interpreters of this know-how, celebrating the value of craftsmanship and making it relevant to the present by designing new products that keep artisanal production alive; contemporary products that are not exclusively local but hopefully global in their appeal, inevitably "glocal".

Geographic (and Cultural) Issues: Design and Craftsmanship in Italy

From the perspective of design practice, therefore, including the teaching of the discipline in schools, the cultural identity of the country in question is a key factor, and the history of craftsmanship and industry in Italy is vastly different to that of England, Holland or other countries. "*Artisanal craftsmanship is one of the distinctive traits of Italy's culture and economy. It is something that identifies the country internationally.* [...] *the competitiveness of our industrial system, and therefore an important part of our economy, is still closely bound up with artisanal* skills that have carved out a niche for themselves in companies of all sizes" (Micelli 2011: 9–10).

For Italian designers, born and trained in Italy, this is a significant factor. Indeed, the relationship between designers, craftsmen and industry is the driving force behind innovative products of great aesthetic value, unique projects that benefit from both high quality manual expertise and the input of machinery and industrial production processes. In this case we are not referring to the "artistic" craftsmanship which is widespread and varied throughout Italy, but rather to that special ability to create high-end products, "a job well done", as Sennet (2008) calls it.

The global economic crisis, and the recession which consequently struck Italian business, has given rise to new scenarios, opening various new fronts and triggering processes which have changed the relationship between designers, craftspeople and industry. The scenario is no longer dominated by industry alone, with its typical rationale and opportunities, its dimension of large-scale production and the global dynamics of the mass market: the local dimension has re-emerged, with its artisanal techniques, limited production runs, and autonomous initiatives, giving designers a stronger, bolder identity, as they become promoters of their work and instigators of new processes.

Designers explore the frontiers of contemporary production in different ways: they collaborate with craftspeople, network, sell online, manage the entire production process—from the concept to the production, promotion and distribution of products—and engage with companies and manufacturers, becoming in some respects entrepreneurs and self producers.

They forge complex relationships between the tangible arena of the project (techniques, materials, details, processes) and those of the market, communications, the story of the process and those involved in it, and the end users. They attempt to bring together the "local" dimension of the project with the "global" universe of the market they operate in, above all when it comes to online sales, which remove all physical barriers to the circulation of products. The world of craft and design is now characterised by a host of different phenomena: self production, self employment, designing one-off pieces for galleries and contemporary art fairs, collectors' items, online sales that bypass the customary dynamics of distribution, technological innovations and 3D printers. All these processes have considerably changed the role of designers and their interactions with the actual makers of the objects.

Where Design Meets Craft

The writer's experience is bound up with the work of a small design school in Sicily, in the shadow of Mount Etna.[1] It was founded in 1992 offering courses in restoration, and became a design school in 2010, training young designers in a region which so greatly needs to look to the future. Though Italy is world renowned for its products and designers, education in this field is not uniformly distributed up and down the country, but mainly concentrated in the northern regions. There are obvious reasons: the schools are located in manufacturing areas, where projects take shape. But the country's non-industrial areas are also crying out for design capabilities: design is a tool which can promote both tangible and intangible assets, strengthen existing concerns and generate new ones, by designing communications, strategy, services and processes. Design has the potential to breathe new life into traditional artisanal craftsmanship and spark new entrepreneurial and cultural processes, bringing craftspeople, small companies and designers together to create new, high quality products.

In our work to date, "teaching" design in a region "*with no design and no designers*" like Sicily, every year we have invited visiting professors, mostly from Milan, to spend a few days with our students,

---

[1]Abadir is a Design and Visual Arts School officially recognized by the Ministry for Education, Universities and Research. In 2010 it opened its Design Department, establishing a three year course in Design and Visual Communications which grants a Level 1 Academic Diploma. In the new department Abadir also offers post-graduate education and extra-curricular activities that promote design culture in Sicily. In partnership with Idlab it has set up a new experimental online training programme and offers a Level 1 Masters in Relational Design, now in its third year. In 2015 Abadir partnered with the Bicocca University in Milan for the MADIM Level 1 Masters in Management and Digital Innovation www.abadir.net.

holding design workshops and sharing their experience as contemporary designers.

Some of these projects offer insight into the contemporary scenario and some of the ways in which design and craft now interact.

In 2012 we invited Giulio Iacchetti, founder of the brand *internoitaliano*, who aims to give a central role to craftsmen, alongside designers, in the production of furniture and decor items which are sold online to keep costs down. As Iacchetti explains: "Right from the start it was clear to us that the role of the craftsmen could not simply be that of bringing the design process to completion. Without their unique expertise and ability to transform matter, all of our work would simply remain on paper. To underline the importance of their role, we decided that the name of each artisan would appear as co-author of the product in question. *Internoitaliano* is a system of designing and producing furniture and decor items with a strong artisanal element which uses the web as a virtual showcase on the global market. The result is a promising initial series of items that spring from an equal partnership between the designer who designed them and the craftsman who produced them. As they are not distributed in stores we do not have the financial constraints of retail mark-up, meaning they can be marketed at a fair price which reflects the value of the work of those who designed and produced each item". In this process of shared authorship the designer also acts as entrepreneur, operating in synergy with local craftspeople.

Giulio Iacchetti came to Sicily curious to explore the potential of volcanic materials, seeing the local area and its distinctive characteristics as a rich seam of experiences and images for the designer to draw on. He visited lava stone quarries, spoke to local craftsmen, studied the properties of the material and the machines used to process it, observed local production and common uses: key steps when it came to reworking this stone in a contemporary key. In this approach the designer needs the input of the craftsman and his manual skills, both at the exploratory stages and during the design process.

Another story of design and craftsmanship that offers a very clear snapshot of the new attitude of contemporary designers and their relationship with craftsmanship is that of Alvaro Catalán de Ocón,[2] who we invited to the school in 2016 for an exhibition entitled "Presente artigiano" (Craftsmanship today).

In 2011, Alvaro Catalán de Ocón travelled to South America where he took part in a project led by Hélène Le Drogou, psychologist and activist who was concerned with the plastic waste contaminating the Colombian amazon. Alvaro's solution to the problem? Engaging the local community to turn the containers for liquids into ceiling lamps. With the help of the Asociación Artisanías de Colombia (an organization dedicated to the preservation of Colombian crafts), Alvaro collaborated with two distinct groups of artisans from the Cauca region who had been displaced to Bogota by guerrilla warfare. Together they have been giving new life and shape to the PET bottle since 2012, which gave rise to Petlamp.org project.

As Alvaro Catalán de Ocón writes: "One of the principal hypotheses out of which the PET Lamp project emerged is the possibility to approach a global problem (the waste from PET plastic bottles) with a local activity (the basket weaving tradition). Basket making is a traditional craft worldwide that can be found in the popular folklore of every culture. This craft works as a vehicle for the transmission of knowledge which facilitates the passing on of the symbols, beliefs and rituals of the culture that developed it. Used since the Palaeolithic, a precursor of pottery and earlier than the textile techniques of spinning and weaving, basket making was a response to the need for receptacles for storing and transporting food. With the aim of materializing this concept, PET Lamp has taken a further step in this direction, by replicating the experience in new countries noted for their tradition, handcraft techniques and latticed society. The objective of this project is not solely to obtain an attractive and desirable contemporary object, but also to be able to establish a method of working laden with anthropological tones" (http://catalandeocon.com/product/pet-lamp/).

[2]After a degree in economics and business administration, Alvaro studied design in Milan and London. With these two disciplines under his belt, he embarked on a career as a design entrepreneur, and the Pet Lamp project is emblematic of his two-fold approach.

Alvaro's work is interesting because the designer has created not just a product but also a process: he has attempted to come up with a solution to global issue, rediscovering the "archaic" craftsmanship of artisans from different countries and inserting them into the production system. He sells, distributes and ships the resulting products, communicates with the press, takes part in exhibitions, and so forth.

The third case study is that of Vittorio Venezia, born and trained in Sicily, who is based in Milan but with one foot always in Sicily, where he seeks out craftspeople to work with on his design projects. His collection *Officine Calderai* set out to preserve the intangible heritage of a master tinsmith, Nino Ciminna, who was aged over 80 when Vittorio met him in his workshop in Via dei Calderai in Palermo. In 2015, the pair came up with a series of lamps entitled *4decimi* (four tenths), designed by Vittorio and entirely made by hand by the old craftsman, who has since passed away. The celebration of manual craft, or perhaps more accurately the joy of rediscovering bygone skills is the *leit motiv* of this series, more so than the functional or aesthetic characteristics of the product which we appreciate not just for the actual object itself, but the story behind it.

Vittorio Venezia has played a key role in teaching design since Abadir's Design Department was first established. He has worked with great passion and dedication, helping students understand the processual nature of design, from the initial concept to the finished product. And this has been accompanied by the manual expertise of craftspeople—wood turners, stone masons, blacksmiths, potters, carpenters and many more—an approach that draws on local resources and celebrates the value of design in a region without industry. Indeed, the latter is by no means a banal concern: just how can designers exist in Sicily if there are no manufacturers? One possible answer lies in reappraising all the local resources which could benefit from an update, to respond to new demands and new horizons.

Many of the projects which came about in our school under Vittorio Venezia's guidance are strongly grounded in the local area and its traditional crafts. They include: a series of modular vases inspired by the old tradition of "mending broken pots", the prototypes for which were produced by a ceramics company in Caltagirone (a Sicilian town known for its ceramics) which subsequently decided to put the vases into production and sell them online; a collection of items made from the Luffa Cylindrica, a species of vegetable sponge gourd that is cultivated in Sicily; a cooking tool which exploits the heat induction characteristics of lava basalt stone; and a terracotta fridge that relies on the insulating properties of sand, also produced by the ceramics firm in Caltagirone.

In these projects, which combine teaching and design, the relationship between the young designers and craftspeople was all-important in terms of forging a design approach based on local materials, artisans and traditions to create new products relevant to the contemporary era.

Our design courses, and courses in materials technology, strategic design and communications have given us the opportunity to sound out the production sector in Sicily, which is characterised by both craftspeople and small and medium-sized companies operating in different sectors, some with advanced technological capabilities, which are gradually carving out a market niche and constructing an identity. This work affords interesting opportunities to meet and interact with the key players in the design universe, and therefore map the panorama of contemporary practices and explore the production scenario present in our region.

In particular, in recent years the school has initiated a sort of survey of the production sector in Sicily by means of a competition entitled *Sicilia felicissima*.[3] The competition aims to highlight examples of design culture in Sicily, which capitalise on our region's tangible and intangible resources and apply a grass-roots approach to the design process. It is a way of bringing together companies, communities and public and private bodies capable of sparking new processes and practices and implementing them, acting as the roots and incubators of a new future for production. In this scenario we believe that designers can play a significant role. Visual communications design in particular has the potential to be a vital tool for promoting the bodies operating in culture, tourism, business and craftsmanship. Fostering synergy

[3]The reference here is to Leonardo Sciascia who ironically describes Sicily, with all its problems and difficulties, as "felicissima"—happy, fortunate.

between talented designers, Sicilian companies, public and private bodies and craftspeople is fundamental when it comes to ensuring a high standard of communications capable of promoting and developing the area. The first edition of the competition offered up a reassuring scenario in which sound, virtuous processes are underway, adding value to the island's economy and cultural development, processes that represent niches of excellence which it is important to promote as best practices in the sector.

The approach we build in the school is based on observing the global panorama, while remaining in touch with the local dimension we live in. We believe in the importance of manual skills for designers, as a resource to deploy during the design process. We believe in high-quality communications to promote existing concerns and boost the region's strengths. We believe in layering different areas of expertise, in the importance of collaborations between different skillsets and the inevitable coexistence of multiple ways of being a designer.

References

Micelli, S. 2011. *Futuro Artigiano*. Venice: Marsilio Ed.

Moore, R. 2013. Hello World: Where Design Meets Life by Alice Rawsthorn—Review. *The Guardian* https://www.theguardian.com/books/2013/mar/10/hello-world-alice-rawsthorn-review.

Muse, Le. 1964. *Enciclopedia di tutte le arti*. Novara: De Agostini.

Rawsthorn, A. 2013. *Hello World: Where Design Meets Life*. London: Penguin Books.

Sennet, R. 2008. *The Craftsman*. London: Allen Lane.

Treccani. 2018. William Morris. Available at http://www.treccani.it/enciclopedia/william-morris/. Last accessed 15 July 2018.

Material Is the Mother of Innovation

Maikel H. G. Kuijpers

Introduction

An interesting situation occurs when an archaeologist is invited to participate in a cultural economic analysis of craft, because archaeology could be just as easily the subject of the analysis. The practical side of archaeology—excavating—is itself a utilitarian craft according to Klamer's scheme (cf. Chapter 10), and the knowledge produced by archaeology above all has cultural value. To make matters even more thought-provoking I opted to write a chapter in the section on the future of craft.

Archaeology is a way of thinking. This thinking can be characterised through three particular foci. (1) A focus on material culture, which is the archaeologists main port of call in terms of data, and through which we gain insight in human behaviour; (2) a focus on big questions about the nature of human societies; and (3) a focus on the long-term, which

M. H. G. Kuijpers (✉)
Leiden University, Leiden, The Netherlands
e-mail: m.h.g.kuijpers@arch.leidenuniv.nl

A. Mignosa and P. Kotipalli (eds.), *A Cultural Economic Analysis of Craft*,
https://doi.org/10.1007/978-3-030-02164-1_20

helps us to understand and detail the slow but fundamental processes that shape human societies (Kintigh et al. 2014; Guldi and Armitage 2014; Barker et al. 2017). In this manner I wish to employ archaeology, exploring the notion of craft in its broadest terms.

A substantive framing of the relevance and contribution of craft to society at large depends on the society we are looking at, and what we think is 'large'. The chapters in this book dealt with contemporary societies, but there is a lot to learn from looking at past societies. In fact, due to the simple reason that large scale societal processes are easier documented from afar than from within, the contribution of craft to society is accessible foremost through disciplines well equipped to study the long-term. The reflection I offer here makes use of this to focus on a big question: what future development may happen *through* craft?

The chapter starts with an attempt to define craft from an archaeologist's point of view. Setting it apart from 'making' on the basis of skill. Following, I address two themes. First, that the history of craft is a long one. This hugely enriches the notion of craft, yet problematises the idea of 'traditional' craft as intangible heritage. Second, that there is an important link to be drawn between skill and cognition, through which I claim that material is the mother of innovation.

Homo Faber

Humans pride themselves as a species of tool- users and makers: *homo faber*. Historically, making tools was even regarded as a uniquely human trait (Oakley 1949; Taylor and Gray 2014). We now know that tool-use, and the somewhat more delimited notion of tool-making, is restricted neither to modern humans, nor humans at all (Shumaker et al. 2011; Bentley-Condit and Smith 2010). Other human species were also exceptionally good at it. Some of the crafts we see today, such as leatherworking, were already practiced 50,000 years ago by Neanderthals, using similar tools (a *lissoir*) and techniques as today (Soressi et al. 2013; Callaway 2013). Chimpanzees are notorious tool-makers and users, and even show cultural traditions (Whiten et al. 2005; Whiten et al. 2007). Crows are able to make a hook from a straight wire and use this to lift a small bucket of food from a vertical pipe (Weir et al. 2002). Clearly, the uniqueness of *homo faber* is a myth that should be laid to rest (Shew 2017; Miller 2018). This, however, does not invalidate the research of how humans go about materials, and why this happens in a different and skilful manner.

A Matter of Skill

The nature of skilful human–material relationships, which are particularly apparent in craft, is what I would like to focus on. Here too there have been claims that human skills differ little from other animals, taking weaving and the nest building skills of the weaver bird as an example (Ingold 2000: 349–361). There are certainly similarities and these are interesting to highlight, but we should not simplify a complex concept to accommodate a false symmetry. We can observe that humans are exceptionally spirited about making things, and that there is undeniably a vast gulf between the complexities of human technologies compared to other species.

One of the differences that needs to be explored further is how to differentiate habit from skill. Although habit is an essential part of becoming skilled, I argue it is the ability to cognize one's actions that distinguishes human skilled behaviour to that of other animals. Craftspeople typically stress the importance of reflecting on practice (Høgseth 2012; Sennett 2009: 50). To understand past practices before reapplying them is one of the most important factors to advance skills. This process is captured in the term *apperception*, which entails the process by which new experience is assimilated to and transformed by the residuum of past experience to form a new whole (Kuijpers 2018: 52–55). Not only is this fundamental to learning processes, it also allows for concepts to be formed and transferred. This is important because concepts are cognitive abstractions of practice. It is on this basis of skill that we might also be able to distinguish a general kind of making from a more particular kind of making that is generally accredited as craftsmanship (Sennett 2009). Let us now look at a specific human–material relation to further explore the relations between craft, skill, and cognition.

Human–Material Relations

Experiencing material realities help to construct cognition. This is a core idea held by group of researchers who think past cartesian cognitive science and argue that cognition extends beyond the brain (Clark 2008; Malafouris 2013; Renfrew 2007; Rowlands 2013; Sutton 2008). Weight, Renfrew (2007: 199) explains, "has first to be perceived as a physical reality—in hands and arms, not just in the brain within the skull—before it can be conceptualised and measured". Not surprisingly archaeologists are drawn to this theory as it emphasises the role of materials. The deeply entangled nature of humans, things, and materials is increasingly recognised and stressed (Hodder 2011, 2012) as these entanglements shape who we are and what we value (Morris 2015). We do not only live in a material world, we have material minds (Boivin 2008). Let me explain this further through the particular example of bronze.

Making Metal, and Bronze Age Minds

From about 2500 BC prehistoric people start to combine copper and tin on a regular basis, making metal known as bronze (Roberts, et al. 2009; Sørensen and Appleby 2018). The invention of bronze as an alloy of naturally occurring minerals had far-reaching consequences for prehistoric societies, both economically and epistemologically. The ores from which these metals could be extracted were found in few regions only, and rarely together. Making bronze meant moving materials over long distances. Connecting sources and end-users and leading to an intensification of trade. For these reasons the Bronze Age is considered to be a "formative epoch" in the formation of Europe, in which we witness the emergence of pan-European exchange networks and large-scale trade (Kristiansen and Suchowska-Ducke 2015). These networks are thought to have set in motion an unprecedented process of unification. Some researchers even speak of "Bronzization", the Bronze Age variant of globalisation (Vandkilde 2016). But there is more to bronze.

The process of metalworking differs markedly from other—earlier—crafts. Objects made from wood or stone *appear* from the mass of raw material used. Making them involves the removal of material, which is why these are known as reductive technologies. In contrast, basketry, weaving, and pottery are additive technologies. The desired object *grows* from the reed, textile, or clay used. Bronze is different in that it is a transformative technology (Sørensen and Appleby 2018). The raw material is melted down to a completely liquid state and poured into a shape, where it solidifies again.

This may not sound very exciting to us but for the prehistoric people involved this must have a been a ground breaking and fundamentally different way of working materials. With bronze, making truly became designing. To illustrate this, consider a flintknapper who wishes to produce an axe from a piece of raw material (a flint nodule). This flintknapper can only conceptualise the axe *within* this nodule, by which I mean that the axe must be present in the shape of the raw material (sensu Heidegger 2011: 253). This is not the case with metal. The shape and form of metal are not set by the raw material itself. Instead, the material in which the desired object is designed is the mould in which it will be casted. Mould-making necessitates that an idea conceptualised in metal as a positive, is detached from this material and transposed to a negative conceptualisation of that idea in a stone or clay mould (Appleby and Sørensen 2018). This is interesting as it implies that along with the development of melting and casting skills, a theoretical skill was increasingly addressed: cognitive abstraction. Moulds were the very first blue-prints, documenting the design of an object to be produced—and reproduced.

When you can cast one axe in a stone mould, you can cast many. This is exactly what Bronze Age people did. Archaeologists have discovered hoards containing up to hundreds of remarkably similar objects like axes, swords, halberds, and neck-rings (Forel et al. 2009; Lenerz-De Wilde 1995; Lenoir 2017). From my own research I observed prehistoric axes that in terms of dimensions and weight are perceptibly identical (Kuijpers 2018), and because we know that imitation leads to variation within 5% of the intended size (Eerkens 2000), these axes should be interpreted as *copies*. This difference between imitation and copies is an important one. Imitation is interpretive, copying is mechanical. The unprecedented sameness between objects as a result of copying would no doubt have made an impact on prehistoric minds (Appleby and Sørensen 2018). Instigated deep epistemological changes with respect to prehistoric notions of reproducibility and affecting ideas about uniqueness, originality, and similarity (Sørensen and Appleby 2018; Sørensen 2012). In short, the Bronze Age was the dawn of the copy (Stockhammer 2017).

Another important affordance of bronze is that it is recyclable. This, together with copying likely guided the development of a proto-currency in the shape of neck-rings that appear in Central Europe in the Early Bronze Age (Lenerz-De Wilde 1995). Perhaps more than anything else, metalworking needs to be understood as a technology for reproduction and standardisation. I am inclined to think that mould-making, and its inherent capability to produce exact copies of a single model, brought about changes of a magnitude comparable to the effect of the photo-camera on the world of art (Benjamin 2008). Bronze casting called upon a kind of design-thinking in which the notion of the prototype becomes relevant, or even *thinkable* (Appleby and Sørensen 2018).

These are but a few examples of how bronze may have guided innovative ways of thinking in the Bronze Age. The point is that specific human-material relationships affected and became part of a Bronze Age 'way of being' and understanding of the world. Bronze created a new world with new possibilities, not only in terms of production and trade, but because it helped people think.

Back to the Future

Having explored the past, we can now move forward and think through how the observations made resonate with the current notion of craft, and the importance of craft for the future.

Craft as Intangible Heritage; Politically Loaded

A popular contemporary notion of craft is to see it as unique, handmade, quality objects, and typically opposed to mass-production. I have shown how this is historically incorrect as large-scale copying was part and parcel of Bronze Age metalworking. Moreover, many of the objects that were produced in large quantities—such as axes—were not of high quality, but 'good enough' (Kuijpers 2018). Of course, it is possible to see Bronze Age metalworking as industrial mass-production, and some have done so indeed (Budd and Taylor 1995). To me this seems anachronistic. Rather, we should recognise that the popular notion of craft is a modern construction and a political statement, which can be rooted in the Arts and Crafts movement. A nineteenth century invention meant to contrast craft to industrial production and to capture a sense of loss (Adamson 2013).

The heritage discourse that revolves around craft is effectively a continuation of this particular sentiment of loss. After all, craft knowledge needs to be "safeguarded" (UNESCO 2018). Framing craft as intangible heritage has the particular shortcoming that it must define craft categorically, and struggles to acknowledge craft as a heuristic device.

Archaeology allows us to see craft outside of the constraints of heritage. Carpentry techniques like the mortise-and-tenon joint still in use today, were already known to carpenters in the 6th millennium BCE (Tegel et al. 2012). The earlier mentioned *lissoir* for leatherworking dates back to 50,000 BC and was used by our nearest cousin, the Neanderthal. Traditionalising and heritagisation of the crafts (Villaroya 2013) simultaneously builds on and ignores these deep time signatures of craft. What tradition does Neanderthal leatherworking, or Neolithic carpentry techniques belong to? The fact they are still used today can hardly be explained as the result of cultural transmission. There is no direct link between French traditional leatherworkers using a *lissoir* and the Neanderthals of Pech-de-L'Aze. This makes the similarity all the more striking, and it is worthwhile to consider whether knowledge of these techniques is at least partly associated with the material rather than a specific group of people. This would mean we need to start thinking of craft knowledge as the heritage of materials.

An Epistemology of Materials

Craft is about making but making is not necessarily craft. Having argued that making is far from uniquely human and does not characterise human behaviour per se, I also made the observation that humans do seem to be particularly good at it and are able to draw upon materials in a skilful rather than purely habitual manner, cognizing their actions and abstracting concepts from their engagement with material. Skill, as a recursive and apperceptive process, creates knowledge from material interactions. On this basis I argue that material—and the skilful handling of it—constitutes an epistemology of its own (Kuijpers 2018: 36–63).

Following, craft should not be seen as a descriptive category, but as a heuristic device. Craft, is a way of exploring and understanding. Like science and art, it guides future development. While the methodologies may differ, all endeavour to make particular claims about the world. The methodology employed by craftspeople is that of experience. Their claim to truth based on the fact that what they make, works.

Material Mentalities

Craftspeople tend to think with the material that they use, but they also think through their material. By this I mean that materials are a rich ground of metaphors through which we understand ourselves and the world, because human thought processes are largely metaphorical (Lakoff and Johnson 1980; McGilchrist 2010; Brück 2004). It follows that the main materials and technologies a society works with shapes not only socio-economic development, but also guides the way people think. I gave the example of bronze and explained how this material affected people's understanding and view of the world, leading to a specific Bronze Age way of being. Effectively, it may be possible to speak of a material mentality. If this is correct, our choice of materials for the future matters.

Defining craftspeople as those who work, shape, and understand materials we should nowadays extend this group to also include designers, scientists, and especially engineers, who might better be seen as craft technologists (Shorter 2015), or craft scientists (Ball 2010: 319).[1]

[1]Interestingly, the idea that engineering is a craft rather than an applied science is gaining traction (Pesch, in review).

These are the craftspeople of today experimenting with new materials. They are doing more than making. They are exploring alternative ways of thinking.

The materials craftspeople work with change over time and this causes more substantial social changes. Leather of the future may well be made from fruit-waste.[2] Algae are the new textiles.[3] Flax and sugar beets are used to create the first biodegradable car.[4] These materials—all organic and grown—affect how we look at the world. These are all small-scale projects, but new materials that may change our future thinking are also developed in labs, by scientists. Graphene, with its extraordinary affordances, will radically transform our world. This is normally explored in terms of the different applications on which it will have an impact (Geim 2009; Singh et al. 2011; Edgeworth 2010). I argue that graphene's fundamental change of society—on the long-term—will lie with the metaphors and concepts that come along with this material. The people most receptive to these new metaphors and concepts are those working closely with the material. It is in this light that I look at the value of craft for the future.

Conclusions

I start this conclusion with a critical note first, so I can end on a positive one. My critique of craft as intangible heritage addressed the tendency to make categorical definitions of craft and phrasing its value in terms of loss. Through heritage, craft knowledge becomes politically charged in an unhelpful manner. There is no reason to define craft as uniquely handmade objects. In fact, prehistory teaches us that this definition is problematic, while history has shown how such a definition will only lead to exclusivity, rhyming the failure of the Arts and Craft movement.

[2]http://www.fruitleather.nl.

[3]http://www.tjeerdveenhoven.com/portfolio_page/algaefabrics/.

[4]https://www.reuters.com/article/us-tech-netherlands-biocomposite-car/dutch-students-grow-their-own-biodegradable-car-idUSKBN1AO1BL.

Instead, I suggested the possibility that craft knowledge is partly based in the material, and therefore might belong to the material, rather than entirely to humans. Recently, the forward-looking architect Thomas Rau made a call to extend human rights to materials, drafting the first Universal Declaration of Material Rights. If materials can be given rights they can be given heritage, and this is exactly what I propose; craft knowledge as the heritage of materials.

Craft is about making but making is not necessarily craft. My attempt to distinguish them was based on the idea of skill as an apperceptive learning process, through which experience is cognized, and concepts are drawn from practice. Following, craft was interpreted broadly as skilful human–material relationships. An example of such relationship was given to show how the affordances of a material guide thinking and affect worldviews. Bronze guided humans into design-thinking, copying, and prototyping. The people most receptive to the concepts that became *thinkable* because of these affordances were the people most familiar with these materials: craftspeople. It is in this manner I believe craft matters for the future. Material is the mother of innovation, and craft a heuristic through which these innovations are brought about.

My last note is on interdisciplinarity, and the invitation to write this chapter. Listening to the tune of craft throughout human history, economists hear the details of the line sung right now, historians describe the carrying bass and guitars, archaeologists focus on the beat set by the drums. Differentiating between them is drawing artificial boundaries in a complex whole that result in each discipline listening to the same repetitive jingle. With the use of archaeology, I have tried to sketch the beat of craft. To make music, all matter.

Acknowledgements I would like to thank Anna Mignosa for her kind invitation to write a chapter for this book, at a very late stage in the process. She convinced me saying that she likes to be academically 'contaminated', which to my mind sounds far more exciting than disciplinary purity. Arjo Klamer is thanked for inviting me to the Values of Craft symposium in Rotterdam. This chapter benefitted from a workshop in Leiden under the same title. Thanks to all the participants of these meetings. Some special thanks are needed for a few people always willing to help, even when it is very late notice. Catalin Popa, Ulrika Botzojorns, Nienke Broekema, and David Fontijn made sure that the chapter was written coherently, despite the slight rush to get it finished on time. Any errors and incoherency left are my doing. Financial support came from the project 'Economies of Destruction. The Emergence of Metalwork Deposition during the Bronze Age in Northwest Europe, C. 2300-1500BC.', funded by the Netherlands Organisation for Scientific Research (NWO project number: 277-60-001).

References

Adamson, G. 2013. *The Invention of Craft*. London: Bloomsbury.

Appleby, G., and M.L.S. Sørensen. 2018. Forming Metal: The Development of Moulds. In *Creativity in the Bronze Age: Understanding Innovation in Pottery, Textile, and Metalwork Production*, ed. J. Sofaer, L. Bender Jørgensen, and M.L. Stig Sørensen, 99–106. Cambridge: Cambridge University Press. https://www.cambridge.org/core/books/creativity-in-the-bronze-age/forming-metal-the-development-of-moulds/3849D210011E5800145FF-970C0879EE2.

Ball, P. 2010. Making Stuff: From Bacon to Bakelite. In *Seeing Further. The Story of Science & The Royal Society*, ed. B. Bryson, 295–320. London: Harper Press.

Barker, G., C. Roberts, C. Gosden, A. Horning, and K. Welham. 2017. *Reflections on Archaeology*. London: British Academy.

Benjamin, W. 2008. *The Work of Art in the Age of Mechanical Reproduction*, trans. J.A. Underwood. Great Ideas. London: Penguin Books.

Bentley-Condit, V.K., and E.O. Smith. 2010. Animal Tool Use: Current Definitions and an Updated Comprehensive Catalog. *Behaviour* 147 (2): 185–32A.

Boivin, N. 2008. *Material Cultures, Material Minds: The Impact of Things on Human Thought, Society, and Evolution*. Cambridge: Cambridge University Press.

Brück, J. 2004. Material Metaphors: The Relational Construction of Identity in Early Bronze Age Burials in Ireland and Britain. *Journal of Social Archaeology* 4 (3): 307–333.

Budd, P., and T. Taylor. 1995. The Faerie Smith Meets the Bronze Industry: Magic Versus Science in the Interpretation of Prehistoric Metal-Making. *World Archaeology* 27 (1): 133–143.

Callaway, E. 2013. Neanderthals Made Leather-Working Tools Like Those in Use Today. *Nature News*. http://www.nature.com/news/neanderthals-made-leather-working-tools-like-those-in-use-today-1.13542.

Clark, A. 2008. *Supersizing the Mind: Embodiment, Action, and Cognitive Extension*. Philosophy of Mind Series. Oxford: Oxford University Press.

Edgeworth, M. 2010. Beyond Human Proportions: Archaeology of the Mega and the Nano. *Archaeologies* 6 (1): 138–149.

Eerkens, J. 2000. Practice Makes Within 5% of Perfect: Visual Perception, Motor Skills, and Memory in Artifact Variation. *Current Anthropology* 41 (4): 663–668.

Forel, B., M. Gabillot, F. Monna, S. Forel, C.H. Dommergues, S. Gerber, C. Petit, C. Mordant, and C. Chateau. 2009. Morphometry of Middle Bronze Age Palstaves by Discrete Cosine Transform. *Journal of Archaeological Science* 36 (3): 721–729.

Geim, A.K. 2009. Graphene: Status and Prospects. *Science* 324 (5934): 1530–1534.

Guldi, J., and D. Armitage. 2014. *The History Manifesto*. Cambridge: Cambridge University Press.

Heidegger, M. 2011. *Basic Writings: Martin Heidegger*. London: Routledge Classics.

Hodder, I. 2011. Human-Thing Entanglement: Towards an Integrated Archaeological Perspective. *Journal of the Royal Anthropological Institute* 17 (1): 154–177.

———. 2012. *Entangled: An Archaeology of the Relationships Between Humans and Things*. Malden, MA: Wiley-Blackwell.

Høgseth, H.B. 2012. Knowledge Transfer: The Craftsmen's Abstraction. In *Archaeology and Apprenticeship: Body Knowledge, Identity, and Communities of Practice*, ed. W. Wendrich, 61–79. Tucson: University of Arizona Press.

Ingold, T. 2000. *The Perception of the Environment: Essays in Livelihood, Dwelling and Skill*. London: Routledge.

Kintigh, K.W., J.H. Altschul, M.C. Beaudry, R.D. Drennan, A.P. Kinzig, T.A. Kohler, W.F. Limp, et al. 2014. Grand Challenges for Archaeology. *Proceedings of the National Academy of Sciences* 111 (3): 879–880.

Kristiansen, K., and P. Suchowska-Ducke. 2015. Connected Histories: The Dynamics of Bronze Age Interaction and Trade 1500–1100 BC. *Proceedings of the Prehistoric Society* 81: 361–392.

Kuijpers, M.H.G. 2018. *An Archaeology of Skill: Metalworking Skill and Material Specialization in Early Bronze Central Europe*. Routledge Studies in Archaeology. London: Routledge, Taylor and Francis Group.

Lakoff, G., and M. Johnson. 1980. *Metaphors We Live By*. Chicago: University of Chicago Press.

Lenerz-De Wilde, M. 1995. Prämonetäre Zahlungsmittel in Der Kupfer- Und Bronzezeit. *Fündberichten Aus Baden-Württemberg* 20: 229–327.

Lenoir, M.L. 2017. The Axe and the Why: A Research into the Occurrence of Metrological Systems and Metric Patterns within Early Bronze Age Axe Hoards of Central Europe. Master thesis, Leiden University. https://openaccess.leidenuniv.nl/handle/1887/52667.

Malafouris, L. 2013. *How Things Shape the Mind: A Theory of Material Engagement*. Cambridge, MA: The MIT Press.

McGilchrist, I. 2010. *The Master and His Emissary: The Divided Brain and the Making of the Western World*. New Haven: Yale University Press.

Miller, G. 2018. Animal Laborans, Homo Faber, or Something Else? *Social Epistemology Review and Reply Collective* 7 (3): 1–4.

Morris, I. 2015. *Foragers, Farmers, and Fossil Fuels: How Human Values Evolve*. Princeton: Princeton University Press.

Oakley, K. 1949. *Man the Tool-Maker*. London: British Museum.

Pesch, U. in review. Making Innovation Public: Imaginaries and Metamorphoses.

Renfrew, C. 2007. *Prehistory: The Making of the Human Mind*. London: Weidenfeld & Nicolson.

Roberts, B.W., C.P. Thornton, and V.C. Pigott. 2009. Development of Metallurgy in Eurasia. *Antiquity* 83 (322): 1012–1022.

Rowlands, M. 2013. *The New Science of the Mind: From Extended Mind to Embodied Phenomenology*. Cambridge, MA: MIT Press.

Sennett, R. 2009. *The Craftsman*. London: Penguin.

Shew, A. 2017. *Animal Constructions and Technological Knowledge*. Lanham: Lexington Books.

Shorter, M. 2015. The Craft Technologist. *Studies in Material Thinking* 13: 1–19.

Shumaker, R.W., K.R. Walkup, and B.B. Beck. 2011. *Animal Tool Behavior: The Use and Manufacture of Tools by Animals*. Baltimore: Johns Hopkins University Press.

Singh, V., D. Joung, L. Zhai, S. Das, S.I. Khondaker, and S. Seal. 2011. Graphene Based Materials: Past, Present and Future. *Progress in Materials Science* 56 (8): 1178–1271.

Sørensen, T.F. 2012. Original Copies: Seriality, Similarity and the Simulacrum in the Early Bronze Age. *Danish Journal of Archaeology* 1 (1): 45–61.

Sørensen, M.L.S., and G. Appleby. 2018. Making Metals: From Copper to Bronze. In *Creativity in the Bronze Age: Understanding Innovation in Pottery, Textile, and Metalwork Production*, ed. J. Sofaer, L. Bender Jørgensen, and M.L. Stig Sørensen, 37–50. Cambridge: Cambridge University Press.

Soressi, M., S.P. McPherron, M. Lenoir, T. Dogandžić, P. Goldberg, Z. Jacobs, Y. Maigrot, et al. 2013. Neandertals Made the First Specialized Bone Tools in Europe. *Proceedings of the National Academy of Sciences* 110 (35): 14186–14190.

Stockhammer, P.W. 2017. The Dawn of the Copy in the Bronze Age. In *The Transformative Power of the Copy: A Transcultural and Interdisciplinary Approach*, vol. 2, ed. C. Forberg and P.W. Stockhammer, 169–189. Heidelberg Studies on Transculturality. Heidelberg: Heidelberg University Publishing.

Sutton, J. 2008. Material Agency, Skills and History: Distributed Cognition and the Archaeology of Memory. In *Material Agency: Towards a Non-Anthropocentric Approach*, ed. C. Knappett and L. Malafouris, 37–55. Berlin: Springer.

Taylor, A.H., and R.D. Gray. 2014. Is There a Link Between the Crafting of Tools and the Evolution of Cognition? *Wiley Interdisciplinary Reviews: Cognitive Science* 5 (6): 693–703.

Tegel, W., R. Elburg, D. Hakelberg, H. Stäuble, and U. Büntgen. 2012. Early Neolithic Water Wells Reveal the World's Oldest Wood Architecture. *PLOS One* 7 (12): e51374.

UNESCO. 2018. *Basic Texts of the 2003 Convention for the Safeguarding of the Intangible Cultural Heritage, 2018 Edition*. Paris.

Vandkilde, H. 2016. Bronzization: The Bronze Age as Pre-modern Globalization. *Praehistorische Zeitschrift* 91 (1): 103–123.

Villaroya, A.A. 2013. The Crafts, Between Heritagisation and Digitalization. *VOCI Annuale di Scienze Umane* X: 11–20.

Weir, A.A.S., J. Chappell, and A. Kacelnik. 2002. Shaping of Hooks in New Caledonian Crows. *Science* 297 (5583): 981.

Whiten, A., V. Horner, and F.B.M. de Waal. 2005. Conformity to Cultural Norms of Tool Use in Chimpanzees. *Nature* 437 (7059): 737–740.

Whiten, A., A. Spiteri, V. Horner, K.E. Bonnie, S.P. Lambeth, S.J. Schapiro, and F.B.M. de Waal. 2007. Transmission of Multiple Traditions Within and Between Chimpanzee Groups. *Current Biology* 17 (12): 1038–1043.

Education for Artisans: Beginning a Sustainable Future for Craft Traditions

Judy Frater

Craft Traditions in India Today—What's Wrong with This Picture?

On the train to Bagalkot, Karnataka, I suddenly noticed that my white cotton/polyester bed sheet was proudly labeled with a "Handloom" tag… and I wondered, what's wrong with this picture?

In Bagalkot I met handloom weavers working for minimal wages under "Master Weavers,"[1] from whom they had borrowed more than they would ever be able to pay back at the wages they earn. Ilkal sari weavers were being pressed through government-supported programs to leave their traditional handlooms and use jacquard looms to make copies of Varanasi saris. Many had power looms back to back with their handlooms. In some villages it was hard to find even one handloom.

[1]A Master Weaver is usually a person who operates a unit under whom weavers work. He does not weave, and is usually also a money lender.

J. Frater (✉)
Somaiya Kala Vidya, Adipur, Kutch, Gujarat, India

A. Mignosa and P. Kotipalli (eds.), *A Cultural Economic Analysis of Craft*,
https://doi.org/10.1007/978-3-030-02164-1_21

And that loom was devoted to plain white cotton/polyester yardage destined to be government school uniforms.

What is wrong with this picture? I wondered again.

The Indian government has a Ministry of Textiles, under which there are Development Commissioner (Handicrafts) and Development Commissioner (Handlooms), and many schemes to uplift craft and artisans. There is a Ministry of Skill Development and Enterprise, and The National Skill Development Corporation. These bodies, all amply funded, aim to upgrade skills to international standards. The intent fits with the Government's "Make in India" movement, launched in 2014. Firmly in the industrial age, India is focused on manufacturing. Meanwhile many NGOs and advocacy groups are concerned that traditional artisans are steadily leaving craft as a livelihood. Artisans leave craft because from their perspective, craft does not generate enough income, nor enough respect for the effort that it requires.

The mismatch between schemes and results arises from the focus on manufacturing. The concept and language of government and non-government schemes, and of the public, indicate that craft is perceived as an antiquated, inferior form of manufacturing that could only survive if propped up with subsidy and mandated orders for railway sheets and school uniform yardage, and that artisans are perceived as skilled laborers.

Craft is not industry. Nor do artisans perceive it that way. Traditional craft in India was not made in large-scale factories or production lines. In Kutch, a desert region in western India on which most of the data of this chapter is based, an individual or family conceived the object to be made, produced or procured the raw materials needed, and created it; it was holistic creation. Nor was craft distributed in mass. The artisan knew the user, and delivered his work to him directly. Each artisan family had its own clientele, and there were often hereditary, personal relationships between makers and users. Traditionally craft was made in a community-based horizontal social structure, in which artisans all held more or less equal economic and social status.

In the 1950s as India began nation building, balancing traditions with modern technology and ideas, it focused on rapid industrialization. With inflation and the influx of cheaper industrially produced products, traditional clients of rural India began to prefer plastics, synthetics, and mill made fabrics to hand craft. At the same time, the concept of design as an entity was introduced to India. Seeking alternative clients, artisans looked to more distant, unknown markets, often through intermediaries such as designers and traders. The commercialization of craft used an industrial model in which the assumed goals are to manufacture faster, cheaper and in a more standardized way.

In Indian languages there is no word for design as a process separate from creation. Artisans understand what they traditionally create as "art," and the relationship between art (kala) and craftsmanship (karigari) is subtle. As four traditional artisans define it:

- Zuberbhai, bandhani artist, "Art exists; craftsmanship is what we do with it."
- Alimahamadbhai, bandhani artist, "Art is the first time, craft is thereafter."
- Ismailbhai, Ajrakh print artist, "Art is imagination, craft is skill."
- Lachuben, embroidery artist, "Everyone does craft, but not everyone does art."

The introduction of design, as "intervention," began a process of separating concept and execution, resulting in the perception of artisan as worker. "Intervention" further comes with an implication of power and hierarchy: that designers have valuable knowledge, while artisans have less valuable skills. Thus also began cultural dis-empowerment. Relegating artisans to worker status results in minimizing value for their work, little to no opportunity for creativity or recognition and, finally, waning interest in craft, particularly among the next generation of artisan families.

Education for Artisans

After many years of studying craft traditions of Kutch, and then many years working with hand embroidery artisans, I began a design education program for artisans. I felt that a new direction was needed.

Crafts were appreciated enough to commercialize them, and yet the process used was to bring professional designers to "intervene." Artisans had designed the craft that attracted interventionists, and clearly demonstrated their ability to innovate appropriately within their own cultural context. When hand embroidery was banned among Dhebaria Rabari women, for example, they invented a whole new art form based on machine application of ready-made trims. This became a fashion trend locally and beyond.[2]

The concept of the design education program is to value traditional craft as cultural heritage, to take traditional knowledge as a prerequisite and provide what is understood as higher or specialized education directly to artisans. The goal is to enable artisans to increase their capacity by utilizing their strength—creativity—as well as labor. Simultaneously, by bringing artisans in touch with contemporary markets and teaching them to innovate within traditions, traditions are also sustained. The intent is that through education artisans gain respect as well as income. Underlying this concept is the belief that money-profit, scaling up, etc., is not the ultimate goal.

I received an Ashoka Fellowship to develop the program. With further support from UNESCO and the Development Commissioner Handicrafts, I launched it in 2005 as Kala Raksha Vidhyalaya (KRV), in Tunda Vandh, Kutch. After eight years of directing KRV I felt that the program had reached its limitation in that venue. To build the program to an institute, I joined forces with the K.J. Somaiya Gujarat Trust to begin Somaiya Kala Vidya.

The design course comprises six intensive two-week courses spread over a year. It teaches artisans to know and appreciate the design of their traditions, and to recognize aspects that make them unique. Then it teaches them to innovate. The strengths of the course are local orientation, and sustained input.[3] The course is conducted in local language, and draws from local traditions. Schedules accommodate cultural practices.

---

[2]Janakidevi, Bajaj Puraskar, "TBI Blogs: From a Village in Kutch, Pabiben Rabari Created a Global Brand to Empower Local Female Artisans," 16 February 2017.

[3]Chatterjee, Ashoke, "Kala Raksha Vidhyalaya: An Evaluation Report," June 2007.

Courses are taught by visiting faculty—professional design educators, in tandem with local faculty who are artisan graduates of the program. Between courses, the local faculty members visit students individually in their homes to insure that they have understood course material and can implement it in practical homework assignments. The year-long duration of the course insures that students learn, retain and use what is taught. Artisan students learn to find their own interpretations of their traditions, looking beyond technique to using technique in visual language. Education enables the individual to emerge. Each person's vision is unique, even when they draw from the same tradition. Among 185 design graduates, there has been virtually no duplication.

After operating the design course for eight years, I realized that to reap full economic benefit, business and management were also needed. So in 2013 with an Executive-in-Residence from Western Union in partnership with Ashoka, I developed a post-graduate course in Business and Management for Artisans (BMA). Both courses end in public events. A fashion show held in Kutch during each graduation program compels artisan communities and other local public to value craft and artisans in other ways. Student-planned and implemented exhibition/sales in higher-end urban venues provide immediate confirmation of increased value.

Impact to Date

Thirteen years of design education have clearly demonstrated success in connecting graduate artisans to new markets and increasing their incomes. About 75% of men graduates say they have increased their income 10–300%. Women increased their income from 10% to six times. All graduates say they have increased their creative capacity.[4] When individuals express their ideas, traditions diversify and the market actually expands. As one small-scale artisan noted, "My income has increased ten times, while the long-time major producer's income

[4] In-house surveys conducted with graduates of Kala Raksha Vidhyalaya and Somaiya Kala Vidya.

has not suffered at all. It is a win-win situation!" Graduates have won the Indian President's and World Crafts Council awards. Three graduates' work was exhibited in the contemporary design section—along with that of Sabyasachi Mukherjee and others—of the major exhibition "The Fabric of India" at the Victoria and Albert Museum in London. In 2017, seven graduates were the first artisans ever to be recognized as designers on the national Lakme Fashion Week ramp. Nine design graduates have participated in the International Folk Art Market|Santa Fe.

In effect, the design course re-imagines traditional systems in an appropriate contemporary form. Master artisan advisors teach students about traditions, as children once learned from elders; teaching weavers, printers and dyers together in classes revitalizes the interdependence of weavers and dyers in producing traditional textiles; and enabling direct interface between artisan designers and urban markets reinvents the system of direct contact with hereditary clients. Most important, education has shaped understanding, attitudes and values. As Ismailbhai, Ajrakh printer, puts it: "Earlier we knew so many things, but we never reflected upon them. Now this education has helped us understand the rationales behind doing what our ancestors were doing." Purshotambhai, Weaver, design and BMA graduate states: "My father did not allow us to be weavers; there is not enough income in this, he said. So, after I left studies I worked with an NGO for twelve years. Then I took the design course. I learned design; everybody learns design. We could create designs with our eyes closed. But I also got confidence. This course not only teaches us design but also gives us confidence to desire progress." Aslambhai, Ajrakh printer, design and BMA graduate affirms: "My father and I were doing job work, meaning we would print on someone else's fabric. When I saw new products created by design graduates, I also felt the urge to create something. After I completed the design course I had a business but not a market. I found SKV's BMA course to be a perfect opportunity. Most important, we learned that we shouldn't copy other products in the market. We must create designs and carve out a new identity for ourselves." Irfanbhai, Ajrakh printer, design graduate and Governing Council member states: "The one year design course brought many changes in the way we work and made creating new designs easy. Because of making new designs we don't have to go to the market looking for new customers; rather customers come looking for us. Many of us work with established brands such as FabIndia, Good Earth, Jaypore. These brands have terms and conditions which artisans have to agree on. Similarly, we artisans should draft our terms and conditions for these brands to agree on."

Perhaps the most significant success is children of artisans in Kutch returning to craft as an attractive livelihood. Dayabhai, Weaver, design and BMA graduate, and SKV faculty asserts: "I asked my younger son to study further, and he said, 'What will I do after graduation? I will probably do a job where only my office staff or my boss will know me, and however much I work I will get a limited salary. It is better to use my education in the craft sector, because in the craft sector the whole world will know me and I will get maximum return from my inputs.'"[5]

Outreach

In 2014, when we could conclude that design education for artisans in Kutch was reaching its goals of increasing income and respect, we began outreach work to explore whether the approach would be applicable in other regions. The pilot project was begun in Bagalkot, Karnataka. With the inspiration of a Kutch weaver graduate, we used an Artisan-to-Artisan approach: weaver design graduates mentored and co-designed with Bagalkot weavers. The goal was for partner artisans to quickly reach better markets, realize that design makes a difference, and be motivated to take a version of the design course tailored for their situation. As hoped, the weavers sold well in their first market experience and were eager to learn design. A condensed, tailored design course was conducted in Bagalkot, in Kannada language, over two years. The participants dramatically transformed from indentured job workers to independent entrepreneurs in just three years. Subsequently we

[5]Quotes taken from the transcription of the seminar "Craft Nouveau: A Decade of Education for Artisans," held by Craft Revival Trust at India International Center, Delhi, 30 November 2016.

conducted a similar project with embroiderers in Lucknow. In 2018, a third project was begun with weavers in Kumaon.

Outreach work has been mutually beneficial. As Dayabhai, Weaver, design and BMA graduate, and SKV faculty states: "Teaching artisans is the responsibility of an artisan, because an artisan quickly understands the language of a fellow artisan, and an artisan trusts another artisan more. There were many barriers in the beginning, be it language or their thinking…so before teaching anything we must address their way of thinking. What do they want to do? What are we going to teach there? If we clearly communicate, we get faster results.

In the beginning the Bagalkot weavers couldn't believe that their sari valued locally at 800 rupees would sell for a fair price of 4000 rupees in Mumbai. And until they participated in the exhibition they couldn't believe that the saris they were making would be appreciated in Mumbai. But when they sold their products themselves, their joy was amazing. I am fortunate that I could be part of this initiative to pave the way for an artisan to help fellow artisans."[6]

Changing Goals and Perspectives

Artisans understand that craft is more than earning a livelihood. They are working to earn a livelihood; simultaneously they are also clearly working for satisfaction. They have choices in means of earning. In institute intake interviews, many artisans have cited the freedom of working independently as an important benefit of earning through craft. They also understand that there are other measures of success. When a group of weaver graduates was recently asked if they considered themselves successful, nearly all of them answered yes. Asked to define success, they detailed the following: "We confidently know good design, we now have our own concepts and identity, we know how to take feedback, we can talk to our customers. Success is having a voice," they said.

[6]Ibid.

"It is using your creativity, decision making power, achieving goals, and taking responsibility."[7]

Strikingly, not one artisan spoke of success in terms of money. "My early goal was money," Dayabhai explained. "My goal was to educate my children. Now, it is to be my own person. My elder son told me not to weave. Now people from all over the world come to my house, so I have value. It's not about just money." Asked if their goals had changed because of design and business education, Prakashbhai laughed. "Before the course, we had no goals!" he said. "Previously there were no choices," Dayabhai concluded. "Now, weavers who continue their tradition do it by choice. We can share our experience with the next generation. Now we can think of the benefit to our community."[8]

Approaching *Creative Craft Culture*—Craft Communities in the Market

The impact of design and business education on artisans of Kutch and Karnataka remarkably resembles what Klamer et al. detail as characteristics of the supply side of a strong and vital creative crafts culture.[9] For artisan design graduates, the demand side of the ideal creative crafts culture perhaps must still be developed.

In Kutch, craft was traditionally exchanged in a barter system. Weavers, printers and dyers gave fabrics to herders and farmers, and in turn received milk, goats and grain. When asked how they insured that goods exchanged were equal in value, Irfanbhai, Ajrakh printer and SKV Governing Council member, said simply, "We didn't." People received what they needed when they needed it. The shift in conception between this traditional valuation system and the commercial market is enormous.

[7]Quoted from a meeting held with Bhujodi weaver design gradates, 20 February 2018.

[8]Ibid.

[9]Klamer, Arjo, et al., "Crafting Culture: The Importance of Craftsmanship for the World of the Arts and the Economy at Large," Erasmus University, June 2012.

Artisan advisors of the education programs recognize the key role that community plays in craft, and that design education reinforces community. Shyamjibhai, Weaver, Advisor suggests: "Previously, when our elders wove they wouldn't just weave warp and weft threads but would also weave in their emotions and affections, and when one would look at those woven textiles one could see this in the designs they had made. This is the legacy that the design students, even today, carry in their work and design, and that makes them think about the larger benefits to the community. Design education not only benefits families but also helps the larger community. When anyone makes a new design, initially he gets to earn the profit on the design. But later other artisans see that design, and in subsequent years they make changes in it and then that design no longer belongs to one person but is rather owned by the community. When the community starts to think this way, everyone benefits."[10]

However, when craft is pushed into the world of not only cash economy but also industrialized scaled-up production, the structure of artisan societies inevitably changes from horizontal to vertical. Economically stronger individuals become "Master Artisans," employ previously equal status artisans as workers, and gain higher social as well as economic status. The perception of the artisan as worker has re-emerged in a new, socially threatening form.

The number of artisan design graduates in the circumscribed Kutch region has grown so that a new genre of art and artisan has emerged: Artisan Designer. Today there is a community of artisan designers, with new perspectives. Dayabhai suggests: "With design education we learned to create new products appropriate to the market. That facilitated the financial growth of the community, which benefited the entire craft sector. It promoted healthy competition. Earlier, artisans were afraid of sharing their work with others, but that has changed. Now each artisan has his USP and his identity, and we share new work and

[10]Quotes taken from the transcription of the seminar "Craft Nouveau: A Decade of Education for Artisans," held by Craft Revival Trust at India International Center, Delhi, 30 November 2016.

ask for feedback. That has made a social change and has promoted a friendlier outlook. Artisans have come closer to one another."[11]

Discussing the persistent issue of copying, artisan designers acknowledged that copying is a universal issue. Designs *will* be copied by artisans who are not graduates, and anyone using the internet. But copying within the group was not an issue, they assured.[12] Artisan designers to date have found clientele through the plethora of direct sale/pop-up shows in Indian urban centers. Nearly all of them are active on Facebook and many sell directly through Facebook and online shops such as Jaypore, Gaatha, India Kala and even Amazon. The question now is, how to develop a market appropriate to smaller scale, highly diversified and higher value production of artisan designed work?

The Craft Consumer and the Human Connection

This task begins with the craft consumer. Returning to the worldwide concern for the decline of craft, one must probe to define the concern. Many solutions imply that the concern is for beautiful products. But if we examine the essence of craft, more emerges. Craft is hand made. It is the creation of the human hand guided by the human spirit. Craft is slow, labor intensive. Craft is limited in production or one of a kind, and full of quirky character. Craft has meaning. It is the expression of cultural heritage and identity. Traditionally, craft is crafted of natural materials, with ecologically sound practices. And finally, craft is produced in rural, remote regions of the world. These characteristics are all diametrically opposed to large-scale production.[13] People who consume craft do not care about mass production. That is why they choose craft. Craft is about meaning and human connection.

An informative study of craft markets done by the Craft Council of England in 2010 elaborates on what craft consumers want. First, in

---

[11]Ibid.

[12]Quoted from a meeting held with Artisan Designers, 14 May 2018.

[13]Frater, J., "Valuing the Unique: Craft Traditions in the Contemporary Market," keynote address for the International Textile and Apparel Association Annual Conference, November 2015.

England craft consumption is significant. 63% of the population consumes £913m/of craft a year. Craft consumers tend to be women, educated, older, culturally active, open and independent thinking. More important, the study defines cultural consumption and it correlates craft buying choices to current consumer trends. English consumers value craft in terms of authenticity, quality, workmanship, and personal touch. In a time termed the Era of Consequences, consumer demand has shifted towards value-centered products that meet emotional as well as functional needs. People buy craft as a unique and also ethical route for consuming objects. They consider craft buying as an experience, and a new way of signaling connoisseurship.[14] In short, scaling up hand craft production will not likely meet the needs of these consumers.

The phenomenal success of the International Folk Art Market|Santa Fe offers a possible direction for developing an appropriate market. Craft products can be purchased locally across the USA, or online. Yet for the past fifteen years, people have flocked to Santa Fe for this weekend event. Arguably the apex of the tradition-based craft market, the International Folk Art Market|Santa Fe boasted in 2017: 21,000 visitors, $3.1 million sales in 21 hours, for 154 folk artists from 53 countries. Average booth sales were over $20,000. This demonstrates great potential for craft with excellent design, production and market readiness, and interest in craft beyond product. As a key aspect of the Market is the presence of artisans selling their work, we may surmise the huge response illustrates a market that values the human connection of craft.

What's Next—Scaling Out

Education can guide craft to realize an identity by virtue of its personal, human character. Dayabhai, Weaver, design and BMA graduate, and SKV Faculty relates: "When I joined the school in 2008 I was asked what my dreams were? I was doing job work and I dreamed of opening my own business. Once I had my personal business, I wanted to participate in an international exhibition. And I wanted to provide good education

[14]McIntyre, M.H., "Consuming Craft: The Contemporary Craft in a Changing Economy," Crafts Council England, 2010.

to my sons. So this education gives us an opportunity to dream. My three dreams came true. And because of my experience in the Santa Fe Market my position in society here has improved, and it is even helpful in the domestic market. That is the power of design education. It can give you what you wish for."

Early experiments in teaching craft skills and cultural context to craft aficionados in a 22-day Craft Traditions course indicate that appreciation for the value of a craft can be deepened through an immersive experience. One woman, learning Ajrakh printing, related that her aesthetics were actually altered. After working closely with Ajrakh, she began to prefer its complexity over the simpler patterns she originally preferred. A woman learning embroidery said that the experience made her realize the difference between perfection and excellence. She felt free of the bonds of perfectionism, she said. She had discovered that craft doesn't have to be perfect to be beautiful.

Educational efforts could begin to generate value for unique hand work. But to insure a sustainable future for artisan designers, a concerted effort is needed. A system of distribution and development commensurate with the increased capacity of the new artisan designers must be realized. The International Folk Art Market|Santa Fe could be an ultra-niche market. Or, it could be the vanguard of a market ready to be tapped or created. But over time IFAM|Santa Fe's focus has shifted to product, statistics and money. Observed in the context of the Indian participants, this encourages selection of "Master Artisan" professionals who can communicate easily in English and fill out online forms. Correspondingly, as stakes are high, applicants for the few spaces at the market have become shrewd and competitive. Significant economic benefit for a few has reinforced the vertical structure in craft communities.

Traditional systems of marketing based on the human connection of craft must be further examined and re-imagined. The traditional system of craft production and distribution in Kutch exemplifies an alternative model of community-based economy with the potential for more equitable distribution and development—a scaling out rather than scaling up. The next frontier of the ideal Creative Craft Culture is to cultivate robust, widely accessible domestic markets that value diverse, smaller scale, artisan-centered creation.

References

Chatterjee, A. 2007. Kala Raksha Vidhyalaya: An Evaluation Report, June 2007.

Frater, J. 2015. Valuing the Unique: Craft Traditions in the Contemporary Market. Keynote address for the International Textile and Apparel Association Annual Conference, November 2015.

Janakidevi, B.P. 2017. TBI Blogs: From a Village in Kutch, Pabiben Rabari Created a Global Brand to Empower Local Female Artisans, February 16.

Klamer, A. 2012. Crafting Culture: The Importance of Craftsmanship for the World of the Arts and the Economy at Large. Erasmus University.

McIntyre, M.H. 2010. *Consuming Craft: The Contemporary Craft Market in a Changing Economy*. London: Crafts Council.

Index

A. Mignosa and P. Kotipalli (eds.), *A Cultural Economic Analysis of Craft*,
https://doi.org/10.1007/978-3-030-02164-1

Printed by Printforce, the Netherlands